HOMO MYSTERIOUS

DAVID P. BARASH

HOMO MYSTERIOUS
Evolutionary Puzzles of
Human Nature

OXFORD
UNIVERSITY PRESS

OXFORD
UNIVERSITY PRESS

Oxford University Press, Inc., publishes works that further
Oxford University's objective of excellence
in research, scholarship, and education.

Oxford   New York
Auckland   Cape Town   Dar es Salaam   Hong Kong   Karachi   Kuala   Lumpur
Madrid   Melbourne   Mexico City   Nairobi   New Delhi   Shanghai   Taipei   Toronto

With offices in
Argentina   Austria   Brazil   Chile   Czech Republic   France   Greece   Guatemala   Hungary
Italy   Japan   Poland   Portugal   Singapore   South Korea   Switzerland   Thailand   Turkey
Ukraine   Vietnam

Published by Oxford University Press, Inc.
198 Madison Avenue, New York, New York 10016

www.oup.com

Oxford is a registered trademark of Oxford University Press, Inc.

Library of Congress Cataloging-in-Publication Data
Barash, David P.
Homo mysterious : evolutionary puzzles of human nature /
David P. Barash.
p. cm.
Includes bibliographical references and index.
ISBN 978-0-19-975194-5 (hardback: alk. paper)
1. Human evolution. 2. Social evolution.
3. Evolution (Biology) 4. Sex (Biology)
5. Sociobiology. I. Title.
GN281.B36 2012
303.4—dc23   2011044302

Printed in the United States of America on acid-free paper

TO ISAAC SANDER BOGAISKY, WHO WILL
DOUBTLESS ENCOUNTER MANY DELIGHTFUL
MYSTERIES AS HE GROWS UP, AND WHO
MIGHT EVEN SOLVE A FEW.

Contents

Acknowledgments

I thank Abby Gross and Joanna Ng, at Oxford, who contributed mightily (probably more than they know) to this project; my wife, Judith, who tolerated (and contributed to) more diversionary discussions than were reasonable; and the many scientists whose work stimulated this book by asking good questions and seeking ever-better answers. I also thank the students in my University of Washington Honors Arts & Sciences 350 class, who helped me chew over and improve the text.

HOMO MYSTERIOUS

CHAPTER ONE

In Praise of Mystery: That's
How the Light Gets In"

*"Mystics exult in mystery and want it to stay mysterious. Scientists exult in mystery for a
different reason: It gives them something to do."*

—*Richard Dawkins*

WE ARE SURROUNDED BY MYSTERIES. Indeed, mysteries
R us. There are more things in human biology than
are dreamt of in our philosophy or—more to the
point—known by our science. But don't get the wrong idea,
Horatio: Mystery is not the same as mysticism, and *Homo Mysterious*
does not refer to some sort of ineffable, spiritualistic claptrap
beyond the reach of natural law or human understanding. Just as a
"weed" is a plant that hasn't yet been assigned a value, the mysteries we shall encounter in *Homo Mysterious*—such biological oddi-
ties as female orgasm, prominent nonlactating breasts, advanced
consciousness, the origins of religious faith, and the making of
art—are simply scientific questions waiting for answers.

It was a stroke of brilliance as well as immodesty when our
species named itself *Homo sapiens*, usually translated as "man the
wise." A better rendering, however, would probably have been

the knowing," since human beings seem more effective at accumulating knowledge than wisdom, although it can be hoped that the former will lead, eventually, to the latter.

In any event, there is no doubt that our collective store of knowledge has been increasing dramatically and that science is largely responsible. At the same time, there is also no doubt that plenty remains to be learned. Although some people gesture toward what has been called "the end of science"—the notion that all the Big Questions have been answered ("mission accomplished" redux), leaving us with mere mopping-up operations—the reality is that there is an awful lot that we still do not know. And ironically, we *Homo sapiens* are both subject and object of much of that unknowing.

"Know thyself"? Easier said than done. Moreover, at the risk of descending into cliché, the more we know, the more we discover how much remains to be learned. Far from discouraging, I hope this will be seen as both a reward for past accomplishments and, no less, a challenge to do more. Who wants to read about a topic when science has already "closed the book" on it? Most books about science, however, are just that: accounts of what has already been learned. This one is different; it's about mysteries, what we don't know—yet.

The *Collins International Dictionary* (2003) defines mystery as "an unexplained or inexplicable event, phenomenon, etc.," which seems reasonable enough . . . until you think about it. For an event or phenomenon to be *unexplained* is one thing, but to be *inexplicable* is quite another. If something is truly inexplicable, it is beyond the possible reach of human understanding and therefore likely to fit a theological rather than a scientific definition of mystery: something unknowable except through divine revelation, such as how wine is "mysteriously" turned into the literal blood of Christ during the Eucharist.

Let me lay my cards on the table here and now. I do not believe in theological mysteries, or rather, I believe that they are simply ways of clothing meaninglessness in gobbledygook. *Homo Mysterious*, therefore, will not be concerned with the inexplicable, but rather with the unexplained, with things about human beings that are currently unknown but that fall within the potential reach of science. After all, the real world poses genuine mysteries aplenty, that is, puzzles that are not *yet* susceptible to understanding, but that we can be confident will be brought to heel, sometime in the future.

Science, of course, is in the business of doing just this, answering questions about the natural world, *Homo sapiens* included. And since nature does not disclose its secrets readily, scientists are understandably proud whenever they solve any of its numerous puzzles. As a result, we teach courses, give lectures, and occasionally write books whose goal is to share these triumphs. They are, after all, hard-won and often immensely useful. No one, therefore, should begrudge us taking a victory lap now and then.

But just as the race is not always to the swift, nor the battle to the strong (Ecclesiastes 9:11), the cheers of the crowd do not always bespeak that the race is over, or the battle won.

I have been teaching science courses at the college and university level for 40 years and am no less guilty than my colleagues of providing what may well be a misleading perspective on science. Like everyone else, I teach what is known, often at the risk of misleading students into thinking that today's science is a catalog of established and comprehended facts: *This* is how cells metabolize carbohydrates; *this* is how natural selection works; *this* is how the information encoded in DNA is translated into proteins. The reality, of course, is that we know quite a bit about how cells metabolize carbohydrates, how natural selection works, and so forth. But another, parallel reality is that there is much more that we do *not* know . . . and very few courses that admit it. (One of these days, I will design a course titled something like "What We Don't Know About Biology," hoping that my colleagues in chemistry, physics, geology, mathematics, psychology, and the like will join the fun.)

But until then, this book will have to do. It is, in a sense, a companion piece to a much more famous publication—or rather, a series of 17 volumes—first published in France between 1751 and 1765 and best known as the *Encyclopédie*, which endeavored to summarize all human knowledge in its 18,000 pages of text, 75,000 different entries, and 20 million words. Its primary editor, Denis Diderot, was one of the heroes of the Enlightenment, and indeed, the *Encyclopédie* represents a culmination of Enlightenment thought, which valued reason, science, and progress—what we know—above all else. Its frontispiece is especially delightful,

Detail from frontispiece of the *Encyclopédie*, published in 1772. Truth is surrounded by a bright light (a frequently employed symbol of the Enlightenment). Reason and Philosophy, on the right, are undressing Truth, by pulling off her veil.

depicting Truth (surrounded by a bright light, the traditional symbol of the Enlightenment itself) as an attractive young woman being disrobed by Reason and "Natural Philosophy" (i.e., Science). The illustration is more than a bit erotic, as Truth is revealed to be both alluring and accessible, albeit appropriately shy.

Just as Diderot's *Encyclopédie* was a paean to Enlightenment values—notably the upside of human knowledge—*Homo Mysterious* is similarly enamored of reason, science, and progress, even though it is superficially dissimilar, and not merely because its goals and reach are much more limited. Nonetheless, in *Homo Mysterious*, we shall continue the tradition of the *Encyclopédie*'s frontispiece, attempting to get a closer look at Truth, but instead of undressing her, we shall proceed nonvoyeuristically, pointing out where, despite the best efforts of Reason and Science, she continues to be at least somewhat clothed. "All women, O, are beautiful," wrote

Theodore Roethke, "when they are half-undressed." The same applies to Truth itself.

Unlike the *Encyclopédie*, which took all knowledge as its subject, in *Homo Mysterious* we shall limit ourselves to human beings.[i] Not only that, we'll be concerned only with certain characteristics of *Homo sapiens* as seen through the lens of evolutionary biology.

The traits in question are fundamental to being human, stubborn stigmata of our species' unique evolutionary heritage, yet their basis is neither understood by scientists nor for the most part even acknowledged by the public as the puzzles that they are. Most people are unaware that female orgasm, for example, or even religion is a biological mystery, simply because nearly everyone takes the most intimate aspects of his or her life for granted, so deeply woven into our substantive human being that they are rarely identified as legitimate perplexities.

We members of *Homo sapiens* are almost literally immersed in mystery; the evolutionary enigmas of humankind are the seas in which we swim. In *Homo Mysterious*, you will be introduced to this ocean of unknowns, as well as to the major hypotheses that currently occupy scientists who are attempting to unravel each puzzle (including some proposed here for the first time). Like science courses, nearly all science books describe what we know, thereby giving the impression that we know nearly everything, whereas the reality is exactly the opposite: We know very little compared to how much we don't. *Homo Mysterious* is designed for readers likely to be challenged by the blank spots on the human evolutionary map, the *terra incognita* of our own species.

At the risk of channeling former Defense Secretary Donald Rumsfeld, there are "unknown unknowns," things we don't understand and that we don't even know that we don't know! Since we can't identify them, "unknown unknowns" are difficult—perhaps impossible—to write about. On the other hand, there are also "known unknowns," things that we don't yet understand but that we at least have the wisdom to acknowledge as such. Prior to Albert Einstein, Niels Bohr, Enrico Fermi, and others, nuclear energy

---

i. It is an interesting and paradoxical testimony to how much we have learned in the intervening 150 years that today, no one could seriously entertain the prospect of summarizing all knowledge in a book, or series of books, or even via the Internet.

was a known unknown, just as evolution was before Darwin. Today, the underlying basis for homosexuality is similarly a mystery—a phenomenon whose scientific basis is unknown—as is consciousness, the cross-cultural universality of religious belief, the evolutionary basis of artistic creativity, and so forth.

Homo Mysterious will examine these and other perplexities from a perspective that many readers will find unusual. Thus, we shall be less concerned with *how* these things came about than with *why*, not "why" in the metaphysical sense, but that of evolutionary biologists. Were we to ask "how" people became bipedal, the answer would involve changes in muscle attachments, bone structure, and nerve growth; to be concerned instead with the evolutionary "why" is to ask about the likely adaptive pressures that must have conveyed a reproductive advantage to those of our ancestors who walked on two legs, regardless of exactly *how* that posture was achieved.

Similarly, we'll be less concerned with *how* religious belief or homosexuality comes about—the nerves, muscles, brain regions, hormones, or specific genes responsible—than with *why* these behaviors, regardless of their underlying mechanisms, appeared and have persisted in the human population, despite their seeming evolutionary disadvantages.

This approach is familiar to evolutionary biologists and, less so, to most anatomists, physiologists, and the intelligent lay public as well. Not that scientists aren't likely to be "evolutionary" in their thinking; rather, they are more prone to ask questions—and to answer them—in terms of immediate causal mechanisms. Instead, we'll raise questions—and answer them—in evolutionary terms. The underlying conceptual theme is, therefore: "In what way has _____ (female orgasm, concealed ovulation, homosexuality, consciousness, religious belief, etc.) contributed to the ultimate reproductive success of human beings, thus in all likelihood explaining why this particular trait evolved?"

One way of conceptualizing this process is to think about what is sometimes called reverse engineering. In normal engineering, a problem is identified, after which some sort of device or structure is engineered as a solution. Reverse engineering operates, not surprisingly, in reverse: A device or structure (or, in the case of *Homo Mysterious*, a behavior) is identified, after which the evolutionary biologist tries to figure out how this particular phenomenon came to be "engineered"—which is to say, why it evolved.

In many cases, the process is straightforward and obvious, so that it is rarely even attempted. Why do we love our children? Almost certainly, ancestors who lacked parental love didn't do a very good job of caring for their offspring and therefore didn't become ancestors. In that sense, love may actually be less mysterious than is generally thought! For all its storied and supposedly enigmatic nature, there are other human characteristics far more mysterious than love; once we identify them, we are faced with the question of "reverse engineering" them.

In nearly every such case, we will identify multiple potential evolutionary explanations—although we'll refrain from coming up with *the* explanation, simply because at this point, despite the world's impressive store of accumulated scientific knowledge, final answers just aren't yet available. Hence the mystery, the pleasure, and, eventually, the illumnation. "There is a crack in everything," writes poet/songwriter Leonard Cohen. "That's how the light gets in."

Just one modification: There are *many* cracks and, when it comes to some of the most interesting mysteries of human evolution, no reason why a single one should necessarily provide the only illumination. *Homo Mysterious* therefore cannot claim to be exhaustive, just scientifically accurate as far as it goes and, I hope, fun.

Consistent with our slightly lascivious reflections on the frontispiece to the *Encyclopédie*, we'll begin our exploration with some human sexual mysteries. Then, we move above the waist. I hope you enjoy the trip and that along the way, you might even come up with a suggestion or two that could help solve some of the evolutionary mysteries we are about to explore together.

CHAPTER TWO

Sexual Mysteries I: Menstruation, Concealed Ovulation, and Breasts

MOST PEOPLE WOULD AGREE that sex is a mystery. But they would probably be thinking of romantic perplexities rather than scientific enigmas. The fact is, however, that when Winston Churchill famously described Russia in 1939 as "a riddle wrapped in a mystery inside an enigma," he could as well have been speaking of some hard-wired aspects of human sexuality. Particularly mysterious, at least from the perspective of evolutionary biology, are some aspects of the sexual biology of women.

The first notable mystery begins when a girl becomes a woman: menstruation. Although a few other species bleed slightly at midcycle, no other organism does so as prominently as *Homo sapiens*. Breast development is another perplexity: Although we take it for granted that women have conspicuous breast tissue even when not nursing, no other mammal is comparably bosomed. Only human beings are blessed (or, in the opinion of some, cursed) with prominent nonlactating breasts.

The mysteries continue. Go to a zoo and take a look at the chimpanzees, gorillas, or baboons (or, indeed, nearly any nonhuman primate). There is no question when an adult female is ovulating.

It is as obvious as the bright pink cauliflower on her behind. Not so for our own species. Given the great importance—socially, biologically, evolutionarily—of reproduction, and thus of ovulation, it is extraordinary and as yet unexplained why even now, in our medically sophisticated 21st century, it is exceedingly difficult to tell something so basic as when a woman is fertile. For reasons unknown, human beings conceal their ovulation and are unique among mammals in doing so. Not only that, but in the great majority of cases, the exact time of a woman's ovulation is even hidden *from herself*. As with menstruation and nonlactating breasts, hypotheses abound, but no one knows the answer.

Ditto for female orgasm. Its male counterpart is a no-brainer (almost literally!), since without ejaculation there would be no fatherhood and thus no evolutionary success. But the data are quite clear: There is no correlation between female orgasm and female fitness in the evolutionary sense. In other words, orgasmic women are no more successful reproductively than their less fortunate, nonorgasmic "sisters." So, why does female orgasm occur at all?

Proceeding along the trajectory of a woman's life, we come to yet another mystery: menopause. By around age 50, a woman can anticipate that she will cease ovulating. Why does reproduction inevitably end, even for the healthiest women, at a time in middle age when many can anticipate several decades of continued and vigorous life? This is especially perplexing since reproductive success is the name of the Darwinian game and simple calculations show that producing just one additional child, compounded over time, would convey a huge evolutionary advantage. Yet menopause is not only a cross-cultural human universal but also one not shared by any other living thing, except possibly for the short-finned pilot whale (but of course, you already knew that).

Let's consider these mysteries and some possible solutions, one at a time.

A Signal?

It has been suggested that all mammals may in fact shed some of their uterine lining between ovulations, but no other species comes close to *Homo sapiens* in the volume of blood flow and amount of tissue disruption, which requires women to literally rebuild their uterine lining with each reproductive cycle. The amount of blood loss—about 40 ml—is not enormous but is enough to force many to take iron supplements. It is as though every sexually competent woman is obliged to suffer an automatic monthly deduction from her metabolic checking account. Not only that, but it seems likely that the shedding of fresh blood, sometimes in copious quantities, would make menstruating women more susceptible to predators, many of which are exquisitely sensitive to cues that indicate potential prey.[i] Given that evolution is a stern task-mistress, constantly sifting and sorting through alternatives to find the most efficient and fitness-enhancing way to accomplish the various tasks of living, why have we signed on to such expensive and possibly even risky monthly taxation? And this doesn't even count the cramps, which in some cases are so severe as to be temporarily disabling.

One might even say that menstruation almost literally deserves its old-fashioned descriptor, "the curse." More scientifically, we would expect that women who did *not* menstruate would have been more successful over evolutionary time than those who did. Yet the opposite has clearly been true, since menstruation is something that all healthy premenopausal women do. It may be an annoyance but it is not an illness or a biomedical problem; rather, prolonged amenorrhea—*failure* to menstruate—indicates that something is wrong.

In addition, about 10% of otherwise healthy women suffer from endometriosis, a painful and potentially life-threatening condition caused when cells of the uterine lining are discharged in the wrong direction, into the pelvic cavity instead of outside the body. And of course, menstruation necessitates that for a particular duration (typically 3 to 5 days), pregnancy cannot occur. This is yet another cost of menstruation, which further italicizes the mystery that it exists at all.

For starters, let's ignore the suggestion, repeated through generations of folk "wisdom," that menstruation indicates the "weeping of a disappointed uterus" that has failed its reproductive role.

---

i. It has been claimed, for example, that menstruating women are more vulnerable to grizzly bear attacks; however, I have not been able to confirm whether this is statistically true.

(This notion is especially foolish since the likelihood is that without menstruation, more cycles would be "successful.") Ditto for the theological assertion that it constitutes part of the punishment inflicted by a vengeful deity upon a disobedient Eve. There are, in fact, several possible scientific hypotheses for menstruation.

For one, it could be a signal by which a woman's body tells her brain that she isn't pregnant. After all, that is how menstruation is "used" today, just as, conversely, a failure to "get one's period" is an early signal that a woman may be pregnant. It would clearly be advantageous for a woman to know her reproductive status, and in a world before pregnancy test kits, it is quite likely that by its presence or absence, menstruation gave the first clue.

Fair enough, but logically unlikely. Why should natural selection have favored such an expensive "all-clear signal," especially one that had to be broadcast each month? Wouldn't it have been far more efficient—and not at all beyond the reach of evolution— to endow pregnant women with a distinctive smell, a unique sneeze, or the rapid blinking of their left eye? It seems like blatant overkill to lose much of your physical self—your uterine lining— just to send the message that you are not pregnant. And even if menstruation serves such a signaling function, why isn't it simply a bit of spotting, as in dogs?

The copiousness of human menstrual bleeding nonetheless suggests that maybe it's a social signal, a message intended for others. In many human societies today, the onset of menses indicates the beginning of adulthood. So maybe menstruation—for all its drawbacks—was selected as a way of informing one's surrounding social network that a girl is becoming a woman and should be taken seriously.

One problem with this hypothesis is that such signaling appears more likely to be *disadvantageous* to the signaler. Even though biologists are agreed that male–male competition is typically more vigorous—even violent—than its female–female counterpart, it is increasingly clear that female–female competition also occurs. More subtle than the male–male version, it nonetheless involves situations in which dominant adult females of a number of species actually attack, intimidate, and often inhibit the breeding of subordinates. Assuming that something comparable occurs in our own species (admittedly, an unproven assumption at present), it would seem to behoove a young woman to, if anything, hide that fact that she is entering reproductive competence, especially since such a signaler would necessarily be young and thus liable to be particularly vulnerable.

The possibility still exists—although a slim one—that menstrual bleeding is not targeted at other women generally, but more specifically aimed at close relatives and others who might be primed to cooperate rather than compete, to render useful assistance to a younger kinswoman once they know of her change in reproductive status. It would be interesting to see if menstrual flow is in any way correlated with presence or absence of potential competitors on the one hand or helpers on the other. At present, however, it is hard to see how menstruation could have evolved as a social signal, especially given that in nearly all human societies today, it is considered awkward, embarrassing, even shameful— the body conveying information that one's mind would prefer to keep under wraps.

A signaling hypothesis for menstruation could still be salvaged, however, if it were directed toward men. But if so, the earlier question repeats itself: Why use such an expensive signaling system instead of, say, employing pheromones? After all, males are sperm makers by definition, and because sperm are cheap and abundant, sperm makers are selected to be highly attuned to indications of fertility on the part of prospective partners.

It is interesting, nonetheless, that in the modern Western world at least, substantial effort is expended to hide the fact of menstruation—which itself paradoxically suggests that in the absence of the "feminine hygiene" industry and its constant efforts to provide women with "protection" from their own bodies, enabling them to hide, suppress, tip-toe around, or otherwise obscure the reality of menstruation, maybe it really did evolve as a signal. In the past it was certainly widely noticed, although generally misunderstood. "Nothing could easily be found that is more remarkable than the monthly flux of women," wrote Pliny the Elder, two millennia ago:

Contact with it turns new wine sour, crops touched by it become barren, grafts die, seeds in gardens are dried up, the fruits of trees fall off, the bright surface of mirrors in which it is merely reflected is dimmed, the edge of steel and the gleam of ivory are dulled, hives of bees die, even bronze and iron are a once seized by rust, and a horrible smell fills the air.[1]

Demeaning and inaccurate as such attention has been, if nothing else it encourages us to look for other explanations.

The Cleansing Hypothesis

Here is one. What if menstruation serves a cleansing function, using periodic blood flow to sluice away potentially dangerous pathogens, including—but not limited to—those introduced during copulation?[2] This "explanation" has pros and cons, like nearly all the perplexities to be considered in the present book, and like most, it has generated fruitful debate. Moreover, it's a nifty idea, not least because it reverses the old canard that menstruating women are somehow unclean or that the phenomenon is a reflection of female weakness, emphasizing instead that the exact opposite is more likely the case: Sperm plus semen are actually more likely to be unclean (not to mention possible pathogens introduced during coitus itself), with menstruation conceivably being a hygienic and even heroic countermeasure.

The reality, of course, is that ovaries and the uterus are internal organs, abundantly outfitted with delicate tissue that is vulnerable to infection. And sexual intercourse necessarily involves introducing foreign material deep inside a woman's body, bypassing most of her traditional defenses. Certain pathogens such as *Chlamydia*—a common cause of pelvic inflammatory disease—hitchhike on the tails of sperm, and bacteria such as *Staphylococcus* and *Streptococcus*, which cause no harm when inhabiting the vagina, can be serious troublemakers when transported via an enthusiastic penis into a woman's upper reproductive tract.

Margie Profet, who developed the "cleansing hypothesis," emphasized that the uterus is "designed to bleed," via its specialized spiral-shaped arteries and arterioles. When these constrict, the uterine lining dies and is sloughed off, presumably taking any unwanted pathogenic invaders along with it. In addition, the resulting copious blood flow essentially "hoses down" the underlying uterine wall. Profet also pointed out that menstrual blood contains a concentration of leukocytes that is about three times higher than normal blood; these white blood cells, brought directly into contact with the uterus, are thus made available to fight any infections.

There are practical implications of the cleansing hypothesis. If, as the hypothesis holds, menstrual bleeding is an adaptive response to infection or potential infection, then it is clearly normal. What about unusually heavy bleeding (menorrhagia) or intracyclic bleeding (metrorrhagia)? These could be symptoms of endometritis, inflammation of the uterine lining, or they could be part of a body's attempt to fight off such infections. Profet, originator of the cleansing hypothesis, points out that assuming the former, and therefore using medications to inhibit such bleeding, would be equivalent to "blaming firemen for a fire."

Convincing as it might be at first blush, the cleansing hypothesis also has problems.[3] Menstrual blood contains nutrients— especially iron—that might actually *encourage* pathogen growth. And in fact, many pathogens are specifically iron deprived, such that surrounding them with blood might provide them with just the nutrients they need! There is also no evidence that menstrual intensity—either in human beings or animals—correlates with pathogen load, which would be predicted. Under the cleansing hypothesis, an already "clean" uterus would be expected to correlate with less tissue loss and reduced blood flow. Were this the case, it would doubtless have been trumpeted by devotees of the cleansing hypothesis as evidence in its favor, so the opposite finding must be acknowledged as evidence against.

Suppose, alternatively, that pathogen invasion is difficult for the uterus to detect, which might in turn prevent adaptive modulation of the cleansing response (in fact, insofar as bodies are able to respond to pathogens by killing them, selection would have favored discreet invaders that gave minimal indications of their presence). Even then, however, another correlation could be expected: between sexual activity—either number of partners or frequency of coitus with the same partner—and menstruation. But the reality, once again, is not encouraging: Although some women have relatively heavy menstrual flows and some much lighter, menstrual intensity also does not vary with the number of different sexual partners or with the nature and frequency of sexual encounters. Another strike against the cleansing hypothesis.

Also, if menstruation serves to diminish the uterus's pathogen load, either by flushing them away or zapping them with white blood cells, then there should be fewer bacteria present after menstruation than before. It is notoriously difficult to assess total bacterial load in a given human organ. However, it is relatively easy to determine how many different kinds of bacteria are present, and when this is done, the evidence points the opposite way: more bacterial diversity *after* menstruation than before.

There is yet more evidence against the cleansing hypothesis. It is well established that women in traditional, nontechnological societies enter menarche later and spend more time pregnant and nursing than do Western women. As a result, they experience far fewer menstrual cycles than do Western women, and therefore, according to the cleansing hypothesis, they should be more susceptible to uterine infections. There is no evidence for this. The cleansing hypothesis would also expect that women with an especially heavy menstrual flow would have a lower frequency of pelvic inflammatory disease; this has not (yet) been evaluated.[ii] It is also problematic that oral contraceptives, which substantially decrease menstrual blood volume, do not increase the risk of uterine infection, even though it could be argued that such contraceptive use is balanced by a possible increase in heterosexual activity . . . which is typically why the contraceptives are used in the first place.

The Efficiency Hypothesis

There is another possible explanation for why menstruation evolved, based on energy efficiency: Calculations suggest that it is metabolically cheaper to slough off the uterine lining (which is energetically expensive to maintain) and then regrow it in preparation for the next cycle of ovulation than to maintain it in a high level of vascularization. In support of this idea, anthropologist Beverly Strassman noted that a postmenstrual uterus consumes only about 14% of the oxygen required by a fully prepared endometrium. Not only that, but a woman's overall metabolic rate during the preovulatory ("follicular") phase of her cycle, when the

---

ii. Unless greater flow was a *response* to greater infection.

uterine lining is regressed, is about 7% lower than during the secretory ("luteal") phase, when it is actively growing.

Efficiency is a less-than-exciting notion, but after all, energy is the basic currency of life, making it not unreasonable that a woman's metabolic economy alternately revs up and down, economizing on the costs of remaining ready to reproduce. The idea is that unlike, say, the lungs or heart, a woman can afford to down-regulate the activity within her uterus, keeping it at a slow idle during those times between ovulations when reproduction is not an option.

On the other hand, the metabolic efficiency hypothesis is not entirely convincing. Why, for instance, isn't the uterus simply kept in a more efficient, low-energy, less vascularized state until needed for nourishing an embryo? That is, why build up a fancy and expensive uterine lining, ready to receive an implanting embryo, only to tear it down every month? Why not just tamp down the endometrium and keep it quiescent until an embryo comes along? That would be more efficient yet.

Part of menstruation's enigma, and the need for all these hypotheses, is that it poses a kind of Sisyphean dilemma. According to Greek mythology, Sisyphus was condemned to spend eternity pushing a heavy rock up a steep hill, only to have it roll back down each time. A menstruating woman finds herself constructing a snazzy, energetically expensive endometrium each month, only to dislodge it again and again. Sisyphus had no choice; ditto for most women. But presumably, evolution did.

A Competence Test?

An alternative explanation is what I have dubbed the "evaluation hypothesis," which derives from the fact that human beings are unique among mammals in how much they invest in each offspring. This makes it especially important that any embryo that is brought to term be an especially capable one. After pregnancy and childbirth comes lactation, followed by years—even decades—of continuing expenditure on behalf of human offspring: spending time and energy, running risks, and so forth. It may therefore be significant that for every successful pregnancy, there are many "spontaneous abortions," caused by the failure of an early embryo to implant successfully.

For anyone with a scientific mind set and who therefore believes that all phenomena have causes, the very word "spontaneous" should set off alarm bells. Maybe in this case a "spontaneous" abortion really means that the embryo or fetus was tried and found wanting or, at least, not deserving of further maternal investment. And maybe the events surrounding menstruation are how a woman's body evaluates her would-be offspring and does so early in the "investment" cycle, thereby minimizing wasted investment in case of a thumbs down.

A key aspect of early pregnancy takes place when an embryo (really, just a fertilized zygote) begins burrowing into the uterine lining and starts secreting a hormone—human chorionic gonadotropin or HCG—that inhibits menstruation. Early in a woman's menstrual cycle, luteinizing hormone, produced by the brain, not only kick-starts ovulation but also keeps a woman's ovaries making its own hormone, progesterone, which in turn keeps the uterine lining in place. If no pregnancy occurs, luteinizing hormone levels decline, which in turn causes a precipitous drop-off in progesterone, which results in the breakdown of the uterine lining and, shortly thereafter, menstruation.

Let's consider, therefore, that menstruation, rather than signaling "no pregnancy," is a way of ensuring its absence. But of course, evolution shouldn't promote nonreproduction . . . except perhaps in a species such as *Homo sapiens*, whose investment in offspring is so great that it pays to establish a kind of competence test, making sure that any would-be fetus and eventual child is sufficiently sturdy to warrant all that expenditure of time and energy and running of risks that are to come.

To ward off menstruation, the newly implanted embryo has to substitute its own HCG for the luteinizing hormone produced by the mother. Molecule for molecule, HCG is more potent than luteinizing hormone, and it actually causes an increase in progesterone levels, which in turn prevents menstruation and maintains the uterus as a rich and warmly receptive receiving blanket for the embryo.

The foregoing leads toward a hypothesis whereby menstruation is part of a regularly repeating competence test. Because HCG is a very large molecule, it cannot pass directly into the mother's body by crossing her cell membranes; it must be secreted directly into her blood. As a result, a human embryo cannot guarantee its survival by simply secreting HCG: It has to get to the endometrium and dig itself in. This Big Dig isn't easy, which might be exactly the point. The process of implantation in human beings is more invasive—and thus more difficult—than in other mammals, consisting of a delicate dance between receptive maternal tissues and a capable embryo. In the earliest stages of pregnancy, it's the embryo that does nearly all the work, struggling to get itself deeply enmeshed in uterine tissue so that it can eventually get nourishment—but first, so that it can secrete HCG to prevent menstruation. If so, then menstruation is a sword held over the head of the as-yet headless embryo.

Implantation itself is a kind of Rubicon. Once crossed, the mother is committed to ongoing investment, and lots of it. This, in turn, may have selected for the mother ensuring that any inadequate early embryos can be weeded out quickly and painlessly. To summarize, perhaps menstruation is essentially a regularly repeating competence test, whereby evolution selects against embryos whose burrowing and secretory abilities are inadequate. Unfortunately for this hypothesis, however, it makes a prediction identical to the cleansing hypothesis, and one that is not supported by reality: Menstruation should be tied to sexual activity. Also, if people have been selected to menstruate as a means of subjecting their embryos to competence testing, then why isn't this the case for other species for whom each offspring also represents a major commitment? Why don't elephants menstruate? Or blue whales, or manatees?

It's a mystery. Period.

Concealed Ovulation: An Evolutionary Shell Game?

Most female mammals are altogether above board when their eggs are ripe and ready to encounter a suitable sperm. In addition to signs of genital swelling, they typically emit characteristic pheromones and their behavior changes as well. Not so for our own species. (Actually, there is growing evidence that women do in fact exhibit subtle behavioral cues as to their ovulatory status, but the key here is *subtle*; it is only in recent years that these indications have been discovered. If they constituted what scientists call a "robust phenomenon," everyone would have known about them long ago.)

The surprising reality is that very few people can tell—and no one with certainty—when their neighbor, friend, relative, lover, or wife is about to ovulate. Not only that, but most women cannot even tell when, or if, they will do so themselves. To some degree, ovulation can be detected by a very small rise in body temperature as well as changes in the consistency of the vaginal mucus, but both assessments are difficult and unreliable. Indeed, the fact that such careful ascertainment must be exercised only further italicizes the extent to which it is not obvious! Even now, we have no reliable "rhythm method" of noncontraceptive birth control, which is to say, no easy way to know when women are ovulating. Pharmaceutical companies make huge amounts of money marketing test kits that provide anxious women the same information that most mammals get for free.

Concealed ovulation, therefore, is a mystery squared: The timing of human ovulation is hidden, and thus a mystery in itself, and furthermore, it is a mystery why it is such a mystery!

It is, of course, possible that concealed human ovulation hasn't been actively selected for, but rather that shout-out-loud, Technicolor ovulation, á la chimpanzees, is the derived condition—and thus the one that needs explaining—with inconspicuousness, as found among *Homo sapiens*, being the evolutionarily irrelevant default state. This is unlikely, for several reasons. Start with the fact that nearly all mammals (including our closest relatives, the chimps and bonobos) announce their ovulation, which itself is strong presumptive evidence that our ancestors, too, were relatively uninhibited about drawing attention to their ovulatory status.

Beyond this, there is essentially no variability with regard to concealed ovulation in our species. If natural selection were indifferent to whether human ovulation was hidden or advertised, then we would expect substantial variability since public ovulators, concealed ovulators, and in-betweeners would all be pretty much equally fit and thus equally abundant. There is, for example, substantial variability in human skin color, eye color, blood type, and so forth, all traits about which natural selection is evidently more or less indifferent. But there are no women whose ovulation is even remotely like a chimpanzee's.

The likelihood, therefore, is that human ovulation isn't just neutral or subtle but that it is actively hidden. Yet a moment's thought suggests that if nothing else, any woman who knows when she is fertile (whether or not she informs others) should be better equipped to become pregnant, or avoid pregnancy, or choose her offspring's father than would someone who hasn't a clue and doesn't give any.

Earlier, when considering menstruation, we considered and for the most part rejected the idea that it might have evolved as a social signal. Could the same be true, but reversed, for concealed ovulation? What of the prospect that human ovulation is concealed as a way of *suppressing* a social signal? It is—pardon the expression—conceivable.

Thus, it could be argued that by concealing ovulation, our early hominid ancestors obscured their reproductive status, thereby limiting possible aggressive competition from other, more dominant women. Consistent with this idea, there is growing evidence that—contrary to the generalizations still popular in evolutionary biology about the exclusive maleness of same-sex competition—females generally and women in particular do in fact compete, albeit more subtly than via the chest-beating, fangs-bared style more characteristic of males. Hence, it might well have contributed to a woman's ultimate evolutionary success if she kept her reproductive status under wraps. Almost literally.

This seems a plausible hypothesis, except that it would be stronger if ovulation were more concealed among women living in more densely interactive social environments and comparatively unobscured when the woman in question was the only show in town. This isn't the case. Similarly, this hypothesis would be more convincing if younger, less dominant women concealed their ovulation, while older, more socially and physically secure women flaunted theirs. But they don't.

It is reasonable to hypothesize that concealed ovulation is essentially an evolutionary shell game whereby women who hid their time of maximum fertility kept "their" men in a kind of sexual thrall. Among species in which ovulation is clearly signaled, males are free to copulate at this time, then essentially abandon their inamorata, often in search of other short-term partners. Such, for example, is the notorious sex life of chimps and bonobos. But in *Homo sapiens*, in which ovulation is concealed, men wanting confidence of paternity are obliged to remain in attendance throughout the female's cycle, engaging in regular sexual relations during the month. A study examining 68 different primate species, looking for correlations between mating system and visible signs of estrus, found that not a single monogamous species was a conspicuous ovulator.[4]

Human beings are also unusual among living things—not just primates—in the extent to which they copulate without much regard to ovulation or the details of a woman's hormonal condition. This further suggests that concealed ovulation may have evolved as a tactic whereby our great-, great-, great-grandmothers made sure that our great-, great-, great-grandfathers kept close tabs on them, instead of (or in spite of) lusting after someone else. One of *Homo sapiens*' signature characteristics is our long period of infancy and childhood dependency, which is why even today, single parenting is difficult. It therefore makes sense that having a devoted mate would enhance the fitness of the woman in question, even if said devotion is purchased via a kind of sexual hostage taking, playing to his unconscious uncertainty rather than his love.

It is certainly possible that if women were more chimplike, men would be, too: copulating avidly with a given partner while she is fertile, but then seeking other and equally alluring "partnerships," bolstered by an unconscious confidence that his prior mate would not cuckold him in the meanwhile, since she obviously is incapable of conceiving. In addition, it is interesting to speculate that by inducing men to keep close company with a given woman, concealed ovulation contributed to making them fathers and not just sperm donors, since one result of all that "mate guarding," as biologists term it, would be greater male confidence that their offspring—or rather, their female partner's offspring—are in fact theirs, too.

But such speculation—compelling as it may be—doesn't prove anything. For instance, the "keep him close by keeping him uncertain" hypothesis assumes that regular sex is a prerequisite for social bonding and biparental behavior, yet there are numerous bird species and even some primates (e.g., gibbons) that commonly go long periods without sexual intercourse and are nonetheless socially monogamous, and some that copulate rarely yet demonstrate notably shared parental duties (e.g., pigmy marmosets, in which fathers carry infants and even reportedly assist with the birthing process). Most of us know people who stay devoted to each other even though the sexual spark may be only intermittent, if not altogether extinguished. And on the other side, human marriages can fail despite intense and satisfying sexual chemistry; sometimes, indeed, this is the only thing that works in a relationship, and if so, it's rarely enough.

Taking Control and Increasing the Options

In fact, there is another possible explanation for concealed ovulation that goes precisely against the grain of the "shell game" or "keep him guessing to keep him close" explanation. Rather than promoting social and sexual bonding (cynics might say "bondage"), ovulation might be hidden in our species because such obscurantism makes it easier for women to have sex with men other than their designated partner. After all, given that women don't identify their precise time of ovulation, even the most dedicated man would likely have a hard time guarding "his" woman so closely as to be able to monopolize her sex life—something that would presumably be more possible if her fertile times were clearly signaled as in so many other primates. By obscuring their exact ovulation, ancestral women might therefore have actually given themselves more leeway to mate with other, more attractive males when and if they chose.

In addition to giving themselves greater potential choice of mates, concealed ovulation may have provided a counterintuitive evolutionary payoff, by enabling them to mate with males who might otherwise be potential murderers of their offspring. It is now well established that among many social species—including, presumably, our own ancestors—strange adult males were a major threat to the survival of infants. This is because after taking over a social unit, male langur monkeys, chimpanzees, gorillas, lions, and so forth often kill lactating infants, which had been sired by their predecessor. Why such carnage? Two reasons: First, these infants had been sired by the *previous* male, so the new harem tyrant has no genetic interest in preserving them. And second, by killing their suckling babes, a newly ascendant male induces nursing mothers to begin cycling once again, thereby making these females potential recipients of the murderous male's sexual attention and, eventually, contributing to his reproductive success.

Not a pretty picture, especially for the victimized infants and their mothers.[iii] But the latter might have a few tricks of their own, including perhaps one inherited by our ancestors: Typically, newly ascendant males spare the offspring of females with whom they had previously copulated, as though they say to themselves, "Isn't that my old flame from several months ago? And just look at that cute little baby, he's got my chin!" It has been suggested, in short, that female choice of multiple male sexual partners—itself facilitated by concealed ovulation—may be a means whereby our great-, great-, great-grandmothers fooled the men in their lives, inducing several to think that each might be the father and thereby taking out a kind of "infanticide insurance."

Here is a related but more cheery hypothesis for why human ovulation is concealed, focusing on benefits to the woman, ultimately via payoffs to her offspring.[iv] It is clearly advantageous to every woman to be fertilized by the best available sperm, which unfortunately might not be provided by her mate/husband. Sadly, the real world of potential sexual and social partners is not like Lake Wobegon, "where all the women are strong, all the men are good-looking and all the children are above average." The average mate of the average woman is, well, average! Since a would-be mother is more likely to be reproductively successful mated to a less-than-perfect male specimen than if she were unmated, she might therefore be predisposed (which is to say, favored by natural selection) to increase her fitness by sticking with her partner—who

---

iii. And a useful lesson for those who think we can derive ethical lessons from evolution. The harsh reality is that evolution by natural selection is a marvelous thing to learn *about*, but a terrible one to learn *from*.

iv. In this as in other similar examples, feel free to translate "benefits to an individual" into "benefits to the genes that underlie the trait in question."

presumably is the best she is able to obtain—while also trying to have sex with more attractive men on the sly.

The assumption here is that attractiveness, which is very much in the eye of the beholder, is likely to be determined by whether the person in question has traits that signal higher fitness to be experienced by his potential offspring: either unusually healthy, for example, or simply possessing traits that—once manifested in their sons—would likely be found attractive by the next generation of women. The possibility therefore exists that by concealing their ovulation, ancestral women were able to obtain desirable genes—as well as perhaps other immediate material resources— from desirable men with whom they mated adulterously, while also retaining paternal assistance from their socially designated but cuckolded partner.

Another way of saying this: By dispensing with estrus (which is essentially equivalent to concealing one's ovulation), early hominid women may have been able to exercise greater control over their choice of a sexual partner. This could have worked in either of two ways. For one, insofar as concealed ovulation facilitated clandestine matings with men other than their designated mate, this needn't only have involved taking out "infanticide insurance." It would also have provided the opportunity for women to engage sexually with men of their choice. And for another, consider that female mammals in "heat" (which is to say, in estrus because they are ovulating) are typically no more rational than their male counterparts. Lacking estrus—that is, having concealed their ovulation—women can remain comparatively cool and in sexual control . . . at least, compared to other mammals.

By foregoing estrus, this particular argument goes, women have become masters of their genetic fate, empowered to pick and choose, deciding (maybe not consciously, but by exercising a degree of judgment nonetheless) among potential suitors. After all, the word *estrus* comes from a Greek term for a parasitic fly that pursues cattle and drives them crazy; a female animal in estrus seems more than a little crazy. By the same token, females who are not in estrus—which is to say, all women, all the time—are more likely to be sane, sober, and capable of better judgment.

In his poem "If," Rudyard Kipling wrote about the merits of being able to keep your head while all those around you are losing theirs. If you can do this, according to his famous poem, "then you will be a man, my son." Maybe by favoring those women able to "just say no" to the tyranny of estrus, natural selection endowed our female ancestors with the ability to reap the benefits of being more discriminating than any animal (and probably more so than most men, to boot). "If you can keep your secret," evolution might have been betting, "while all those around you are divulging theirs, then you will be a reproductively successful woman, my daughter."

Concealed ovulation could also have adaptively paved the way for women to enjoy greater mating control by reducing the intensity of male–male competition. Think of it this way: If women were only sexually receptive for a day or so each month, at which time they broadcast their availability by sudden, seductive signals of sight, smell, and sexual interest, men might respond by huffing and puffing and blowing each other away—even more than they do now—leaving women little choice, perhaps, but to accept the victor. Dominant males may be desirable sperm donors, if only because their sons may also turn out to be dominant and/or desirable males: This is the so-called sexy son hypothesis (about which more later). But such males may also be terrible fathers, more interested in beating other males over the head than in caring for their own children. By keeping their ovulation secret, and thereby dampening the competitive ardor of men, women might have given themselves the opportunity of choosing men who may be less pushy but more paternal.

At this point it is worth noting that even though women neither broadcast dramatic ovulatory messages like chimpanzees nor behave in a manner commensurate with estrus in other animals, research has shown that women's behavior does indeed undergo subtle but substantial changes during their menstrual cycle. When they are ovulating, women are especially likely to wear clothing that is comparatively sexy and reveals more skin, to speak with greater fluency and creativity, to prefer images of men who are especially "manly" as well as favoring male voices that are lower pitched, to be perceived by both men and women as more facially attractive, to have a heightened sense of smell, and literally to move around more.[5]

Moreover, evidence is also accumulating that men are able to perceive at least some of these changes, albeit unconsciously. Thus, in a series of renowned "dirty T-shirt" experiments, researchers got female college students to sleep alone wearing the same T-shirts for several days during their fertile phase, and again wearing different shirts when postovulatory. Young men were then presented with these pairs of shirts, each worn by the same woman but at different reproductive phases. Sure enough, they preferred the ones worn during the follicular phase (just prior to ovulation) in 75% of the cases.[6] In addition, when the women had been taking hormonal contraceptives, which suppress ovulation, this preference disappeared.[7]

Most dramatic are some findings involving lap dancers. A number of these hard-working women were asked to keep track of two things: their ovulatory cycles and how much money they made on tips while dancing on any given night. The results were staggering, even for people who might have anticipated an effect. During a 5-hour shift while maximally fertile, the women averaged $355; when in the luteal phase (so-so fertility), they brought in $260; and while menstruating, they made a paltry $185.[8] Perhaps these women were sending pheromonal signals to which their male customers were unconsciously responding, or perhaps they unintentionally behaved more sexily as a function of their fertility; either way, they were doing something different and men were responding.

Evidence of this sort has led biologist Randy Thornhill and psychologist Steven Gangestad to claim that women do in fact experience genuine estrus like other mammals.[9] I am dubious, if only because typical mammalian estrus is so obvious that it calls to mind the comment made to someone considering purchase of a Rolls Royce: If you have to ask how much it costs, you can't afford it. If you have to debate whether estrus is occurring, it isn't. On the other hand, although human ovulation is concealed from our conscious awareness, this doesn't mean that it is totally, 100% hidden. Perhaps we should talk about an oxymoronic "cryptic estrus" or some neologism.

In any event, recent findings that women show a sexually and evolutionarily consistent suite of behavior when they are most fertile comports nicely with the "keeping control" hypothesis, described earlier, in that ironically, by concealing their ovulation— even as fertility is influencing their behavior—women might succeed in keeping control without being aware of the control that they are exercising!

As a general rule, male animals trade resources for sex, whereas females trade sex for resources. Imagine a prehistoric hominid woman who, like females of many different species, is prepared to exchange sex in return, let's say, for food. If, chimplike, she made it anatomically obvious when she was fertile, it would also be clear when she wasn't, and as a result, she might have lost some leverage otherwise available. The male might well be uninterested unless her anatomy or pheromones made her interesting. Such a female might then find herself forced to have sex with him, thereby possibly getting his genes, when all she really wanted was his banana.

On the other hand, if she didn't give obvious cues as to whether or not she was fertile, our same great-, great-, great-grandmother could get the banana and eat it, too, and even if she had to comply sexually as part of the deal, she wouldn't necessarily be committing her precious eggs into the bargain.

Sexual Liberation?

It may seem paradoxical, but by losing full-blown estrus, women may also have set the stage for having more sex, not less. Estrus-based sex is largely, if not entirely, reproductive. By severing the link between sexual intercourse and fertilization (or at least obscuring that link), concealed ovulation provides opportunities for nonreproductive sex.

This, in turn, might be part of the biological reason for concealed ovulation, if it enables couples to bond together especially tightly, to express and enhance their love via "liberated sex." But, we might ask, *why* are sex and love so tightly connected? Why don't romantic partners express and enhance their love by picking each other's lice (many primates do just that), or via beautifully coordinated, mutually satisfying bouts of highly choreographed hiccupping? One guess is that people find shared sex reinforcing to the "pair bond" for a particular reason. Hints of why can be glimpsed in other species.

Look at it this way: Why do people—and certain other animals—copulate so often? The answer may seem distressingly practical, even cynical. When we look at those other species that have frequent sex, some even more often than do human beings, we find that many (bonobos, chimpanzees, some species of dolphins, and lions excepted) are "socially monogamous" but prone to being sexually *un*faithful. Certain birds—for example, goshawks, osprey, white ibises, and acorn woodpeckers—copulate hundreds of times for every clutch of eggs. And they don't limit those copulations to their designated partners.[10]

The possible connection is as follows. When males are separated from their mates for a substantial part of each day, they risk having their female partners copulate with someone else, after which they could end up rearing another male's offspring. The sexually adventurous female, by contrast, would be risking little. After all, she is guaranteed to be the mother of her offspring, no matter how many partners she may have. But the male, by contrast, has no such automatic confidence: "Mommy's babies, Daddy's maybes." Accordingly, males who spend substantial time away from their female partners may be especially inclined to copulate frequently when they are at home, to increase the chances that their offspring are in fact theirs. We might conclude that they "love" their mates all the more when given the opportunity to make love with them. Moreover, the more loving they do, the more love they feel, with "love" in such cases defined as a powerful inclination to remain with and be devoted to one's partner. In biological terms, the greater is the confidence of shared genetic investment, the greater is the love.

Now, let's take the female's perspective, and say that the lady osprey, goshawk, or white ibis is occasionally inclined to have sex with males in addition to her mate, perhaps because her extracurricular partner is particularly able or inclined to invest in her offspring or because his genes are especially fitness enhancing. At the same time, however, she dearly wants to retain the parental assistance of her social mate. It would make sense in such cases for the female to indulge her social partner's sexual inclinations and to copulate often, if only because by assuaging his unconscious anxieties, she is more likely to obtain his continuing assistance and commitment while still remaining free to indulge her own extra-pair inclinations when her mate isn't around.

Maybe all this has nothing to do with human beings. But it is probably no coincidence that other species among which pairs copulate frequently are particularly likely to do so outside the pair bond as well. The prospect looms, therefore, that the remarkably high frequency of in-pair human sex isn't so remarkable after all, considering that human beings are more than a little prone to sexual dalliance.

So perhaps we don't advertise our ovulation, at least in part, because to do so would be to invite an unacceptably high level of sexual jealousy and obsessive mate guarding on the part of the male at these times. This would be all the more biologically awkward for females in proportion if they are somewhat inclined to infidelity . . . which they are. Women would accordingly be more fit if they didn't incite their social mates to keep too-close tabs on their sexual activities. Lacking a powerful peak of sexual desire—and of desirability—women would also have been liberated to have sex with other males, and not just their designated mates. This possibility is a variant on the earlier notion of keeping control by keeping him guessing, and it emphasizes the sexual liberation of women, but it differs in paying attention to each woman's payoff, benefits that needn't involve purchasing infanticide insurance or even sire choice, but rather, covering her tracks. Not only that, but such liberation might also free a woman to have abundant sex with her designated partner as well, in the process keeping him sexually satisfied and also less worried about his paternity—perhaps less worried than he ought to be.

Had enough? For better or worse, the above suggestions do not exhaust the many possible explanations for concealed ovulation. It has been suggested, for example, that concealed ovulation has been selected for as a means of keeping the peace. Imagine, if you will, the situation in an otherwise staid commercial office, university, or bank—or Pleistocene campfire or Ice Age cave, for that matter—if the women regularly underwent a dramatic and readily apparent transition each month when they became fertile. The resulting chaos and heightened competition might well be so disadvantageous as to give an advantage to those women whose reproductive status remained demurely incognito.

This may seem compelling, but actually it is not persuasive to most evolutionary biologists, for the simple reason that under such conditions, any benefit derived by a concealed ovulator would be shared by everyone, including those whose reproductive status was public. On the other hand, if the payoff of concealing one's ovulation rests upon keeping the peace, then presumably those who weren't thus concealed would have gained something by going public—and yet, they would be the only ones to profit as a result, while the costs of chaos would largely extend to everyone. Therefore, although concealing one's ovulation might have benefited society as a whole, it is difficult to see how it would have been selected for at the level of individuals and their genes, which is pretty much the only way natural selection works.[v]

Self-Deception and the Headache Hypothesis

There is yet another important hypothesis that remains to be considered. It is especially intriguing for several reasons. For one, it brings in a seemingly independent evolutionary mystery, namely, consciousness.[vi] For another, it confronts one of the enduring puzzles about concealed ovulation: It is one thing for ovulation to be hidden from others, but why in Darwin's name should such important, biologically crucial information be kept from the woman herself? Why is this such a deep, dark secret, one that cannot even be shared with the person who presumably has—if not a legal or moral right to the information—at least a deep personal stake in obtaining it? And finally, this last hypothesis is somewhat counterintuitive and therefore great fun to examine.

It was first suggested by Nancy Burley, an evolutionary biologist currently at the University of California, Irvine.[11] Let's assume that far enough back in the human evolutionary line, there was a range of self-awareness when it came to one's own ovulation, as there is for most things: Some women could tell when they were fertile, others—at the other extreme of the distribution—had little or no idea, and in between there was a range of ovulatory self-consciousness. Add to this the fact that among many traditional peoples today (hunter-gatherers and other members of nontechnological societies), women want fewer children than men do, mostly because of the downsides of pregnancy and childbirth, especially in an environment

---

v. We'll confront the related question of "group selection" later, in Chapter 7.

vi. More about this in Chapter 9.

lacking biomedical sophistication. The result is the following prospect: If, like today's hunter-gatherers, our ancestral grandmothers disagreed with their mates in wanting fewer offspring, then those who detected their own "time of the month" might well have made special efforts at those times to fend off the advances of our would-be ancestral grandfathers. Call it the headache hypothesis.

By succeeding in limiting their reproduction, such women would unknowingly have sabotaged the self-awareness system in which they participated. Who would have gotten pregnant? Not those who could detect their own ovulation, but those who couldn't, who were unaware of what was going on inside their own bodies. A case of matter over mind. Our maternal ancestors would thus have been those who didn't reveal cues as to whether they were ovulating but who also couldn't even tell, themselves.

Breasts: Outlining the Mystery

Next, our attention turns to breasts. In the process, we have plenty of company. Whereas the mystery of ovulation is why it is so secret, the breast question is exactly the opposite: Why so obvious? Whereas ovulation is mysterious because something so important is so hidden, breasts are mysterious because something so unimportant (most of the time) is so prominent (most of the time) and gets so much undeserved attention (nearly all the time).

The most straightforward explanation for why women have prominent breasts even when not lactating is that they signal capacity to nourish offspring, so that bustier women would have been preferentially chosen by would-be fathers. But why hasn't a similar process operated in other mammals? Except for human beings, there are no mammals in which nonlactating females sport prominent mammaries. Moreover, there is no correlation between the size of breasts, while not lactating, and the eventual ability to produce milk. This is because what appears as breast tissue is actually made up of fat; glandular structures only develop during pregnancy. But breast development among human beings occurs in conjunction with sexual maturation, and quite differently later when needed as milk producers. Why, then, do women possess such prominent additions to their anatomy?

As we have seen when talking about menstruation, even though its precise adaptive significance is still a mystery, most biologists agree that it occurs for some down-to-earth reason: to remove pathogens, maximize energy efficiency, eliminate subpar embryos, and so forth. By contrast, there does not appear to be any practical connection between the fat-filled breasts of nubile, nonpregnant, nonlactating women and their eventual role as purveyors of milk. The fat residing in human breasts is not readily mobilized into milk; under severe calorie deprivation, nursing women are far more likely to (figuratively) reach into their hips, thighs, and arms.

So, if breasts are not functionally mandated, why are they there? Or rather, why don't they develop only during pregnancy, then recede when not needed, as in all other self-respecting mammals? The most likely answer is that prominent nonlactating breasts owe their evolutionary existence in our species not so much to the off-spring they might help nourish but to men that they attract. I write this fully aware that indignant readers might complain, "There you go again, how like a man, assuming that our breasts must be pointing at them." But in fact, they probably are.

Note, for starters, that breasts are extraordinarily diverse, from huge and pendulous to small and taut, bilaterally symmetrical or not at all. Ditto for nipples, which vary in size, shape, color, and so forth. Given this remarkable structural variety, the likelihood is that breasts are not unidimensional in their biological role; otherwise, selection would almost certainly have narrowed their anatomical range.

Considering that human breasts have a very high ratio of fat to glandular tissue, a "reverse engineer" would have to conclude that milk production was not the goal. On the other hand, it is worth noting that in every human society (including avowedly bare-breasted ones), men find breasts erotically interesting, which suggests that somehow, male–female interactions—sexual selection, as Darwin termed it—must be involved.

But how? Some downright silly ideas have been advanced, one of the most notorious by British ethologist Desmond Morris in his best-selling book, *The Naked Ape*. According to Morris, conspicuous breasts evolved in part because natural selection favors emotional intimacy between men and women, as a result of the need for devoted biparental care of offspring. Most mammals mate dorsoventrally ("doggy style"), which—although feasible for human beings, too—is less personal and thus less likely to generate emotional bonding than is face-to-face intercourse. To induce ventral–ventral, face-to-face lovemaking, then, evolution supposedly favored conspicuous bilaterally paired breasts, which essentially mimic the buttocks of "normal" quadrupeds and assist in the transition from dorsoventral to frontal copulation.

I wish I could embrace such a creative idea. Frontally. But the problems are too great. For one, there is no evidence of a correlation between women's degree of breast development and their partner's preferred sexual position. In addition, many nonhuman primates—including bonobos, gorillas, and orangutans—copulate in a variety of positions, including ventral–ventral, yet in all these cases, females are flat-chested. The supposed connection between sex while looking into each other's eyes and devoted monogamy also appears to be sheer fantasy. Monogamy is rare among mammals, but when it occurs, in some species of foxes, beavers, otters, the California mouse, pygmy marmoset, and certain oddballs including the fat-tailed dwarf lemur and Malagasy giant jumping rat, the pairs mate dorsoventrally. So prominent breasts aren't necessary for frontal mating, and frontal mating isn't needed for pair bonding.

It is also difficult to imagine that males of any species, including our own, have ever needed the visual image of female buttocks to feel horny. Behavior and pheromones are more than sufficient. Not only that, but mammalian buttocks aren't naked, rounded globes but rather flattened and hair-covered . . . in short, not very breastlike.

For another exercise in foolishness, author Elaine Morgan has long championed the bizarre idea that people evolved as "aquatic apes," with breasts evolving as flotation devices.[12] After all, during World War II, sailors called their life vests "Mae Wests." Floating babies might have clung to their mother's breasts as to water wings. And presumably men would have done the same; even now, they do so whenever they can! Seriously, however, if breasts evolved as life preservers, then men ought to have evolved them, too. Let's return to reality.

Maybe human breasts evolved as calorie storage sites, a kind of pantry that preceded refrigeration. If so, then the ample breasts of Earth Mother Goddesses would certainly have been preferred over those of today's anorexic fashion models. There is a generally close correspondence between what people find sexually appealing and what ultimately leads to reproductive success, and so, it is not unlikely that our male ancestors preferred sexual partners whose well-upholstered bosoms suggested the ability to survive hard times, not to mention promising abundant nourishment for any eventual offspring.

But there are problems here as well. For one thing, breasts are unlikely to have evolved as storage sites; if calorie storage was evolution's intent, it would have been far more efficient to use the hips, butt, or upper arms, where tissue could have been wrapped securely around bone instead of being left unsupported. (Any physically active woman will confirm that breasts are often a distinct liability.) Moreover, as we have already seen, fatty breast tissue doesn't contribute to making milk and nonlactating breasts—whose prominence we are trying to explain—are composed almost entirely of fat.

A Question of Deception?

This leads to the fascinating, albeit dispiriting, proposition that breasts evolved as a kind of biological deception, with women taking advantage of male obtuseness by promising an amply-stocked, milk-soaked delicatessen that they may or may not be able to provide. Since breasts do in fact increase dramatically in size while lactating, it is not unreasonable that prehistoric men noticed and were readily persuaded to mate preferentially with women whose anatomy suggested more nourishment for the consequence of their mating. Even if guilty of false advertising, such a system could have worked, assuming that there was competition among women for access to the most desirable men and that these men, in turn, preferred big-busted women, even if such women likely promised more than they delivered.

Even under this scenario, men would not have been entirely helpless. To minimize being completely beguiled by the substitution of fat for gland, men have evidently evolved a fondness for the classic female "hourglass" figure, with narrow waist and relatively wide hips. Since fat does accumulate in the waist, a comparatively high waist-to-hip ratio indicates overall body fat, and it turns out that cross-culturally, men prefer a waist-to-hip ratio of 70% or even lower.[13]

There are a few exceptions, including an Andean population in which men prefer more "tubular" women, but the overall world-wide preference is remarkably consistent. There has even been constancy over time. Measurements of ancient statues and paintings have confirmed that whether the societal norm favored a well-upholstered female form, á la Rubens, or absurdly slender, like current Western supermodels, the preferred .70 ratio has remained quite steady.[14]

These findings, however interesting and suggestive, do not prove anything. In particular, the fact that men prefer "shapely" women does not necessarily tell us how they got to be shapely in the first place, which is our goal. If women's body shape evolved for some entirely separate reason, it is plausible—indeed, likely—that men's preference would have gone along, simply because men who invested preferentially in women with those traits would have been rewarded with greater reproductive success—of which one consequence would be yet more women constructed that way.

On the other hand, breasts might nonetheless provide accurate information, indicating a woman's ability to accumulate and store calories. Pleistocene-era women who already had enough nutrition on board to readily expand their breasts—even if simply via fat deposition—would have been the most likely to stimulate males to provide yet more. This idea is especially compelling because it hints at a possible explanation for why prominent nonlactating breasts are so characteristic of human beings and not other mammals. The "explanation," if valid, makes use of another trait that is especially characteristic of *Homo sapiens*: our intellect and imagination. Thus, it seems almost certain that prehistoric men would have noticed that lactating women develop enlarged breasts, and not unlikely that human cognition would therefore have made an association between large breastedness and effective milk production (even though such a correlation, as we have seen, turns out to be spurious).

And so, an early hominid female in a position to benefit from storing fat somewhere on her body might as well have done so via her breasts, to stimulate additional male investment . . . all the more so insofar as men would have been predisposed to prefer women with relatively prominent breasts.

This brings to mind what has been called the "banker's paradox," so named because banks are least favorably disposed toward those prospective borrowers who especially need a loan, because the more needy the would-be borrower, the more liable he is to be a poor credit risk. Conversely, they eagerly bestow funds upon the wealthy, who need it least. In short, those who have, and don't need much more, get. Something along these lines may have induced evolution to exaggerate the breasts of early female hominids, because those thereby endowed would have profited from the increased self-interested largesse of men, inclined to "lend" resources to a prospective mate deemed to be a good investment— whether or not they really are.

Honest Signaling?

We turn now to breast evolution as an example of honest signaling. Happily, for anyone predisposed toward telling the truth, it may well be that honesty is the best policy, not just ethically, but also evolutionarily. There are, in fact, several ways in which human breasts may have evolved in the service of honest sexual selection.

A variety of hypotheses revolve around the concept that breasts evolved because they accurately signal the genetic quality of the woman bearing them (or, baring them). For one, they are prominently displayed, left and right, and thus readily judged as more or less symmetric. A spate of research has shown that among many nonhuman animals and human beings as well, sexual and romantic desirability correlates with degree of body symmetry: Attractive bodies and faces are those in which the left and right sides match closely.[15] This makes sense, because body symmetry itself correlates with a low level of deleterious mutations and parasites, raising the possibility that pronounced breast development was favored as a kind of "honest signal" whereby women displayed their symmetry (and hence, their health) to men.

Recent studies, interestingly, have lent support to this conjecture: For example, women with symmetrical breasts have greater

fertility than do their less balanced counterparts.[16] Men who preferred women with symmetrical breasts could well have experienced an evolutionary benefit as a result, and such a male preference
could have impacted female anatomy, especially if the preference
was manifested by men who were themselves likely to confer added
fitness upon their preferred sexual partners.

An interesting wrinkle here is that larger breasts are more
likely to be asymmetric than are smaller ones,[17] a finding that is
difficult to interpret: Is it because whatever causes enhanced
asymmetry also generates increased size? Or might it be that
greater size is simply more likely to reveal any underlying differences? Either way, just as men frequently worry about penis size,
women often obsess about whether their breasts are suitably
symmetrical. Indeed, one typically unmentioned but nonetheless
genuine cosmetic payoff of brassieres is to obscure underlying
breast asymmetries.

But why might women have gone along with being judged and
evaluated in this way? Wouldn't they be better off obscuring any
imperfections rather than presenting them conspicuously and
literally right up front, side by side for everyone to see? For one
thing, if attractively symmetrical women displayed their charms,
whereupon men insisted on making a similar assessment when it
comes to making a sexual choice, then other women may have had
little alternative but to go along, at least if they wanted a chance
with the more desirable men.

Even then, increased breast size could have evolved as part of a
female counterstrategy. Consider two very small breasts on the
same woman; one has a volume of 75 ml and the other, 100 ml.
Such a 25% disparity would be readily apparent. By contrast, if
the breasts in question were expanded to, say, 475 and 500 ml, the
asymmetry between them would be significantly obscured. The
evolution of women's breasts may accordingly have involved
making it more difficult for men to assess their breasts by, paradoxically, making them *more* prominent.

It is also possible that breasts evolved as a way of signaling female
quality and desirability, independent of symmetry. At issue in this
approach is what the great evolutionary theorist R. A. Fisher called
"residual reproductive value,"[18] which is essentially an individual's
future breeding potential: For women, residual reproductive value

is highest in the early stages of reproductive capability. It then declines with age and eventually approaches zero at menopause. Not coincidentally, sexual attractiveness as subjectively measured by people's judgment closely tracks objective measures of residual reproductive value.

It can be predicted with some confidence that when it comes to a one-night stand or equivalent, men would prefer females at peak immediate fertility, as is the case among most mammals. (Among human beings, this would be at about age 21.) On the other hand, with the prospect of long-term bonding, we would expect males to prefer females with maximum reproductive value, that is, who are just entering maturity and have the largest possible reproductive future ahead of them. Too young? She isn't yet ovulating. Too old? She's no longer ovulating. The ideal is just right.[19]

Given that women conceal their ovulation, how are men to know when a prospective romantic partner is old enough to be a reproductive prospect? Maybe by her breasts, which are as anatomically prominent as her ovulation is hidden. And how are men to know when a prospective romantic partner is probably too old? Once again, maybe by her breasts: After all, mature women ruefully acknowledge that feminine aging mandates a progressively failing battle against gravity.

It seems a bit strange that men should be so obtuse as to need ripening breasts to announce reproductive competence. Among other species, males have little or no difficulty telling who is and who is not sexually mature. But then again, our sense of smell is retarded as mammals go, and given that ovulation itself is notoriously concealed in our species, perhaps breast development has evolved to fill the gap and provide information not otherwise available.

Crucially important for what I dub the Goldilocks hypothesis is that such a signal would be difficult to fake[vii]: Undeveloped breasts clearly indicate sexual immaturity, whereas sagging indicates age. If so, then men should prefer breasts that are relatively plump and that therefore provide comparatively honest information as to sexual maturity. As with the symmetry situation, women would to some extent be constrained to go along, especially insofar as the

---

vii. At least, during the eons that preceded the invention of "push-up bras" and cosmetic surgery.

most desirable men (those likely to contribute positively to a woman's reproductive success) were turned on by breasts—and, by extension, their owners—that are not too young, not too old, but just right, prominent but not too droopy.

Larger breasts will naturally sag over time. Hence, it is easier to judge the age of a large-breasted woman than one whose bosom is less "developed." This in itself could have induced men to prefer larger breasts, since they provide more reliable information. Breasts that were protruding but also firm would be one way that women could advertise their youth, thereby attracting a larger number of admiring males from which they could then choose. Older women would accordingly be better off having smaller breasts, since this would help them obscure their age. But there is no getting around the fact that connective tissue stretches and weakens with the years, and, moreover, it appears to be anatomically impossible to go from large firm breasts when young to smaller, equally firm and perky ones in old age. In addition, selection wouldn't work against a trait that conveys substantial benefit early in one's reproductive career even if it becomes costly later, when an individual wouldn't be able to breed in any event.

From Sexy Sons to Doughty Daughters

Finally, my favorite hypothesis, which I confess to admiring for reasons that go beyond scientific plausibility. For one thing, it is my own. And for another, it makes use of two important ideas in evolutionary biology—ideas that so far have been used to explain certain male traits—and turns them around, applying them to women.

The first is known as the "sexy son hypothesis."[20] It has emerged as a cornerstone of sexual selection theory, which—ever since Darwin—has struggled to explain the existence of bizarre, exaggerated male traits. The problem is that such characteristics as the elaborate, gaudy tail feathers of a peacock appear to constitute an evolutionary liability rather than an asset. Feathered finery requires a lot of metabolic energy to grow and maintain, while also subjecting its owners to such risks as getting tangled in vegetation and making their possessors more apparent to predators.

Sexual selection theory was developed to explain the peacock's tail and other comparable anomalies; its key concept is that if a trait makes its owner sufficiently attractive to members of the opposite sex, this can more than make up for any detriment to survival, so long as the bottom line—genetic representation in future generations—remains positive.

But biologists still needed to explain why females should be endowed with such preferences. It isn't sufficient simply to claim, as Darwin did, that members of the "fair sex" are naturally possessed of greater aesthetic perceptiveness. Enter the sexy son hypothesis, which says that the peahen was selected to prefer fancy-plumed peacocks because this would increase the chances that her male offspring would inherit a comparably impressive tail and would therefore be especially attractive to the next generation of peahens. Females who mate preferentially with sexy males would become the mothers of sexy sons, who would reward their mothers' preferences by providing more grandchildren.

What about applying the sexy son hypothesis, inverted, to human beings? Instead of peahens choosing peacocks, substitute men choosing women, and instead of fancy tails, make it prominent nonlactating breasts. Instead of sexy sons, think doughty daughters.

The original sexy son hypothesis did not speak to what originally started the process, what first induced females of a given species to prefer a particular plumage, wattle, or bright color pattern among males. It simply emphasized that once such a preference developed, whatever its source, it could be maintained and even enhanced via sexual selection. On the other hand, I have already suggested several different factors that might have initiated the evolution of at least slightly pronounced nonlactating breasts. Whatever started things off, male preference for ample-breasted women could in theory have maintained and even enhanced female breast size if the doughty daughters thereby produced would themselves have been somewhat more attractive to the next generation of men. Inverting the sexy son hypothesis, men who preferred women with conspicuous nonlactating breasts would have fathered daughters who also had prominent breasts; if the succeeding generation of men exhibited preferences like their fathers, such doughty daughters would have rewarded their fathers' preferences via increased numbers of grandchildren produced by those daughters once they grew up to be sexually enticing and thus reproductively successful young women.

Enter, now, the second relevant idea from evolutionary behavioral biology. Called the "handicap principle," it suggests a particular reason why males—of any generation—might be selected to include prominent breasts among those female traits found to be sexually enticing. The handicap principle is a powerful and important concept, which speaks to one of the often-unappreciated complications of animal communication: the problem of truth versus lies, of honesty versus deceit.[21]

In the past, biologists assumed that animal communication was simply a matter of one individual—the sender—attempting to convey accurate information, and another—the receiver—figuring it out. Fair enough, it seemed, until biologists began unraveling the evolutionary process and came to realize that natural selection operates most powerfully at the level of individuals and their constituent genes. Although there might be a payoff for all concerned if communication proceeds smoothly, there is no inherent reason for a sender to tell the truth. Instead, his or her goal is to do whatever it takes to enhance the success of his or her genes, which might well involve manipulating the receiver rather than providing accurate information.

This, in turn, would place a premium on communication that cannot be faked, that possesses a "reliability component." For example, an additional reason for peahens to preferentially choose peacocks with fancy tails—besides the prospect of thereby begetting sexy sons—might well be, ironically, that these tails are such a handicap. In order to thrive *despite* so much feathered finery, according to the handicap principle, the male in question must be quite a guy! He might simply claim to be unusually sturdy or mutation-free, but talk is cheap. By functioning effectively despite being encumbered by this handicap, the elaborately ornamented peacock proves his quality.

The handicap principle could help explain the evolution of prominent breasts if we add it to the doughty daughter concept. The idea is that when not lactating, developed breasts may in fact be a handicap, which might be just the point. Like the peacock's tail, perhaps breasts signal an ability to function effectively *in spite of* having to grow them and then carry them around. A woman who shows herself capable of surviving and prospering despite her mammary handicap—who was, in a sense, so genetically "wealthy" that she could grow wasteful and troublesome breasts for no survival benefit at all—must be a quality individual indeed. If chosen by high-quality males, her daughters would then likely be similarly endowed, not just with breasts, but also with the ability to flourish in spite of them.

Here is a further consideration, something that initially appears to be a problem with the doughty daughter hypothesis, but which can perhaps be reconciled after all. In the original sexy son version, these sons don't only inherit their fathers' presumed greater viability, but they also get the handicap. If so, and if along with a viable genotype, one's offspring is also encumbered by some sort of elaborate secondary sexual trait (such as the peacock's tail), where is the payoff? One way around this difficulty is if the immediate beneficiaries of a sexy son process aren't those sons, but the daughters, who are likely to gain their father's superior genes without having to cope with his sexually selected handicap (a weirdly fancy tail, or whatever, which only shows up in males). By the same token, it is possible that when men chose elaborately ornamented women (i.e., those with conspicuous nonlactating breast tissue), their sons would have been the real beneficiaries since they would have inherited their mother's ability to flourish despite those awkward mammaries, without the handicap of actually having to produce or cart them around.

There is yet another problem with converting the sexy son hypothesis into its doughty daughter equivalent: Those sexy sons are especially likely to convey a fitness reward to their parents because in most species, males have a particularly high variance in reproductive success. A small number of successful sons can have a disproportionate effect on their parents' fitness since some males have more than their share of offspring, while others have less. By contrast, there is less difference between the most successful females and the least. As far as we know, this is why males are overwhelmingly the more sexually selected sex.

But human beings might be different, at least somewhat. There is no other species of mammal in which the male contributes so much to rearing successful offspring. As a result, it behooves women to be attractive to men, and not just vice versa, as in most traditional evolutionary models of mate selection. The greater the significance of male investment for the success of offspring, the more important it is for females to signal their quality to any prospective mates. And maybe growing full breasts (regardless of what may have initiated this trend) might be one way they accomplish this.

Female sexuality undoubtedly offers a range of evolutionary mysteries, with each mystery susceptible to a variety of explanations. In the next chapter, we examine two more such mysteries, as well as exploring some of their male counterparts.

Notes

1. Murphy, T. (Trans.). (2004). *Pliny the Elder's natural history*. New York: Oxford University Press.
2. Profet, M. (1993). Menstruation as a defense against pathogens transported by sperm. *Quarterly Review of Biology, 68*(3), 335–386.
3. Strassmann, B. J. (1996). The evolution of endometrial cycles and menstruation. *Quarterly Review of Biology, 71*, 181–209.
4. Sillén-Tulberg, B., & Möller, A. P. (1993). The relationship between concealed ovulation and mating systems in anthropoid primates: A phylogenetic analysis. *The American Naturalist, 141*, 1–25.
5. Thornhill, R., & Gangestad, S. W. (2008). *The evolutionary biology of human female sexuality*. New York: Oxford University Press.
6. Singh, D., & Bronstad, P. M. (2001). Female body odour is a potential cue to ovulation. *Proceedings of the Royal Society of London B, 268*, 797–801.
7. Kuukasjärvi, S., Peter Eriksson, P. J., Koskela, E., Mappes, T., Nissinen, K., & Rantala, M. J (2004). Attractiveness of women's body odors over the menstrual cycle: The role of oral contraception and received sex. *Behavioural Ecology, 15*, 579–584.
8. Miller, G. N., Tybur, J. M., & Jordan, B. D. (2007). Ovulatory cycle effects on tip earnings by lap dancers: Economic evidence for human estrus? *Evolution and Human Behavior, 28*, 375–381.
9. Thornhill, R., & Gangestad, S. (2008). *The evolutionary biology of human female sexuality*. New York: Oxford University Press.
10. Barash, D. P., & Lipton, J. E. (2002). *The myth of monogamy: Fidelity and infidelity in animals and people*. New York: Henry Holt.
11. Burley, N. (1979). The evolution of concealed ovulation. *The American Naturalist, 114*, 835–858.
12. Morgan, E. (1997). *The aquatic ape hypothesis*. New York: Penguin
13. For example, Singh, D., & Randall, P. (2007). Beauty is in the eye of the plastic surgeon: Waist–hip ratio (WHR) and women's attractiveness. *Personality and Individual Differences, 43*, 329–340.

14. Gangestad, S. W., & Scheyd, G. J. (2005). The evolution of human physical attractiveness. *Annual Review of Anthropology, 34,* 523–548.
15. For example, Möller, A. P., & Thornhill, R. (1998). Bilateral symmetry and sexual selection: A meta-analysis. *The American Naturalist, 151*(2), 174–192; Rhodes, G., Yoshikawa, S., Palermo, R., Simmons, L. W., Peters, M., Lee, K., et al. (2007). Perceived health contributes to the attractiveness of facial symmetry, averageness, and sexual dimorphism. *Perception, 36,* 1244–1252.
16. Byrd-Craven, J., Geary, D. C., & Vigil, J. (2004). Evolution of human mate choice. *Journal of Sex Research, 41*(1), 117–144.
17. Moller, A. P., Soler, M., & Thornhill, R. (1995). Breast asymmetry, sexual selection, and human reproductive success. *Ethology and Sociobiology, 16,* 207–219.
18. Fisher, R. A. (1958). *The genetical theory of natural selection.* New York: Dover.
19. Marlowe, F. (1998). The nubility hypothesis: The human breast as an honest signal of residual reproductive value. *Human Nature, 9,* 263–271.
20. Weatherhead, P. J., & Robertson, R. J. (1979). Offspring quality and the polygyny threshold: "The sexy son hypothesis." *The American Naturalist, 113,* 201–208.
21. Zahavi, A., Zahavi, A., Ely, N., & Ely, M. P. (1999). *The handicap principle: A missing piece of Darwin's puzzle.* New York: Oxford University Press.

CHAPTER THREE

Sexual Mysteries II: Female Orgasm, Menopause, and Men

NEXT: FEMALE ORGASM. What is *that* all about?

There is a Spanish expression, "Hay que gozar mucho para desquitarse de la vida" (*You need to have a lot of fun to get even with life*). Whether or not you agree, it isn't enough to say that female orgasm exists because it is great fun, or a gift from a benevolent God with an assist from a satisfying partner—when not self-induced—along with a delightfully cooperating personal physiology. Life throws us a lot of curveballs, making it tempting to conclude that some of the good stuff, like orgasms, are simply there to make up for it. Not so fast.

There is no doubt that orgasm feels good. Think of Meg Ryan's famous simulated orgasm-in-the-restaurant scene in the movie *When Harry Met Sally* (after which a middle-aged diner says to the waiter, "I'll have what she's having"). We'll look at fake orgasm later; for now, our point is simply that the real thing cannot simply be written off as good fortune or a surprising culinary consequence of choosing the right menu item while having a meal with Billy Crystal. Nowhere in the biological world is pleasure bestowed cheaply or randomly or out of mere cosmic generosity.

When asked, many women say that orgasm is a great tension reliever. True enough, but this doesn't mean that tension relief is the *reason* for orgasm, since if sexual tension hadn't accumulated in the first place, it wouldn't have needed releasing. And why do it that way?

The reality is that female orgasm is a contentious, unsolved mystery among evolutionary biologists, simply because its adaptive significance—its biological payoff—is obscure.

Events on the male side pretty much speak for themselves. Even though orgasm (a subjectively experienced phenomenon) is technically different from ejaculation (expulsion of semen from the body), it occasions no great surprise that for men the two are tightly connected, and that evolution has doubtless contrived to use the former as a carrot, inducing men to engage in the latter. But what about women?

Why Orgasm Is a Womanly Mystery

Of course, not all women experience orgasm, and that is part of the mystery, although not as one might think: The enigma of female orgasm is *not* why some women don't climax but why some *do*. The data are quite clear that unlike its male counterpart, female orgasm isn't necessary for reproduction; among the many complaints of nonorgasmic women, inability to conceive is not one.

For generations, old and young wives' tales—husbands', too—along with scores of Victorian romance novels claimed that there was some sort of connection between a woman "really giving" herself and finally becoming pregnant. And to be sure, it is easy to speculate how female orgasm might facilitate fertilization, especially if the waves of muscular contraction provide greater access of sperm to egg. The problem, however, is that most of these contractions go in the wrong direction! It has alternatively been claimed that uterine contractions during orgasm literally generate a suction effect, which draws semen up toward the fallopian tubes. There may yet be some truth to this rather inelegantly named "uterine upsuck" hypothesis, which was generated by heroic laboratory research in which a radio telemetry device was inserted into a uterus, thereby revealing a vacuum cleaner–like negative pressure following orgasm.[1] This "finding," however, was based on an unacceptably small sample size: one woman!

Moreover, even if uterine upsuck turns out to be a valid phenomenon, it is far from what scientists call a "robust" one, or else it would have been noted previously. More to the point, it would have generated a cause-and-effect relationship between female orgasm and subsequent pregnancy, which simply does not exist.

It has also been suggested—although again, the data are inconclusive—that orgasm reduces the amount of "flow-back" (the leakage of semen out of a woman's reproductive tract), thereby increasing the likelihood that fertilization will be achieved by the partner who helped induce that orgasm.[2] But this, too, is controversial, based on a very small sample of remarkably cooperative couples.

Although there are, in theory, many ways by which female orgasm could facilitate fertilization (including a range of possible biochemical effects along with physical assistance to sperm or egg), there is currently no evidence that orgasmic women produce more babies, or better ones, than their less fortunate "sisters." And of course, in vitro fertilization further italicizes that when it comes to baby making, female orgasm is simply not a physiologic or anatomic prerequisite.

On the other hand, female orgasms are unquestionably real and are, if anything, more dramatic than their male counterparts, especially given a woman's capacity for multiple orgasms. Given that there are no free lunches in biology, the question presents itself: Why orgasm?

Some Easy-to-Exclude Hypotheses

The redoubtable Desmond Morris, whose fertile imagination gave us the "buttocks mimic" hypothesis for the evolution of breasts, unburdened himself of yet another howler, proposing that orgasm is natural selection's way of keeping a woman horizontal after sex, which in turn supposedly makes fertilization more likely. This "knock-down" hypothesis has problems. For one, despite substantial efforts, it has never been demonstrated that postcoital positions influence fertilization. And if they did, there are lots of possible ways of inducing individuals to remain prone, or supine, or on one's side, etc., such as reducing blood pressure after sex, without any particular subjective bells and whistles. Moreover, if our upright posture somehow necessitates such an intervention, then other upright animals should behave similarly, yet kangaroos and wallabies pop right up and hop about immediately after copulating.

It might similarly be suggested that under more "natural" conditions, orgasm would have made a postcopulatory woman less conspicuous to predators, perhaps by making her somewhat less physically active following sex. The problem here is that if the strategic goal is to remain below the perceptual horizon of potential predators, who might have been attracted to all that commotion in the bushes, it would be far more efficient to eliminate female orgasm altogether, which seems likely to have contributed significantly to the ruckus in the first place. If our ancient ancestors were being prodded by natural selection to keep from being detected—by potentially jealous conspecifics as well as predators— they would seem better advised to keep quiet and minimally aroused all along.

Another possibility, superficially plausible but ultimately unconvincing, is that orgasm is an evolutionary tactic to induce women to copulate at all. The biggest problem here is that there are many animals that lack anything resembling the bells and whistles of female orgasm, and for whom copulation is a dutiful but unexciting act. Instead, they copulate with the same resignation (occasionally mixed with moderate enthusiasm) with which they might build a nest, feed their offspring, or defecate. Orgasm clearly isn't a prerequisite for copulation. Why should we, more than any other species, require profound waves of cataclysmic ecstasy to do what other animals do simply as a matter of course, like scratching when they itch?

Maybe our extraordinary development of female orgasm—and although it is not unique to *Homo sapiens*, it is without doubt uniquely elaborated and more fully developed in our species than in any other—has something to do with that other uniquely human trait, consciousness. In the previous chapter we considered the hypothesis that concealed ovulation might have evolved because prehistoric women were aware of the downsides of pregnancy, causing natural selection to favor those women who couldn't tell when they were fertile. Isn't it also possible that this same awareness, on the part of ancestral women, would have made them hesitant to engage in sex at all?

With great insight comes great reluctance. If so, natural selection might well have favored orgasm as a reward, a tactic getting women to make love when—being in a sense too smart for their own evolutionary good—they otherwise might have declined. Maybe in the distant past evolution favored women who found sex especially rewarding—that is, orgasmically so—even if these days, for whatever reason, the connection has been loosened.

Philip Larkin once defined sex as an attempt to get "someone else to blow your own nose for you," a perspective that is provocative, even comical, but that may ultimately tell us less about sex than about Mr. Larkin himself (who was, by all accounts, as despicable a human being as he was admirable as a poet). It seems unlikely that sexual relations among two emotionally healthy human beings are motivated solely by each seeking to get his or her nose blown by the other, just as it seems highly likely that by virtue of his egocentric self-concern, Larkin was a lousy lover.

In this regard, it would be interesting to see whether orgasm actually motivates sex: whether those who are orgasmic engage in more coitus than those who are nonorgasmic, and whether multiply orgasmic women are more sexually active than one-at-a-timers. Even if this turns out to be the case, it wouldn't necessarily mean that orgasm evolved to get women to engage in intercourse. In a renowned essay titled *Knight's Move*, literary theorist Viktor Shklovsky pointed out that "If you take hold of a samovar by its stubby legs, you can use it to pound nails, but that is not its primary function." Shklovsky went on to note that during the Russian civil war,

> With my own hands I stoked stoves with pieces of a piano . . . and made bonfires out of rugs and fed the flames with vegetable oil while trapped in the mountains of Kurdistan. Right now I'm stoking a stove with books. . . . But it's wrong to view a samovar with an eye to making it pound nails more easily or to write books so that they will make a hotter fire.[3]

Almost certainly, it is equally wrong to view the female orgasm as designed to induce sexual intercourse, just because it may provide an occasional payoff for doing so. The question of orgasm's "primary function" remains open.

A Nonadaptive By-Product?

Also open is an important possibility, analogous to what scientists call the "null hypothesis," which is to say, the possibility that nothing especially interesting is going on. Much of evolutionary biology involves searching for the adaptive significance of things, whether structure, physiology, or behavior. But we must always consider the chance that a trait in question has no adaptive significance at all, that it does not owe its existence to the direct action of natural selection.

This prospect has been raised with regard to female orgasm, first by anthropologist Donald Symons,[4] then by paleontologist/author Stephen Jay Gould,[5] and later by philosopher of science Lisa Lloyd.[6] Their argument is that female orgasm does not owe its existence to any biological payoff associated with it, but rather to the fact that it is a nonadaptive tag-along trait, unavoidably linked to what really matters, namely, male orgasm. It is a claim that must be taken seriously, if only because to be sure, not all traits have been selected for in themselves; some occur simply because of an unavoidable connection with something else (in which case the "something else" typically *is* adaptive).

At first blush, it might seem absurd and demeaning of women as well to claim that women's orgasms are merely secondary by-products to the Real Thing—namely, orgasm in men. Indeed, it is reminiscent of Simone de Beauvoir's contention that women are the "second sex," an eternal Other compared to men who are genuine Subjects, where the Real Action resides. The "by-product" hypothesis points, however, to a powerful metaphor: the case of male nipples. Men don't lactate, so why do they have nipples? The classic and almost certainly correct answer is: because women have nipples, and they do lactate, and the complex developmental pathway during human embryology that eventually gives rise to nipples in women necessarily engenders nipples in men, too, where they are unnecessary, unselected for, and even downright silly. Although no one claims that orgasms are silly, those who deny adaptational status maintain that they are like male nipples, without biological significance in themselves, and that they exist only because they are tightly bound to something strongly selected for in the opposite sex.

The by-product hypothesis has a superficial plausibility. Embryonic development is typically a package deal, with various traits dependent on preceding stages. Since male and female embryos undergo a common developmental pathway, it would be a major fitness burden to interfere and redesign an unnecessary independent pathway that led to nipple-less men. After all, if nipples don't do any good, at least they don't do any harm, so presumably they are simply along for the ride. If they caused trouble, perhaps if they frequently became cancerous or if they required a lot of metabolic energy to create and maintain, they doubtless would have been selected against, but they ain't broke—merely irrelevant—so evolution hasn't fixed them. The same applies, or so it is claimed, to female orgasm.

This idea isn't quite as ridiculous as it seems. Just as male orgasm and ejaculation occurs when the penis is suitably stimulated, female orgasm is intimately linked to stimulation of the clitoris, and the penis and clitoris both derive from the same undifferentiated embryonic tissue, called the genital ridge. Both penis and clitoris are therefore richly endowed with nerves and with parallel brain mechanisms that respond—orgasmically—to enough of the right input from them. It's just that in one case (men) that response is adaptive, whereas in the other (women) it is essentially an evolutionary hitchhiker.

Although the by-product hypothesis deserves respectful attention, it is almost certainly incorrect. For one thing, a potential parallel with male nipples proves nothing. Men's nipples are small and inconspicuous, as befits a by-product upon which selection has been reduced. By contrast, female orgasm is complex, highly elaborated, and downright Technicolor compared to its relatively feeble male counterpart. Rather than existing as an insignificant, pale imitation of where the genuine action is supposed to be (in men), female orgasm shows every sign of having been structured and fine-tuned by evolution. Given its multidimensional intensity and repeatability, it seems downright absurd to relegate female orgasm to the role of mere tag-along hitchhiker while crediting male orgasm as the Real McCoy.[i]

For another thing, women's orgasms are unlike men's nipples in that they aren't always there. There are no nipple-less men, but lots of anorgasmic women. Nor are there any men who develop nipples some of the time, although there are lots of women—the great majority—who experience orgasm only sometimes. Male nipples, by all accounts an unavoidable consequence of human embryology, are persistent, albeit nonfunctional. Female orgasms are not consistent; paradoxically, as we shall see, this may be part of their ultimate functionality.

As to the clitoris, it has, by some estimates, more than 8,000 nerve endings, exceeding that found anywhere else in the human body and approximately double that of the penis. Its only known function is sexual sensation and orgasm. If the clitoris (and thus the orgasmic consequence of stimulating it) exists merely as an unavoidable by-product of selection to produce the penis, why is the former *better* endowed neuronally than the latter? In fact, a case could be made that male orgasm isn't nearly as necessary as many people assume; there is no reason, for example, why ejaculation couldn't be as unexciting as, say, urination—something biologically necessary and which is therefore prompted by feelings of urgency but without any orgasmic *sturm und drang*.

It has also been claimed that women's orgasm couldn't possibly be adaptive since it isn't consistently evoked during heterosexual encounters. Indeed, according to a recent study, about one third of women report never being orgasmic during sexual intercourse, compared to only about 20% during masturbation; in other words, about 67% *are* orgasmic, at least on occasion, during intercourse, whereas 80% regularly experience orgasm as a result of masturbation.[7] This rather inelegantly named "intercourse-orgasm discrepancy" supposedly bespeaks the evolutionary irrelevance of orgasm,

---

i. One of my biological colleagues has suggested that anyone who seriously thinks of female orgasm as merely an evolutionary shadow of male orgasm is either a woman who has never had one or a man who has never been with a woman who has had one.

but as we shall see, it actually relates quite well to the second "evaluation hypothesis," which we shall meet in just a moment.

For now, note that plenty of things that occur intermittently are nonetheless adaptive. Wolves don't always succeed when they initiate a hunt—sometimes the moose gets away—but going hunting is clearly adaptive for a hungry wolf! In fact, psychologists understand that a degree of unpredictability actually adds to the effectiveness of a stimulus: So-called "intermittent reinforcements" are often more potent than is a guaranteed payoff. The fact that some orgasms "get away" doesn't make them any less biologically relevant.

For many women orgasms are more reliably evoked digitally or orally, rather than by an inserted penis, and primarily via the clitoris rather than the vagina. This, too, supposedly makes it less likely that orgasm evolved with heterosexual intercourse in mind. But in fact, it is entirely consistent with biological reality for a trait, having evolved in one context, to function also in another. The fact that orgasm is more readily induced by oral, digital, or mechanical stimulation of the clitoris than by a penis entering the vagina suggests, among other things, that evolution isn't always maximally efficient, not that orgasm isn't an adaptation.

If the clitoris were lodged inside the vagina instead of just outside, then women would doubtless find themselves more inclined to climax as a result of vaginal penetration. But because of embryologic constraints, the genital ridge—which eventually differentiates into either clitoris or penis—doesn't end up there. So, resourceful human beings (as well as several species of nonhuman primates) have discovered other, more efficient ways to stimulate their clitoris, thus achieving an outcome also available via other means. In short, female orgasm is indeed not well designed to be reliably elicited by penile–vaginal intercourse. Under various scenarios, it might be more adaptive yet—and certainly, more convenient for those involved—if women could achieve orgasm by hearing music, wrinkling their noses, eating chocolate, and so forth, but insofar as orgasms are keyed to penises and clitorises, that's what natural selection has had to work with. Penis and vagina are a nice lock-and-key pair, satisfying both evolutionarily and personally. The fact that for women, fingers or tongue upon clitoris are typically even more satisfying doesn't undermine the adaptive significance of either heterosexual intercourse or of the female sexual response, however evoked.

Many women don't achieve orgasm, but perhaps they could, in the right circumstances. Some, presumably, cannot do so at all. This, too, doesn't mean that orgasm isn't an adaptation. Most people can run and jump, whereas some can't—and of these, some probably never will. But this doesn't mean that the capacity to run and jump isn't adaptive, and that the suite of anatomy and behavior enabling most healthy people to do so hasn't been produced by natural selection. It turns out that women experiencing sexual dysfunction are liable to have substantially reduced clitoral innervation via the pudendal nerve.[8] Accordingly, just as there are natural athletes and the rest of us—even though a degree of athleticism has almost certainly been promoted by evolution—there may well be natural sexual athletes, too. And, unfortunately for them, there are those whose neuronal functioning is suboptimal, not necessarily because evolution doesn't favor the higher performers, but rather because many biological traits are distributed across a continuum. Not everyone is an Olympic champion; indeed, as we shall soon see, those who are—that is, women who achieve orgasm with every sexual encounter—are probably less likely to be the focus of natural selection than are those who fall in the "sometimes" category.

An Inducement for Polyandry . . . or Monogamy?

Let's make the reasonable assumption that female orgasm is not an evolutionarily irrelevant by-product or hanger-on, and that by contrast, it is adaptive, which is to say, it evolved. But why?

Earlier, we considered Sara Hrdy's suggestion that concealed ovulation may have evolved to facilitate females' mating with multiple male partners, so as to take out infanticide insurance. Dr. Hrdy has also interrogated female orgasm, noting that "there is a disconcerting mismatch between a female capable of multiple sequential orgasms and a male partner typically capable of one climax per copulatory bout,"[9] and concluding that one potential consequence of this "mismatch" is that females would be inclined to seek multiple partners to achieve their orgasmic potential. This could be yet another clause in a would-be infanticide insurance policy, a proximate mechanism spurring females to ultimately enhance the likely survivorship of their offspring.

As Hrdy put it,

> It is possible that as in baboons and chimps the pleasurable sensations of sexual climax once functioned to condition females to seek sustained clitoral stimulation by mating with successive partners, one right after the other, and that orgasms have since become secondarily enlisted by humans to serve other ends (such as enhancing pair-bonds).[10]

Picture your great-, great-grandmother studiously going from one sexual partner to the next, motivated by unsatisfied sexual tension while transitioning among males, egged on in her search for "sustained clitoral stimulation" by the hope that the next guy will finish the job that the previous one hadn't quite managed. Or maybe if she had already climaxed, she might nonetheless be inspired to encounter multiple males by the simple fact that female orgasm is rekindlable (whether or not a word, it is certainly a bona fide phenomenon).

Such a prospect is intriguing enough. It is also consistent with the hideous practice of female circumcision, still widespread in much of northern and eastern Africa, which is based on the notion that female sexual desire could lead to multiple partners, so that for a woman to be considered marriageable, it is necessary to guarantee her fidelity by curtailing her orgasmic potential, if not eliminating it altogether.

Equally intriguing is Hrdy's suggestion, made at the end of the quote reprinted above, that female orgasm could have been "secondarily enlisted" to enhance an existing pair bond—which leads to precisely the opposite consequence in terms of sexual partnering. There is some evidence that women are more likely to reach orgasm with familiar partners, because they are more likely to feel (and to be) safe, and thus comfortable, relaxed, able to make their needs and preferences clear, and more likely to have them met.[11] Put this all together and a case might be made that rather than being an inducement for polyandry, as Hrdy proposed, female orgasm is an evolutionary sweetener for its opposite: monogamy . . . as Hrdy also proposed! In this regard, it is altogether consistent to have it both ways, since, as already noted, a trait can evolve for one reason, then be employed for another.

A Woman's Body Speaking to Her Mind?

In his poem "Of the progress of the soul," John Donne once eloquently described a young lady he admired (one Elizabeth Drury), by observing that

> Her pure, and eloquent blood
>
> Spoke in her cheeks, and so distinctly wrought
>
> That one might almost say, her body thought.

Of course, bodies don't actually think. Brains do. And should bodies think, they can be expected to do so in silence, as befits good thought. Mr. Donne, moreover, a now-dead white male writing four centuries ago, was probably not gesturing toward female orgasm in any case. By contrast, the 20th-century writer and feminist icon Anais Nin definitely was, when she referred to "Electric flesh-arrows . . . traversing the body," noting how "a rainbow of color strikes the eyelids. A foam of music falls over the ears. It is," she announced, "the gong of the orgasm."[12]

With or without an accompanying gong, orgasms may sometimes appear to speak, at least to the person who occupies that body's brain and who might stand to gain from the information thereby acquired. More than 30 years ago, the idea occurred to me that female orgasm might be a way by which a woman's body speaks to her brain, saying something positive about her current sexual partner. I had been studying the sexual behavior of grizzly bears and was struck by the differences between subordinate and dominant males. While copulating, the former constantly swivel their heads from side to side, looking out for a dominant boar who might displace them. Not surprisingly, they ejaculate quickly, something that the sow grizzly may or may not find disappointing but which, under the circumstances, is entirely understandable and likely adaptive as well. By contrast, dominant males take their time.

I don't know if female grizzlies experience orgasm, but if they do, with which partner would you expect it to be more likely? And is it surprising that premature ejaculation is also a common problem of young, inexperienced men lacking in status and self-confidence? Or that women paired with such men are unlikely to be orgasmic?

Interestingly, a study of Japanese macaque monkeys found that the highest frequency of female orgasms occurred when high-ranking males were copulating with low-ranking females, and the lowest when low-ranking males were having intercourse with high-ranking females.[13] So maybe a woman's orgasm isn't elusive because it is a vestigial by-product, fickle and flaky, sometimes on and sometimes off like a light bulb that isn't firmly screwed into its evolutionary socket. Maybe, instead, it is designed to be more than a little hard to get, adaptive precisely *because* it can't be too readily summoned, so that when it arrives, it means something.

The evaluation hypothesis is even compatible with the fact that orgasm is more reliably evoked by masturbation than by sexual intercourse; potential partners warrant evaluation, whereas there is no comparable pressure to assess one's own masturbatory technique. Moreover, any information made available in the former case can certainly be used to fine-tune the latter. Masturbation almost certainly is not an adaptation for reproduction in either sex; rather, it occurs just because the wiring exists—in both males and females—for orgasm based on stimulation, even in the absence of a sexual partner.

The evaluation hypothesis yields some testable predictions. One that seems so obvious as to be unworthy of testing is that women should find orgasms not only pleasurable but also important in the context of a sexual relationship. Don't scoff: If a woman's climax is merely an irrelevant, tag-along by-product, then it needn't be accorded any more attention than men do their nipples. In a survey of 202 Western women of reproductive age, 76% reported that experiencing orgasm with a partner was between somewhat important and very important; only 6% said it was somewhat unimportant to very unimportant.[14]

If orgasm helps women evaluate their partners, then it helps make sense of the otherwise perplexing fact that female orgasm is notoriously inconsistent: It wouldn't be much good as a means of partner evaluation if it occurred every time and with every partner. The evaluation hypothesis would also seem compatible with an attitude of control and independence. In much of the world, women tend to associate sex with submission, and interestingly, the more they do so, the more they experience impaired arousability and reduced orgasm frequency, suggesting that orgasms have something to do with autonomy and selfhood, but in an erotic context.[15]

Another prediction: Compared to their socially subordinate fellows, dominant men should be better lovers, that is, more likely to evoke orgasms in their partners. And for women, experiencing orgasm with a particular partner should lead to preference for that partner. In short, after having had an orgasm, a woman would likely want more and would therefore be (adaptively) predisposed to have additional sex with the partner in question. The evolutionary outcome is that, in the absence of reliable birth control, a woman would increase the probability of being impregnated by this person. Preference for sex with a sexually satisfying lover seems so obvious that it, too, might appear a foregone conclusion, but just because it is obvious doesn't make it any less true, or significant. In addition, it is at least possible that causation actually runs the other way: Once a woman has a preference for a particular partner (for whatever reason), she might be more likely to be orgasmic with him or her. It might be possible to disentangle these factors, but not easy.

A Way of Communicating, or Manipulating?

Thus far, we have focused on those individuals who experience female orgasm directly, namely, women. But what about those who encounter it second-hand: men? Most lovers—of either sex—are interested in whether their partner experiences an orgasm. Sometimes it becomes an obsession, such that "Was it good for you?" has become a much-satirized query, susceptible to satire precisely because it is asked so often. This leads to the interesting possibility that orgasm may be important not merely for the information it provides to the woman in question, but also as a way of communicating to the partner.

And what would it communicate? The fact that many people take a partner's orgasm as important information may itself speak to an unconscious realization that sexual response inevitably includes an evaluation component. If so, then female orgasm may help reassure one's lover that he (or she) has passed the test, and that accordingly there is less reason to worry about infidelity.

After all, a sexually satisfied woman is presumably less likely to look for additional gratification with someone else. Although probably true, this leads to another, more cynical consideration, which may or may not be true; namely, it generates the prospect of fake orgasms.

It isn't clear how many women fake their orgasms, or how often. But doing so could be in their interest in several circumstances: For one, it can speed up the partner's response, useful if she simply wants to "get it over with." For another, it could be used benevolently to enhance the other's confidence, although such deception is likely to be erosive in the long run. Lastly—and most cynically—faking orgasm could be a ploy to mislead the partner, inducing him (or, in the case of lesbian relationships, her) to think that the woman is sexually satisfied and thus unlikely to seek other partners, as a result of which the deceived individual is predisposed to let down his or her guard, giving the faker greater leeway to pursue other relationships (in which her orgasms presumably wouldn't be fake).

In short, women might use orgasm not only as a means of evaluating prospective partners but also as a way of manipulating them.

Returning to the more straightforward evaluation hypothesis, even though such assessment may seem limited to his or her sexual technique, ability to induce an orgasmic response could also be a cue that serves as a proxy for a more significant, ultimate evolutionary payoff: indicating something deeper about the partner's personality and inclination toward the woman. Thus, male mammals are, in a sense, roving inseminators. Since sperm are abundant and cheap to produce, males are generally primed by natural selection to be quick on the draw and not terribly selective as to targets. ("Bim, Bam, thank you ma'am!") Male grizzlies do not contribute to rearing their offspring. Men do—or at least, they can.

We've already noted that human beings are unusual in the degree to which they benefit from committed biparental care. Accordingly, perhaps an additional reason why human evolution has employed female orgasm is intimately tied to the fact that women are somewhat slower to rouse, often requiring extensive foreplay and direct, focused attention to the clitoris, which, since it isn't within the vagina, isn't likely to be stimulated by a hurried and selfish male focus on penile penetration and ejaculation. This, in turn, could have set the stage for a woman to assess whether her partner demonstrates an inclination to be lovingly generous, predisposed to help meet *her* needs, rather than selfishly focus only on his pleasure. If so, then maybe he'll also be inclined to clean up the family cave, and—a few tens of thousands of years later—mow the lawn and help put the kids through college.

Menopause: Some Unlikely Hypotheses

Last among sexual mysteries in this chapter as in life, we come to menopause. Less engaging than orgasm, less obvious than breasts, menopause shares more with menstruation than its first three letters (which don't refer to male human beings, but to "month"). Like menstruation, menopause is semisecret and hormonally underwritten. It is the matching bookend to a woman's reproductive life: from menarche to menopause. And like menstruation, menopause can also be downright troublesome, substituting hot flashes for monthly cramps.

Biologists, too, are discomfited by menopause, since it presents us with yet another evolutionary conundrum. We've already noted that reproduction is the *sine qua non* of evolutionary success, which makes it especially perplexing that women's reproductive spigot is turned off at what seems an inappropriately early age. Most animals do not experience a prolonged life stage during which they are alive yet nonbreeding. So long as they draw breath, they typically release eggs. But women stop ovulating within just a few years of age 50, when they may still have a few decades of vigorous and for the most part healthy life ahead of them.

Men keep producing sperm into their eighth and even ninth decades. For women, it isn't even a question of making eggs, since every girl is born with all the eggs she will ever have, roughly 400; they simply have to mature and then be released. The "how" of menopause is well understood. A woman's reproductive spigot is literally turned off by a dramatic reduction in endocrine hormones, notably estrogen. But this is proximate causation. What about the "why"? Why has selection evidently favored women whose endocrine machinery runs down when it does? What are the ultimate, evolutionary reasons?

There is no reason to suppose that age and eggs are necessarily incompatible: Female African elephants breed into their 60s and blue whales into their 90s. Not only that but in *Homo sapiens*, eggs—unlike sperm—aren't produced de novo throughout life. Maybe that's the answer: At some point, each woman just runs out of eggs.

This "explanation" turns out to be no explanation at all, however, since once again it confuses proximate with ultimate causation. If there were a reproductive payoff to reproducing in one's 50s, 60s, or 70s, you can rest assured that girls would be born with 500, 600, or 700 eggs, instead of their current 400 or so. Not only that, but women who use birth control pills—which inhibit ovulation—and who therefore only release one half to one third of the lifetime egg supply nonetheless enter menopause just like everyone else, despite having all those unused eggs, and no later than their sisters who supposedly became menopausal because they'd used up all of theirs.

More important, eggs eventually go "bad," causing the risk of genetic defects to increase with maternal age. According to the March of Dimes, for example, a 25-year-old woman has about a 1 in 1,250 chance of having a baby with Down syndrome; a 30-year-old has a 1 in 1,000 chance; a 35-year-old, 1 in 400; a 40-year-old, 1 in 100; and a 45-year-old, 1 in 30.[16] These are impressive numbers, showing that a 45-year-old woman is more than 40 times more likely to produce a baby with Down syndrome. Looked at in terms of actual risk, however, the data are much less overwhelming: Even a 45-year-old has a 29 in 30 chance of giving birth to a child who does *not* have Down syndrome! Whereas there is a genuine genetic risk to reproducing in one's fifth or sixth decade, sheer mathematics nonetheless suggests that the potential genetic payoff greatly exceeds the possible downside.

Perhaps menopause is a result of those darned, new-fangled, increased life spans. Thus, what if menopause itself is an aberration rather than an adaptation, a consequence of the fact that our reproductive biology—including the number of eggs built into a newborn baby girl—was tuned to prehistoric times, when people simply didn't live as long as they do today? After all, if most of our ancestors were dead before age 50, it is no surprise that our bodies haven't evolved with an eye toward making productive use of those additional, tacked-on decades. There is, however, a big problem with this explanation: Even in prehistoric times, many people lived into their sixth, seventh, and eighth decades. *Average* life span was shorter in those times, but because infant and early childhood mortality was very high, not because there were hardly any old people. If, for example, one newborn baby died for every person who survived to fourscore, the "average life span" would be 40.

Although life expectancy at birth for contemporary hunter-gatherers is only 30 to 35 years, this, too, is due to high infant and juvenile mortalities, leaving plenty of opportunity for natural selection to act upon the seniors. Having reached age 20, life expectancy for today's nontechnological foraging people extends about 20 years beyond menopause. So why don't they—and we—keep reproducing?

Maybe an older female body simply isn't up to the rigors of pregnancy and lactation. But assisted reproductive techniques have proven to a no-longer-surprised world that women in their 50s and even 60s can sustain pregnancy and bear healthy babies. So clearly the female "infrastructure" can be up to the task. Basic statistics plus the "magic of compound interest" suggest that selection should have favored those individuals who gave it a try, if only because some would have succeeded—and these would have contributed disproportionately to the current population. Natural selection should have favored women who attempted to bear just one more child, no matter how old they were and even if most of them died trying, because any who succeeded would be a step ahead of the competition.

Finally, if menopause is simply the biologically mandated consequence of increased age, an accidental consequence of modern technology keeping our bodies going beyond their usual and allotted life span, then why is it merely the female reproductive system that poops out? Why isn't it the kidneys, heart, or liver that throws in the towel? Looking simply at the debility of old age, evolutionary theory strongly suggests that all systems should fall apart at about the same time, since as soon as any one began to malfunction first, selection would no longer operate to maintain the others.

Here is a metaphor that might help: It is said that Henry Ford once commissioned an engineer to examine junked Model Ts to determine which parts wore out and which were still functional. He learned that the kingpins remained in good shape, even when the pistons, driveshafts, and so forth showed substantial wear. Ford then ordered that the kingpins be manufactured to *lower* specifications.

It isn't that all human reproduction ceases at menopause, but specifically human *female* reproduction. ("Male menopause" is a myth; certainly it does not exist with anything like the clear-cut biological specificity of its female counterpart. Although male fertility declines with age, it does so pretty much at the same pace as the aging of other organ systems, whereas female fertility and only female fertility stops abruptly.)

One explanation—ingenious but unlikely—has been dubbed the patriarch hypothesis.[17] It is the menopausal equivalent of the by-product hypothesis for female orgasm: namely, that the trait in question (this time, menopause) is a tag-along trait, present in women merely because its counterpart has been selected for in men. The idea is that since human beings are primitively harem forming, a small number of highly successful men have long been able to reproduce disproportionately, often into middle age and beyond, ceasing only when they are felled by illness or injury. Selection would therefore have favored extending male lives accordingly. If any such genetically based longevity factors were present on the Y chromosome, they would be unable to influence female biology, since females are XX. However, if genes for extended life span appeared on any of the other, "autosomal" chromosomes, they would be inherited by women, too, whose enhanced life expectancy would have been "dragged along" by its fitness payoff in men.

Not so fast. First, no such longevity genes appear to exist. And second, if this hypothesis were valid and women's life spans have been "artificially" enhanced because of a breeding payoff to elderly patriarchs among whom selection would presumably have favored their extended sperm production as well, then why weren't women similarly selected for continued reproduction, too?

This should help bring our attention back where it belongs, to women.

Prudent Mothers

Women get pregnant, not men. Women give birth, not men. And women lactate, not men. All of these are demanding, biologically crucial activities, the costs of which fall entirely upon women. Maternal mortality can be distressingly high. Paternal mortality? The phrase doesn't even exist. Add to this the regrettable reality of senescence, the fact that as bodies grow older they become less viable and more breakable than their younger counterparts, and it isn't surprising that at some point as they grow older, women stop bearing children.

But it isn't quite that simple. Why should it matter to evolution if women kept reproducing, or trying to do so, until they died in the process? After all, this is precisely what happens among nearly all other species, which typically breed unto the bitter end. It must somehow be the case that women who, having reached a certain age, desisted from reproduction actually ended up leaving more genetic descendants than did those who kept on keeping on.

But how?

What follows are some ideas about why natural selection might have favored early termination of women's fertility. First comes simple prudence, as negatively modeled by Jane Goodall's famous chimpanzee matriarch, Flo. Chimps do not undergo menopause, and Flo—well known to those who have followed Dr. Goodall's detailed studies of free-living chimpanzees in the Gombe Stream Reserve of Tanzania—kept breeding into advanced old age. It must have seemed a near miracle when Flo became pregnant for what turned out to be the last time, since she was obviously dilapidated in every respect. Here is the sad story, reported by the Jane Goodall Institute:

> Flo gave birth to at least five offspring: Faben, Figan, Fifi, Flint, and Flame. She was a wonderful, supportive, affectionate and playful mother to the first three. But she looked very old when the time came to wean young Flint, and she had not fully succeeded in weaning him when she gave birth to Flame. By this time she seemed exhausted and unable to cope with the aggressive demands and tantrums of Flint, who wanted to ride on her back and sleep with her even after the birth of his new sister. She still had not weaned Flint when Flame died at the age of six months, and at this point stopped even trying to push

Flint to independence. Flint therefore became abnormally dependent on his old mother. When Flo died in 1972, he was unable to cope without her. He stopped eating and interacting with others and showed signs of clinical depression. Soon thereafter, Flint's immune system became too weak to keep him alive. He died at the age of eight and a half, within one month of losing his mother Flo.[18]

Flo wasn't really a failure, since she produced at least three flourishing offspring. But the likelihood is that if she had been just a wee bit more reproductively prudent—if she had refrained from that last breeding attempt—she wouldn't merely have survived longer (which, after all, isn't an evolutionary payoff in itself), but so, too, would the unfortunate Flame and perhaps Flint as well. Maybe, therefore, we shouldn't speak of Flo's failure, but rather, her folly. And maybe human menopause is a way that evolution has outfitted our own matriarchs with a way to avoid Flo's folly by being reproductively prudent and getting her body to "just say no."

Even in medically sophisticated societies, a 40-year-old woman faces seven times more risk of dying in childbirth than does a 20-year-old. Hard-nosed evolutionary biologists might be nonetheless unimpressed, however, pointing out that as with the payoff of reproducing despite the increased risk of genetic anomalies, selection would still favor a woman who tried, even if she failed, simply because it would favor any who succeeded. But this omits another important consideration, somewhat valid for chimpanzees but more so for human beings: the extent to which offspring survival (and thus parental fitness) depends on parental investment in those offspring. Since children depend so heavily on their parents, human parents may well have been under especially strong selection pressure to be prudent rather than go with the Flo.

In the poker game of breeding—in which maximizing your fitness substitutes for maximizing your pile of chips—just as there is a payoff for betting successfully on one's breeding potential, there is a cost to betting too high, like Flo did. Similarly, it would be suboptimal to be too prudent and bet too low—that is, to quit breeding too soon—thereby underplaying one's hand. As in Kenny Rogers's song *The Gambler*, "you got to know when to hold 'em, know when to fold 'em, know when to walk away and know when to run." The prudent mother hypothesis is that menopause tells women when to fold 'em. But it's not the only game in town.

Another is called the grandmother hypothesis.

Grandmothers to the Rescue?

The basic idea is simple enough, although hidden within is a crucially important revision in our current understanding of evolution and, indeed, of the very nature of living things. First, consider that a woman begins to experience menopause at about the time when her own children, born perhaps two decades or so earlier, are themselves likely to become parents. That is, she may well be—or is about to become—a grandmother. The grandmother hypothesis, then, is that by foregoing reproduction, especially at a time when the cost of reproductive "imprudence" is rising—higher risk of morbidity and mortality during pregnancy and childbirth along with increased prospects of genetic anomalies in any offspring actually produced—a middle-aged woman might be freeing herself to contribute to the eventual success of her grandchildren. By doing so, she is actually being genetically selfish as much as altruistic, since the beneficiaries of her personal reproductive restraint include not only the grandchildren themselves but also their genes—which is to say, the grandmother's, too.

It could be mere coincidence or—more likely—part of evolution's design that around the world, grandparents in general and grandmothers in particular pitch in and help out. Not only that, but those who do so typically end up with more grandchildren than those who don't. The grandmother hypothesis does not preclude the hypothesis of prudent mothering, however, since once a mother is no longer encumbered with dependent children, it makes social as well as biological sense that she would be inclined to help out with her kids' kids.

Once again, our species' unusually long period of profound juvenile dependency may also be involved, insofar as such neediness would confer a special benefit to assistance rendered by others beyond the parental pair. Consistent with this, Sarah Hrdy has proposed that humanity may well have evolved in the context of extensive cooperative parenting.[19] And who would be more qualified, and also better positioned to gain biologically as a result, than grandmothers?

Detailed studies by anthropologist Kristen Hawkes and her colleagues have found that among the Hadza, modern hunter-gatherers of Tanzania, the men hunt while the women gather and forage and (ta da!) the most energetic and productive foragers of all are postmenopausal women.[20] A young mother, no matter how healthy and hard-working, is necessarily constrained while burdened with a baby, making such assistance nothing to sneeze at. Sure enough, Hadza grandmothers give their bounty to their children and grandchildren, whose body weights vary directly with their grandmothers' food-gathering efforts. It is doubtless significant that among the Hadza studied by Hawkes and her colleagues, every nursing mother had a postmenopausal helper.

The technical term for cooperative breeding is "allo-parenting" (*allo* = "other") and its likely importance in our evolution should give pause when we consider the extent to which modern Western societies—with their assumption of the "nuclear family"—make it impossible for grandparents to make the kind of social and biological contribution that might well have been crucial for 99% of our biological past. Although multigenerational households can certainly introduce their own forms of stress, it can hardly be denied that children, parents, and grandparents (perhaps grandmothers in particular) have also gained greatly from the interaction.

How much, we cannot tell. But the basic pattern, in which hard-working grandmothers contribute significantly to the success of their grandchildren, has been confirmed by other anthropologists studying other human groups.[21] All of this makes it increasingly likely that grandmothers owe their nonreproductive status to the payoffs that—at least in the past—they were able to convey, and the genetic recompense they received as a result.

An interesting twist to the grandmother hypothesis also merits our attention. It is deservedly popular to point to "win–win solutions" by which everyone in a competition—better yet, an interaction—comes out ahead. The sad reality, however, is that life is often a zero-sum game in which benefit to one participant necessitates some cost to another. The simple act of reproducing, and more to the point successfully rearing one's offspring, is often zero sum, especially when resources are scarce. So perhaps we should consider the role of menopause as a way of minimizing reproductive competition, something particularly relevant when one individual's baby making can depress that of another.

The "competition avoidance" hypothesis argues that menopause is how middle-aged women avoid competing with younger women—by opting out altogether.[22] Once again, they need not be doing so out of genuine altruism, since those younger women who benefit are typically either the menopausal woman's daughters or daughters-in-law, so that in either case, the woman whose ovaries say "no" may well be saying "yes" to her genes, each of which is likely, with a probability of .25, to be present in her grandchildren.

According to the grandmother hypothesis, among the payoffs received by grandmothers themselves are benefits that go beyond emotional gratification and satisfied love and that include evolutionary payoffs received by the menopausal woman's genes. Taking a "gene's eye" view of evolution, natural selection does not proceed with the individual in mind, but rather, the gene. As biologist Richard Dawkins has pointed out so cogently, bodies aren't the bottom line in evolution; genes are.[23] Bodies don't last beyond a single generation; genes do. And so, when at a certain age women forego reproducing (i.e., when they commence menopause) and also begin being helpful grandmothers, their genes are "selfishly" looking out for copies of themselves, genes "for" menopause that get projected into the future via those additional grandchildren that are benefited.

Sarah Hrdy tells of a particular langur monkey, "old Sol," who had ceased cycling and thus might have been quasimenopausal, in a sense. She was obviously decrepit and marginalized within her group, living a sad, solitary, and—it appeared—increasingly useless end of life until a strange adult male invaded the langur troop and attempted to work infanticidal mayhem. Writes Hrdy,

> It was Sol who repeatedly charged this sharp-toothed male nearly twice her weight to place herself between him and the threatened baby. When the infanticidal male seized the infant in his jaws and ran off with him, Sol pursued the attacker and wrested the wounded baby back. With danger momentarily past, and the wounded infant once again in his mother's arms, old Sol resumed her diffident attitude. That an arthritic old female would become marginalized with age is

scarcely surprising. More curious was Sol's transformation from decrepit outcast to intrepid defender.[24]

It doesn't diminish Sol's courage to point out that by defending youngsters, some of whom may be her own grandchildren, Sol and other warrior grandmothers may literally be justifying their own postreproductive existence, or—to put it differently—their genes are acting out their own payoff.

Even then, the grandmother hypothesis is not literally proven. It seems likely, however, that menopause may serve to keep middle-aged women from reproducing at a time when their personal risk is increasing (higher mortality) and payoff is decreasing (greater danger of producing genetically defective offspring), so that these women are more fit in the evolutionary sense if they care for those children already produced (prudent mothering) as well as contributing to their own successful grandmotherhood. Even women who have no children would presumably be influenced by the same basic evolutionary pressures, since for most of our species' history, intentional childlessness was not an option. In addition, once our conceptual focus has shifted to what is presumably natural selection's focus as well—the gene rather than the individual—it isn't strictly necessary for someone to have children to receive an evolutionary benefit.

An Inclusive Fitness Approach

Biologists refer increasingly to "inclusive fitness" as the real focus of evolution. This differs from simple Darwinian fitness in that it includes somewhat more: not just the production of successful offspring, but the enhanced success of copies of one's constituent genes as represented in all genetic relatives, with the importance of each relative devalued as he or she is more distantly related—which is to say, as the probability declines that these individuals share genes by common descent. By this accounting, children are important, but so are nieces, nephews, grandchildren, cousins, and so forth. As a result, we can see how by maximizing an individual's inclusive fitness, natural selection could have favored older individuals contributing to their genes' eventual success whenever they contributed to their network of genetic relatives.

Even a childless, postmenopausal woman could therefore enhance the long-term success of her genes by contributing to them in the bodies of her various relatives, among whom grandchildren are likely to loom large, but not exclusively. In many pre-literate societies, elderly individuals contribute to their fellow group members (many of them genetic relatives) by serving as a source of useful information, especially in times of crisis: where to find water during a once-in-a-lifetime drought, how to prepare certain food for long-term storage, what to do with troublesome tribe members. In such cases, it might not matter that the person in question is unable to get pregnant, since she is already a repository of potentially life-saving, gene-promoting wisdom.

In today's rapidly changing technological world, in which youngsters are needed to translate their grandparents' email, program their cell phones, and unravel the mysteries of iPods and MP3s, it sometimes seems like information and assistance largely flows from the young to the old. But historically, and to a large extent even now, the elderly have been priceless sources of trans-generational wisdom, something far more precious than mere technique. As a result, this gives us reason to ask whether human beings *ever* become truly postreproductive, insofar as, this side of the grave, they can contribute—not merely to the lives of their offspring but also to others within their long, inclusive reach.

It may even be that such "selfish beneficence" on the part of the elderly—or, if you prefer, their genes—has enabled our species to luxuriate in prolonged childhood, which in turn is intimately connected to our having evolved such large brains. So if you like being human—which is to say, being smart—thank grandma!

Fancy Females and Other "Manly Mysteries"

There are also "manly mysteries," but for some reason, these aren't as sexy or prominent as their womanly counterparts. Here, therefore, is yet another mystery, a recursive one insofar that it is a mystery about mysteries: Why are there so many sex-related womanly mysteries and, comparatively speaking, so few male ones? And why are the manly mysteries so trivial by contrast?

Among those pallid male enigmas are: Why are men so much hairier than women? Furthermore, why is this hirsuteness distributed as it is, especially prominent on the face (beard and mustache) and, to a lesser extent chest, the arms and legs? And given that men are generally more hairy than women—whatever the reason—why is this difference reversed on top of the head? For all their hairiness, why are men so much more prone to go bald? It is well known that testosterone is intimately involved here, along with genetics, but this doesn't explain why the outcome—which presumably has been favored by natural selection—is what it is. "Male pattern baldness," for example, is a description, not an explanation.

Most evolutionary biologists would likely suspect that the answer has something to do with social signaling, but exactly what? It doesn't seem that there has even been any interesting speculation. Yet.

There are some other mysteries that aren't really "male." Rather, they exist in the context of comparing male with female, men with women. And they aren't so much "sexual" as they emerge along a dimension contrasting the two sexes. For starters, many animals are "sexually dimorphic," which means that males and females are easily distinguished, and not simply by their genitals. In such cases, males are almost inevitably the gaudy, fancy sex while females are relatively dowdy and unprepossessing. Among human beings, this situation is reversed: It is the women not the men who are especially concerned with their looks and who characteristically adorn their bodies with all manner of bright, showy, attention-grabbing accoutrements.

Earlier, seeking an evolutionary basis for one aspect of female "anatomical ornamentation" (conspicuous nonlactating breasts), we discussed the "sexy son" hypothesis along with the handicap principle. In that case, we looked at male choice of females, itself an inversion of the far more common phenomenon in the animal world: female choice of males. It is this process of female choice that appears responsible for the evolution of traditionally elaborate male secondary sexual characteristics such as feathers, wattles, horns and antlers, manes, ruffs, and so forth.

To be sure, even in modern Western societies, men invest in their dress and appearance, but women outdo them by an order of magnitude, sporting the equivalent of a peacock's tail, only one that is constructed culturally rather than anatomically.

Unlike, say, the case of woodland warblers in which males are brightly colored jewels while females are for the most part drab and distressingly difficult to tell apart, looking strictly at the anatomical endowment of naked men and women, it isn't obvious which sex is fancier. At the same time there is no question that if we admit the role of local culture and technology, women are fancy and men, plain. There is also no question that the matter of female adornment is the "least biological" of all those traits we shall be considering in *Homo Mysterious*. Moreover, as befits something that is so strongly influenced by local cultural traditions, there are exceptions: Among certain New Guinea societies, for example, men adorn themselves with pig tusks and bird-of-paradise plumes, and among many Australian and African aboriginal people, men, not women, are elaborately painted for most ceremonies.

But the pattern nonetheless holds, and is quite robust, especially in the West and in societies influenced by occidental culture: Just consider the comparative expenditure on female versus male cosmetics—nail polish, lipstick, eye liner, hair care products of all description *versus* aftershave cologne, or the female rainbow of brightly colored dresses, shoes, handbags, jewelry, and other accessories *versus* the visually tedious sameness of "men in suits." Fancy females are pretty much a cross-cultural universal,[25] with women being consistently more decorated; this calls for explanation, especially because an evolutionary perspective suggests that the cosmetics and fashion industries did not *create* a demand for female ornamentation so much as *respond* to it.

Not unlikely, this demand on the part of women derives from the adaptive value—to themselves—of creating demand (for themselves) on the part of men. Mammals are unusual in that females are specifically adapted to nourish their offspring via breast milk. As a result, paternal care is rare among our mammalian relatives. But human beings are exceptional mammals in that—because of our prolonged juvenile dependency—males have quite a bit to contribute. Consequently, unlike most animals, in which female choice is the rule, the evolution of *Homo sapiens* has placed a premium on women making themselves attractive to males as well, thereby giving them an advantage when it comes to mating with males who may be especially able to invest in them and their offspring.

In this regard, it is of more than passing significance that around the world, women are drawn to cultural practices and technology such as breast enhancement, lipstick, hair and skin products, and clothing that "flatters the figure," all of which exaggerate traits characteristic of healthy youth, with its subliminal promise of reproductive potential. Women, in short, are trying to make themselves more attractive—no surprise here, except when we consider that this basic pattern goes contrary to the typical situation among most animals, in which males especially "try" to be attractive, which means, of course, that natural selection has particularly favored those that do so.

There is a deeper underlying pattern here, one that is found in other species and is entirely consistent with women's "artificial" ornamentation in our own: The sex investing more tends to be the one doing most of the choosing. This is essentially because the greater the investment on offer, the greater the eagerness to gain sexual access to such individuals, and this eagerness by one sex (in most animals, the males) provides leverage to the other (in most animals, the females). As the more heavily investing sex, females therefore typically have the opportunity to choose among males, who seek to be among the chosen. Human beings do not quite reverse this "differential investment," since their eggs, pregnancy, and subsequent lactation[ii] induce women nearly always to invest more in their offspring than do men. But to a degree highly unusual among mammals, men, too, invest in their offspring, which sets up the potential for them, too, to be choosy.

An interesting parallel is offered by the unfortunately named "Mormon crickets," which are neither crickets nor devotees of the Church of Latter Day Saints. They are, however, among the few species in which males invest more heavily in offspring than do females, since male Mormon crickets produce a large, nutrient-rich spermatophore, which is transferred to the female at mating. As a result, in this species males are sexually reticent and choosy, whereas females are pushy and self-advertising, a reversal of the

---

ii. Further abetted by the fact that women, not men, can be confident that they are genetically related to their offspring.

traditional male–female pattern. In the case of Mormon crickets, females display their desirability by literally climbing on the backs of males, who prefer to mate with those that are heaviest (indicating they have the most eggs).[26]

It is possible that early proto-hominid men preferentially chose women who, like egg-laden female Mormon crickets, were somewhat rotund. These days, however, women are more likely to use clothing, cosmetics, and so forth to display and enhance their desirability. They aren't merely choosy, as befits females of pretty much any species, but they also seek to be chosen. And toward this end, they use adornment, creams, emollients, hair-dos and don'ts, eye shadow, lipstick, rouge, powder, nail polish, depilatories, and eye-catching dresses, tights, bracelets, necklaces, and earrings.

It is true, of course, that kangaroos, kingfishers, and cobras couldn't apply mascara or wear high-heel shoes even if they wanted to, but the likelihood is that people—and especially women—do such things not simply because they can, but because doing so is consistent with natural selection. There is also the possibility that women's penchant for public adornment corresponds, as well, to a private fondness for polyandry, that is, mating—perhaps on the sly—with more than one man. Recall our earlier consideration of the various potential evolutionary payoffs to concealed ovulation, a private hiddenness that might combine especially well with public attractiveness.

Carry this thought a step further: What if, rather than women having been selected to conceal their ovulation, chimpanzees and the like were selected to conspicuously signal theirs? Why, you ask, should evolution have favored female chimps announcing their sexual availability? Perhaps to attract the attention of the dominant male. This would seem an especially adaptive tactic among species in which male genetic quality and/or inclination to be a good parent varies substantially among individuals. If there were a big difference of this sort among males, females should be selected to do what they can to increase their chances of "getting" the better ones.

So what about this hypothesis: Women, biologically more camouflaged than chimps, make use of culturally created, man- and woman-made ornaments to achieve the same effect that chimpanzees get with their flagrant and presumably fragrant anatomy?

This would make particular sense if women's penchant for polyandry is recently developed, so that natural selection hasn't had time to evolve overt physical traits such as the chimpanzee's gaudy genitals, and/or because of the various other payoffs that presumably come with being biologically more discreet.

Just as biologically generated traits have fitness costs—it is metabolically expensive and probably also dangerously predator attracting for a peacock to grow his fancy tail—it is often financially costly for people to ornament, adorn, and augment their bodies. But such costs are evidently seen as worthwhile: Clothing, cosmetics, and other personal adornment make up a large proportion of the budget of many people who might seem to have "better things to do" with their limited resources. For a species that is deeply, biologically concerned with sexual signaling, however, there can be evolutionary logic behind such expenditures.

Sex Differences in Life Span

For another mystery, not quite sexual but intimately linked nonetheless to maleness and femaleness, think about longevity. Women consistently outlive men, suggesting that even though men are stronger when it comes to measures of brute force, women are "biologically stronger." Why?

Maybe it's a result of hormones. Thus, there is some evidence that testosterone inhibits the human immune system, and that mentally retarded men who had been castrated in childhood live more than a decade longer than similar, intact men.[27] Such an explanation, if confirmed, is nonetheless proximate only; it leaves unanswered the deeper "why" question. In addition, hormones alone don't seem sufficient since boys are significantly more mortality prone than are girls even during their first decade, before "raging hormones" become relevant.

Or maybe genes are involved, not so much that women have better ones, but rather more of them. Aside from the sex chromosomes, there are no genetic differences between men and women. But don't forget that women are XX and men, XY, and that the Y chromosome is a real slacker, almost lacking in useful genetic material. As a result, women have literally more DNA upon which they can draw, a difference that might be consequential since a woman possessing a deleterious gene on one of her X chromosomes might find its harmful effect overridden by a more fitness-generating gene on her other X. (Contributing to this prospect is the fact that health-promoting genes tend to be dominant.) By contrast, men are stuck with an "unprotected" X, because their underachieving Y chromosomes cannot compensate for anything disadvantageous on the X. Men may therefore be more vulnerable to genetically related troubles, or simply they may have a shallower genetic "bench" when called upon to deal with life's slings and arrows.

This would suggest that as a general rule, the "heterogametic sex" should have a shorter life span than the "homogametic" one, yet it turns out that among birds, in which females are heterogametic while males have a duplicated, and accordingly protected, sex chromosome, the latter still have shorter life spans. So much for the role of protected versus unprotected sex chromosomes.

Alternatively, maybe women are protected, not by their genome, but rather by cultural traditions and social expectations, which make it far more likely that men will engage in exhausting, physically dangerous, and likely life-threatening activities, whether job related or recreational. It is men, after all, who are prone to be coal miners, farmers, animal herders, construction workers, and soldiers. This undoubtedly accounts for some of the male–female differences in longevity, but not all. It doesn't explain, for example, why the same consistent 7-year difference in male–female life span has been found when comparing cloistered monks and nuns, both of whom are isolated from the hurly-burly of modern life and who do much the same things.[28]

This leads us to another hypothesis for why women outlive men, based once more on evolutionary considerations. The point is that human beings show all the signs of being polygynous, that is, biologically inclined toward harem formation: Men are typically larger and more aggressive than women, and they become sexually mature significantly later (to be successful in mating with numerous partners requires defeating a comparable number of same-sex competitors, and selection therefore rewards would-be harem masters who enter into the reproductive fray when somewhat older and larger). In any event, it is characteristic of mildly polygynous species such as *Homo sapiens* for males to be more likely than females to engage in vigorous same-sex competition, which typically manifests via huffing and puffing and sometimes literally trying to knock each other down, as well as engaging in show-offy behavior—all of which are, quite simply, risky.

To be sure, natural selection has dictated that for males generally and men in particular, such risks are worth running, if only because to a great extent for males—and not necessarily at all for females—evolutionary fitness is a zero-sum game. A woman is likely to become pregnant regardless of what transpires for other women; by contrast, reproductive success by a man is liable to occur at the expense of another man's evolutionary fitness, since the reproductive potential of many women can be monopolized by a relatively small number of men.

Not only are men and boys more violent, but they are also more prone to risk taking, more inclined to take greater chances, because for them, the payoff to success is greater, as is the consequence of failure. As sperm makers and potential harem keepers, males simply play for higher stakes, and this, in turn, may help account for the higher morbidity and mortality that they experience.

This hypothesis is closely allied to one of the better-established theories in evolutionary biology, concerned with the question of senescence generally. One might ask (as many evolutionary biologists have), Why do organisms get old? More precisely, Why do they "senesce," that is, experience higher morbidity and mortality over time? The most widely accepted explanation, first proposed by the great theorist George C. Williams, concerns the genetic phenomenon known as pleiotropy.[29] Genes are pleiotropic when they influence more than one character. Accordingly, imagine a gene that contributes to an individual's fitness early in life but which also has detrimental effects that show up only later, when the individual is postreproductive. Such a gene would on balance be selected for, since it would contribute to survival and reproduction, but would be only weakly selected against at the other end of life, when selection is greatly reduced or even absent altogether. Another way of looking at this is that selection is generally more potent early in life than later, resulting in accumulated costs that reveal themselves late in life.

This pleiotropic theory of senescence applies to all living things, not just human beings, and to both sexes. Thus, by itself, it doesn't explain the male–female disparity in life span. However, combined with the other male–female differences just described, Williams's concept could be insightful indeed. Since males have been selected to engage in male–male competition to a degree not found in females, selection for success in such competition—especially when young—would likely have been stronger among men than among women. If so, then men would be more vulnerable to comparatively early death not only as a direct result of their more risk-prone, competitive behavior, but also because genetic tendencies would be favored that generate reproductive success early in life, albeit at the expense of eventual longevity. Men, in a sense, have evolved to "live fast, love hard, and die young," with younger dying being a consequence of the faster living and the harder loving.

Here is a final possible evolutionary explanation for the male–female life span discrepancy. Maybe it's not a matter of evolution favoring men whose behavior shortens the average male life span, but of selection acting primarily on women, extending *theirs*. Think back to the grandmother hypothesis for the evolution of menopause, and view it from a different perspective: Instead of women having been selected to cease reproducing at a certain age, we might say that selection has acted upon women, more than upon men, to extend their postreproductive life, because of the genetic payoffs they can accrue, especially via their grandchildren. If so, then maybe women who are middle-aged and older can thank their grandchildren—and evolution, too—for their own longevity, no less than for their nonreproductive status.

The Mystery of Sex Itself

Finally, let's conclude with yet another mystery, one that surrounds sex itself, rather than being bounded by considerations of women and men as such. This one is among the major unsolved enigmas of evolutionary biology more generally: Why does sex exist at all?

At first glance, the question seems foolish, since sex serves reproduction, and without reproduction there would be no evolutionary success and perhaps no life itself. But in fact, it is quite possible for living things to reproduce *asexually*, and quite a mystery why so few actually do so. Sex, after all, is a hassle. It requires that a would-be reproducing individual encounter another individual of the same species and the opposite sex and, moreover, that both be similarly motivated. It mandates that sexually reproducing individuals subject themselves to potentially dangerous intimacy with someone else, rendering themselves vulnerable to injury and illness, not to mention the risk of being deceived or exploited. By contrast, as we know from the numerous creatures that do so, asexual reproduction can be accomplished with safety, a high success rate, and without wasting all that time and energy on courtship and copulation.

The largest cost of sexual reproduction hasn't even been mentioned: The fact that whereas a strawberry plant or amoeba who reproduces asexually produces offspring containing 100% of its genes, sexual breeders have to settle for a mere 50%, since each partner gets an equal, one-half share in the outcome.[iii] This is a whopping twofold cost of sex, and in a biological world in which "selection differentials" as small as one tenth of 1% have been shown to drive considerable evolutionary change (see the next chapter), it is exceedingly difficult to understand why natural selection favored sexual reproduction in the first place.

Such considerations drove the great evolutionary theorist George C. Williams to conclude glumly that sexual reproduction is probably not adaptive, at least not for large, complex, slow-breeding creatures such as human beings.[30] It may, on the other hand, have evolved initially among small, simple, rapidly breeding organisms among whom sexual reproduction could have been advantageous. But now subsequent generations are simply stuck with it, essentially because having proceeded down that particular, peculiar anatomic and physiologic avenue, it simply wasn't possible to turn back.

The issue is complex and fraught with arcane mathematical analysis as well as theoretical fine points, and of course, it isn't

---

iii. Technically, I should say that in the case of asexual reproduction, there is a 100% probability that any given gene present in a parent will also occur in every offspring, whereas with sexual reproduction, that probability drops precipitously, to 50%.

limited to human beings. But let's gesture, at least, toward what seems a likely answer: the payoff of variety.

When a strawberry plant reproduces by sending out a runner, or an amoeba splits in two, the offspring are genetically identical to the parent. By contrast, sexual reproduction gives each parent, in a sense, a glass half full—as described above, this is perhaps the most formidable downside to sex. But it may also suggest a very large upside, since although each offspring is only "filled" with one-half the genotype of a given parent, it also contains one-half the genotype of the other parent, and, moreover, these genes will have been randomly reshuffled when eggs and sperm were produced and then combined. As a result, sexually reproducing individuals produce offspring who are different: from each other and from their parents. The benefit of this seems to be that when environments change, as they always do, parents who reproduced sexually end up with offspring that are genetically diverse rather than mere clones of the previous generation. Among such offspring, there is an enhanced likelihood that at least some individuals will find themselves well equipped to deal with the novelties ahead.

By analogy, if you were buying lottery tickets, it would be pretty foolish to purchase a dozen tickets all with the same number; this is essentially the strategy followed by asexual breeders.

Another, related argument has also been raised on behalf of reproducing sexually. Instead of focusing on external environmental changes (in climate, food availability, potential predators and prey, and so forth), let's turn our attention to a living thing's internal environment, including notably its pathogens and parasites. There is a constant arms race between free-living organisms (such as ourselves) and our various fellow travelers (viruses, bacteria, protozoa, nematode and trematode worms, etc.). These creatures, just like their "hosts," are also evolving, "trying" to take advantage of our immune defenses while we seek to evolve ways of keeping the invaders at bay. If host bodies remain genetically unchanged from generation to generation—as happens with asexual reproduction—this makes it relatively easy for pathogens and parasites to home in on their characteristics, evolving ways of breaching their defenses. Sexually reproducing organisms, by contrast, are genotypically moving targets, whose offspring differ from each other and from their parents, and are therefore more difficult to attack successfully.

An especially intriguing evolutionary principle is known as the Red Queen Effect, after the scene in Lewis Carroll's *Through the Looking Glass*, in which the Red Queen grabs Alice's hand and insists that they run. It soon becomes apparent, however, that they aren't getting anywhere:

"Well, in our country," said Alice, still panting a little, "you'd generally get to somewhere else—if you run very fast for a long time, as we've been doing."

"A slow sort of country!" said the Queen. "Now, here, you see, it takes all the running you can do, to keep in the same place. If you want to get somewhere else, you must run at least twice as fast as that!"

Biologists seized upon this image to describe the need of organisms to be constantly evolving so as to keep up with changes in their ecological niche. It could well be that the Red Queen Effect is particularly active with regard to the evolution of sex itself, with our understanding of ecological niche expanded to include not just the "outside" environment, but also the various pathogens and parasites residing inside everyone's body. As primatologist Allison Jolly pointed out in a delightful limerick, this gives new meaning to the expression "keeping up with the Joneses":

Your kids must keep up with the Joneses;

relaxation's forever denied you.

For the reasons you've kids and not clones is,

the Joneses are living inside you[31]

A research report titled "Running with the Red Queen: Host-Parasite Coevolution Selects for Biparental Sex" provided evidence for just this sort of competition between free-living organisms and their internal, parasitic "Joneses." The biologists took a species of nematode worm that can reproduce sexually as well as asexually and infected it with some nasty bacteria that digest their "hosts" from the inside out. Two different populations were compared: one infected with the bacteria and another that wasn't. Over time, the infected population of worms evolved to engage in significantly more sexual reproduction. In addition, obligately asexual populations infected with the bacteria went extinct quite rapidly, whereas those that were capable of sexual reproduction persisted over time, presumably because they were able to remain at least one genetic step ahead of their lethal fellow travellers.[32]

Next, we turn to yet another human sexual mystery, one that is limited to a minority of the population but that is nonetheless among the most perplexing of all.

Notes

1. Fox, C. A., Wolff, H. S., & Baker, J. A. (1970). Measurement of intra-vaginal and intra-uterine pressures during human coitus by radio-telemetry. *Journal of Reproduction and Fertility, 22,* 243–251.

2. Baker, R. R., & Bellis, M. A. (1993). Human sperm competition: Ejaculate manipulation by females and a function for the female orgasm. *Animal Behaviour, 46,* 887–909.

3. Shklovsky, V. (2005). *Knight's move.* Champaign, IL: Dalkey Archive Press.

4. Symons, D. (1979). *The evolution of human sexuality.* New York: Oxford University Press.

5. Gould, S. J. (1987). Freudian slip. *Natural History, 96,* 14–21.

6. Lloyd, E. (2005). *The case of the female orgasm.* Cambridge, MA: Harvard University Press.

7. Dunn K. M., Cherkas, L. F., & Spector, T. D. (2005). Genetic influences on variation in female orgasmic function: A twin study. *Biology Letters, 1,* 260–263; Dawood, K., Kirk, K. M., Bailey, J. M., Andrews, P. W., & Martin, N. G. (2005). Genetic and environmental influences on the frequency of orgasm in women. *Twin Research and Human Genetics, 8*(1), 27–33.

8. Connell, K., Guess, M. K., La Combe, J., Wang, A., Powers, K., Lazarou, G., et al. (2005). Evaluation of the role of pudendal nerve integrity in female function using noninvasive techniques. *American Journal of Obstetrics and Gynecology, 192*(5), 1712–1717.

9. Hrdy, S. B. (1979). Infanticide among animals: A review, classification, and examination of the implications for the reproductive strategies of females. *Ethology and Sociobiology, 1,* 13–40.

10. Hrdy, S. B. (2000). *Mother nature.* New York: Ballantine Books.

11. Komisaruk, B. R., Beyer-Flores, C., & Whipple, B. (2006). *The science of orgasm.* Baltimore: Johns Hopkins University Press.

12. Nin, A. (1970). *The diary of Anaïs Nin* (Vol. 2). New York: Harcourt, Brace, Jovanovich.

13. Troisi, A., & Carosi, M. (1998). Female orgasm rate increases with male dominance in Japanese macaques. *Animal Behaviour, 56,* 1261–1266.

14. Eschler, L. (2004). The physiology of the female orgasm as a proximate mechanism. *Sexualities, Evolution and Gender, 6,* 171–194.

15. Kiefer, A. K., Sanchez, D. T., Kalinka, C. J., & Ybarra, O. (2006). Sex roles how women's nonconscious association of sex with submission relates to their subjective sexual arousability and ability to reach orgasm. 55, 83–94.

16. March of Dimes. Retrieved from http://www.marchofdimes.com/ professionals/681_1155.asp.

17. Marlowe, F. (2000). The Patriarch Hypothesis: An alternative explanation of menopause. *Human Nature, 11,* 27–42.

18. The Jane Goodall Institute. Retrieved from http://www.janegoodall.org/ chimp_central/chimpanzees/f_family/flo.asp.

19. Hrdy, S. B. (2005). Cooperative breeders with an ace in the hole. In: E. Voland, A. Chasiotis, & W. Schiefenhoevel (Eds.), *Grandmotherhood: The evolutionary significance of the second half of female life* (pp. 295–317). New Brunswick, NJ: Rutgers University Press.

20. Hawkes, K., O'Connell, J. F., & Blurton Jones, N. G. (1997). Hadza women's time allocation, offspring provisioning and the evolution of long postmenopausal life spans. *Current Anthropology, 38,* 551–578.

21. For example, Sear, R., Mace, R., & McGregor, I. A. (2000). Maternal grandmothers improve the nutritional status and survival of children in rural Gambia. *Proceedings of the Royal Society of London, B, 267,* 1641–1647.

22. Cant, M. A., & Johnstone, R. A. (2008). Reproductive skew and the evolution of menopause. In: R. Hagar & C. B. Jones (Eds.), *Reproductive skew in vertebrates.* Cambridge, UK: Cambridge University Press.

23. Dawkins, R. (1989). *The selfish gene.* New York: Oxford University Press.

24. Hrdy, S. B. (1999). *Mother nature: Maternal instincts and how they shape the human species.* New York: Ballantine.

25. Saad, G. (2004). Applying evolutionary psychology in understanding the representation of women in advertisements. *Psychology and Marketing, 21,* 593–612.

26. Gwynne, D. T. (1981). Sexual different theory: Mormon crickets show role reversal in mate choice. *Science, 213,* 779–780.

27. Hamilton, J. B., & Mestler, G. E. (1969). Mortality and survival: comparison of eunuchs with intact men and women in a mentally retarded population. *Journal of Gerontology, 24,* 395–411.

28. Dingard, D. L. (1984). The sex differential in morbidity, mortality and lifestyle. *Annual Review of Public Health, 5,* 433–458.

29. Williams, G. C. (1957). Pleiotropy, natural selection, and the evolution of senescence. *Evolution, 11,* 398–411.

30. Williams, G. C. (1975). *Sex and evolution.* Princeton, NJ: Princeton University Press.

31. Jolly, A. (2000). *Lucy's legacy: Sex and intelligence in human evolution.* Cambridge, MA: Harvard University Press.

32. Morran, L. T., Schmidt, O. G., Gelarden, I. A., Parrish II, R. C., & Lively, C. M. (2011). Running with the Red Queen: Host-parasite coevolution selects for biparental sex. *Science, 333,* 216–218.

CHAPTER FOUR

Sexual Mysteries III: Homosexuality

H OMOSEXUALITY, "THE LOVE THAT dares not speak its name," speaks loudly indeed when it comes to posing an evolutionary mystery. The mystery is simple enough; its resolution, however, is not yet in sight. First, the mystery.

Partitioning the Puzzle

The *sine qua non* for any trait to have evolved is for it to connect positively with reproductive success, more precisely, with success in projecting genes relevant to that trait into the future. So, if homosexuality is in any sense a product of evolution—and it clearly is, for reasons to be explained—then genetic factors associated with same-sex preference must enjoy "positive selection pressure," which is to say, some sort of fitness advantage. The problem should be obvious: How can natural selection have favored any genes whose phenotypic outcome (anatomy, physiology, or behavioral inclination) results in its own diminished success? By definition, they should be selected against. And pretty much by definition, homosexuals should experience less reproductive success than their heterosexual colleagues. Yet, as we'll see, same-sex preference clearly has a genetic component, which is to say, it must have evolved. But how?

The paradox of homosexuality is especially apparent for individuals whose homosexual preference is exclusive, that is, who have no inclination toward heterosexuality. But the paradox persists even for those who are bisexual, since it is mathematically provable that even a tiny difference in reproductive outcome can drive substantial evolutionary change. One of the giants of evolutionary theory, J. B. S. Haldane, made the following calculation in 1927 (it loomed large in the about-to-emerge "synthetic theory of evolution," which crucially combined genetics and natural selection).

Haldane suggested that we imagine two alternative forms of the same gene—that is, two "alleles"—call them A1 and A2.[i] Lets say that the initial frequency of A1 is 0.1% and that of A2 is 99.9%. Imagine, further, that A1 produces 101 successful offspring for every 100 produced by A2; that is, A1 enjoys a very slight fitness advantage of just 1%. Despite the fact that it starts off being so rare that its numbers seem downright insignificant (merely one A1 allele for every 1,000 A2s), and despite the fact that it does only 1% better than its rival, in just 4,000 generations the situation would have reversed, with A1 now making up 99.9% of the population and A2, a mere .1%.[1] Such is the power of compound interest, and of natural selection.

For our purposes, the implication is dramatic: Anything that diminishes, even slightly, the reproductive performance of a given allele should be vigorously selected against. And homosexuality certainly seems like one of these things. Gay men, for example, have children at about 20% the rate of heterosexual men.[2] I haven't

---

i. Think of an allele as a playing card, say, the jack of spades. In this case, there are four different alleles—spades, hearts, diamonds, and clubs—four different manifestations in which the gene for "jack" can appear. In a biological system, these four alleles (the four suits) are competing with each other at any given place on a chromosome, and evolution will favor the one or ones that generate the highest fitness. For an example more connected to human biology, there are three alleles that determine blood type, A, B, and O, and two alleles for the Rh factor, Rh+ and Rh−, and so forth.

seen reliable data for lesbians, but it seems highly likely that a similar pattern exists.

Of course, many homosexuals are actually bisexual, and as a result, they reproduce heterosexually, at least some of the time. True enough. In fact, Alfred Kinsey and his collaborators developed a useful 7-point scale concerning human sexual preferences, ranging from exclusive heterosexuality to exclusive homosexuality. They emphasized that when it came to human beings, same-sex and opposite-sex preferences do not constitute two distinct and nonoverlapping populations. "The world," Kinsey et al. pointed out, "is not divided into sheep and goats."[3]

But Haldane's demonstration is nevertheless convincing, and relevant: Just a small difference in fitness is capable of driving huge differences in ultimate success, and it seems more than likely that someone who is bisexual, who occupies any of the intermediate points in the Kinsey scale, would be at least somewhat less fit than another person whose romantic time and effort is devoted exclusively to the opposite sex. Remember, a difference of merely one part in a thousand is sufficient to cause a monumental difference in outcome, such that anything less than a full commitment to opposite-sex preference would have to be strongly selected against. Not only that, but it is also true that some people, at least, are pretty much entirely "sheep" or "goats"; that is, they are exclusively homosexual in their preferences. Indeed, numerous studies have confirmed the common-sense assumption that homosexuals have lower lifetime reproductive success than do heterosexuals.[4]

A basic bio-economic model shows that the puzzle is more puzzling yet. Thus, every behavioral or physical trait can be associated with an average benefit—its positive contribution to reproductive payoff—as well as a cost, its negative effect. Obtaining food, for example, conveys a benefit in terms of calories added, as well as a cost, measurable, for example, as time, energy, and risk expended while foraging or hunting. Natural selection works to adjust such traits so as to generate the largest possible ultimate fitness payoff, which economists would describe as maximizing "utility" by favoring the largest difference between benefits and costs.

Clearly, heterosexual reproduction is costly, requiring time and energy in courtship as well as the act of mating itself. But although evolutionary biologists have long wondered about the adaptive value of sexual reproduction as opposed to its asexual alternative,[5] no one seriously questions that once a lineage has opted for sexual reproduction, the actual costs of heterosexual behavior are more than compensated by its fitness benefits. Although sex itself remains an evolutionary mystery (compared to reproducing asexually, which generates twice the genetic payoff per parent), it is nonetheless clear that among individuals already specialized for sexual reproduction, the balance sheet is positive. That is, the accumulated evolutionary benefits of interacting with an opposite-sex partner on balance exceeds the sum total of costs.

What about homosexual interactions? They, too, are costly, even if measured strictly in terms of time and energy.[ii] Economists would have to conclude that at a minimum, same-sex courtship and consummation impose an above-zero "opportunity cost" on the participants, if only in that time and energy budgets are finite, and whatever is expended on homosexual relationships cannot be available for direct, heterosexual reproduction or simply for self-maintenance. The problem, therefore, isn't merely one of sexual preference, but also time and energy.

The plot thickens.

Is Evolution Relevant Here?

On the other hand, it is still possible to negate much of the evolutionary mystery if it can be argued that homosexuality is disconnected from genetics—which turns out to be a very difficult case to make. One possible route, however, would be to emphasize the uncertainty of the designation "homosexual." It could be pointed out, for example, that for some people, bisexuality is a stable state, whereas for others, it is part of a life-course transition from one preference to another.[6] Moreover, what sorts of acts are necessary to qualify as homosexual? Holding hands? Back or shoulder rubs? Kissing? Fondling genitals? Mutual masturbation? Oral sex? Anal sex? Dildos? Even more confounding: What about people who

---

ii. Disease transmission, too, but it is unclear how heterosexually transmitted diseases such as syphilis and gonorrhea compare in their fitness consequences with the best-known disease associated with homosexual transmission, namely, AIDS.

acknowledge having occasional same-sex hankerings but who do not actually *do* anything? And what of those cases—notably, from same-sex prisons—in which the overt behaviors are clearly within the range of "traditional" homosexual acts, but whose participants often maintain that they are not in fact homosexual, but rather, are simply acting out of social dominance, subordination, or loneliness, combined with a dearth of heterosexual partners? Moreover, among many nonincarcerated men in a wide range of societies, those who take an active, mounting, inserting role relative to other men are typically considered fully masculine. In short, where do we draw the line?

One way of dealing with the definitional dilemma is to speak about "men who have sex with other men" and "women who have sex with other women," which neatly gets around the difficulty of nonexclusivity. After all, a man who has sex with other men doesn't necessarily refrain from sex with women, on occasion. But this simply introduces yet another problem: namely, the meaning of "have sex." And in truth, this definitional folderol is largely besides the point, tantamount to a squid or octopus emitting lots of ink in an effort to confuse its pursuers.

In the pages to come, I'll refrain from drawing any lines or squirting excessive ink, but I will focus on the agreed fact that homosexuality exists, that in its various manifestations it differs from exclusive heterosexuality, that it is present in nontrivial frequency, and that, regardless of the precise details, it therefore requires some sort of evolutionary explanation. Or maybe not.

Thus, we must consider the possibility that homosexuality is entirely a function of proximate causes, devoid of evolutionary substructure. Homosexuality could conceivably be an illness, as argued in 1886 by the sexologist and psychiatrist Richard von Krafft-Ebing in his highly influential book, *Psychopathia Sexualis.*[iii] Astoundingly, reverberations of this view persisted in the *Diagnostic and Statistic Manual of Mental Disorders* (DSM) of the American Psychiatric Association until 1974, when the DSM no longer classified homosexuality as a mental disorder. Aside from its hurtful social impacts, the perception of homosexuality as an illness flies

---

iii. Krafft-Ebing was the first to introduce the terms *homosexual* and *heterosexual*, as well as *masochism* and *sadism*.

in the face of the high and persistent cross-cultural existence of same-sex preference.[7]

There is actually an early history of categorizing homoeroticism as nonpathological, beginning, not surprisingly, among the ancient Greeks. Perhaps the best known "hypothesis" for the origin of same-sex preference occurs in Plato's *Symposium*, where it is enunciated by the comic playwright Aristophanes. According to this story—clearly intended as myth rather than a serious explanation—the founding human beings were remarkable creatures known as Androgynes, who sported four arms and four legs, as well as the sexual apparatus of both male and female. Great was their power and glory, but they grew insolent. Zeus responded—as was his habit—with thunderbolts, splitting each offending creature into two, each one equipped with what we now take to be the traditional two arms, two legs, and one paltry set of genitals, either male or female. (Fortunately, the Androgynes abated their insolence at this point, for if they had not, Zeus was apparently prepared to split them yet again, which would have resulted in beings who hopped about on one leg . . . and with sex organs that can scarcely be imagined.)

According to Aristophanes, the human search for emotional and carnal union ever since is simply a continuing attempt to re-establish our species' prior, androgynous wholeness, each person seeking to reunite with his or her missing half. Since there were originally three kinds of Androgynes—male–female, male–male, and female–female—this story conveniently explains not only the origin of men and women, as two distinct sexes, but also the source of male and female homosexuality as well.

A Pathology?

It appears that the first effort at a scientific explanation for same-sex preference was by Karl Heinrich Ulrichs (1825–1895), considered by many the first gay rights activist. He suggested that male homosexuals were actually *anima muliebris virili corpore inclusa* ("a woman's psyche trapped in a man's body") and that lesbians were the inverse. In 1870, Ulrichs gestured toward likely biological underpinnings of homosexuality as an argument for gay rights, arguing that a male homosexual has inalienable rights. His sexual orientation is a right established by nature. Legislators have no right to veto nature, no right to persecute nature in the course of its work, and no right to torture living creatures who are subject to those drives nature gave them.[8]

However, since this "inversion model" claims that homosexuality derives from a mismatch between sexual anatomy and sexual preference, it nonetheless implies that homosexuality is pathological. It found favor with many early sex theorists, including Freud, von Krafft-Ebing, and Henry Havelock Ellis. Yet the picture is muddled. A historical overview of the psychoanalytic perception of homosexuality begins as follows:

> As the founder of psychoanalysis, Freud entertained complex and inconsistent views about homosexuality. In a famous letter to the mother of a homosexual, he stated that homosexuality is neither a vice nor an illness. He spoke out against persecution of homosexual people and pointed out that many great men, among them Plato, Michelangelo, and Leonardo Da Vinci, were homosexual. He also observed that it was generally not possible to change sexual orientation with psychoanalysis. In a letter to Ernest Jones, Freud affirmed the right of homosexual people to become psychoanalysts.[9]

At the same time, Freud believed that the Oedipus complex was both biologically determined and normal, which led many analysts to question how a man could in his youth be sexually attracted to his mother, then become attracted to men as an adult and yet all the while be "normal." And for a truly stunning example of seeming to embrace simultaneously a pathologized as well as a normalizing view of homosexuality, consider this observation by Freud:

> By studying sexual excitations other than those that are manifestly displayed, it has been found that all human beings are capable of making a homosexual object choice and in fact have made one in their unconscious. Indeed libidinal attachments to persons of the same sex play no less a part as factors in normal mental life, and *a greater part as a motive force for illness*, [my emphasis] than do similar attachments to the opposite sex.[10]

So, everyone is constitutionally bisexual, capable of homoerotic no less than heteroerotic unconscious choices, of which the former are as consequential as are heterosexual preferences in normal life . . . but even more important when it comes to mental illness!

Comparable foolishness is found in a hypothesized identification with the opposite-sex parent, rage toward same-sex siblings, castration anxiety, an unconscious fear of heterosexuality, a faulty sense of gender identity, and so forth—all emphasizing early developmental experiences and more or less based on the assumption that *normal* development leads to heterosexuality.

The view that homosexuality is pathological is currently held almost exclusively by right-wing ideologues and religious fundamentalists; at present, it is the overwhelming view of unbiased scientists that same-sex preference, when it occurs, is no less "natural" than its opposite-sex counterpart. Some of the evidence for this comes from the widespread distribution of homosexuality among animals. Once a species is observed long enough, nearly always it eventually reveals instances of homoeroticism, usually via male–male and/or female–female mountings, often with genital contact and pelvic thrusting. In most cases, these interactions take place in the context of bisexuality, typically by juveniles.

What is uniquely human, or nearly so, is the existence of at least some individuals for whom homosexuality is an *exclusive preference*, that is, individuals occupying the far end of Kinsey and colleagues' 7-point scale. To my knowledge, the only other mammal species of which this is true are domestic sheep, *Ovis aries*, among whom some rams appear to be homosexual exclusivists, regularly ignoring ewes in heat and preferring to mount other rams.[11] Some rams are heterosexual (55–75%, depending on the study), some bisexual (18–22%), some exclusively homosexual (7–10%), and some asexual (12–19%). The homosexual rams, interestingly, are masculinized; that is, they are the mounters rather than the ones mounted. It seems plausible that these individuals have experienced intrauterine influences upon their sensory receptors and/or brain mechanisms, rendering them sensitive to male pheromones rather than female.[12]

It is difficult to identify what might be uniquely shared by domestic sheep and human beings, such that they, alone among other animals, exhibit exclusive homosexuality. Dominant male baboons will on occasion accept what appear to be sexual advances from subordinate males, but I do not know any instances in which male–male pairs establish a close social and sexual relationship while ignoring nearby fertile females. There is, of course, no reason to believe that such examples won't eventually be identified, among mammals in general, or primates in particular. If current speculation proves correct, they would likely correlate with a complex cascade of hormonal events. Thus, it is generally accepted that hormones, especially circulating sex hormones, can activate existing neural patterns and predispositions. It was thought for a time that gay men were "that way" because their testosterone levels were lower than that of heterosexuals, with bisexuals in between, just as lesbians were supposed to be "androgenized" relative to straight women. Such "findings" were never confirmed, but nonetheless penetrated into much popular consciousness.[13]

What is somewhat newer, however, and for our purposes more important, is the idea that in addition to being *activational*, hormones also have an *organizational* role, influencing the establishment of brain systems and structures beginning early in embryology. Even here, however, some sort of genetic involvement seems necessary, even if merely permissive rather than directly causative.

Perhaps the strongest argument for a biological underpinning to same-sex preference is a simple generalized one, deriving from how remarkably widespread it is in the biological world. In one of the earliest such reports, published in 1979, anthropologist Linda Wolfe presented detailed data on the sexual behavior of a troop of 60 adult female Japanese macaque monkeys, within a troop composed of 140 animals overall.[14] Wolfe described a substantial frequency of female–female mountings, results that essentially were not believed—at least, not initially. But as further observations accumulated from a wide array of species, the conclusion became inescapable: Homosexuality is a common fixture in the lives of many animals, perhaps most.

More than 30 years after Wolfe's pioneering observations, same-sex pairing and attempted copulation have been described for a vast array of animal species, including all the major vertebrate groups as well as mollusks, insects, even nematode worms, and among free-living individuals as well as under captive conditions. Moreover, it is likely that the actual frequency of homosexual behaviors among animals is higher than reported, simply because when sexual behavior is observed among "monomorphic" species (those in which male and female look similar), it is typically assumed even now that the interaction is heterosexual.

Natural Exuberance?

A popularized book titled *Biological Exuberance: Animal Homosexuality and Natural Diversity* described a wide range of same-sex behaviors among 470 different species.[15] This number should be taken with a grain of salt, however, since in his eagerness to overcome what he perceived as a pro-heterosexual scientific bias and to "document" the full range of animal homosexuality, the author, Bruce Bagemihl, seems to have deviated in the opposite direction, uncritically accepting nearly any account of same-sex sociability as indicating homoerotic behavior. Moreover, his explanation for the existence of animal homosexual behavior is downright silly: that nature is simply abundant, surprising, and—his word—exuberant.

In one respect, Bagemihl is altogether correct: Nature really *is* abundant, surprising, and wonderfully exuberant, but this is simply a description of how it appears to us. In no way does the word "exuberance" explain anything at all, just as Aristotle didn't really explain why objects accelerate when they have been dropped by claiming that they become increasingly "jubilant" as they approach the ground. There is something delightfully liberating about exuberance generally, and perhaps sexual exuberance in particular, but it is bone-headedly unscientific to maintain that gay and lesbian sexuality, for example, simply result from nature's profligate fondness for variety as such.

It is doubtless more pleasant to revel in diversity—whether of human or nonhuman sexuality—than to morosely deny its existence. Moreover, it must be challenging for religious fundamentalists to maintain that homosexuality is contrary to God's law and therefore a mortal sin once it is seen to be widespread in the natural world. Alternatively, perhaps there is simply a widespread prudish disinclination to look honestly at animal sexuality in general and at homosexuality in particular, discernible in the shocked surprise evoked when the facts are made clear. In 2005, for example, the blockbuster movie *March of the Penguins* was widely embraced by the viewing public in general and by Christian fundamentalists in particular as testimony to the potency of monogamy in nature. Shortly thereafter, considerable media attention, seasoned with outright disbelief, followed publication of the fact that male chinstrap penguins form long-standing pair bonds . . . with other male penguins![16]

To be sure, the situation among animals could be illuminating for *Homo sapiens* as well, especially when it comes to possibly revealing certain generalizable evolutionary pressures. At least, this seems to be a fear on the part of many biologists, most of whom are constitutionally disinclined to extrapolate from their animal-based research to the human condition, as well as for antigay activists, who worry that animal studies will somehow "naturalize" what they see as immoral behavior. Thus, those male chinstrap penguins at the Central Park Zoo successfully fostered a chick and also gave rise to a best-selling children's book, *And Tango Makes Three*. For several years running, this book has exceeded all others as the one most requested to be banned from libraries, a situation that does not seem to have been ameliorated by the fact that after constituting a male–male unit for 6 years, one of these male penguins ran off with a female named Linda.

Animal research, applied indiscriminately to human beings, can be misleading. There have, for example, been numerous research findings dealing with same-sex courtship in that long-time favorite of research geneticists, the fruit fly, genus *Drosophila*. Several different mutations have been identified that induce males to court other males instead of females.[17] Sexual behavior in these animals is very strongly controlled by pheromones and how the fruit fly's brain responds to them. Behavior geneticists have known for decades of a particular mutation—appropriately known as *fruitless*—that induces males to court other males. Others have also been identified. But nothing as clear-cut applies to human beings: It is simply not the case that gay men prefer sex with other men because they are unable to distinguish them from women.

So let's turn briefly to some of the evidence for homosexual genetics among human beings in particular before we consider various hypotheses as to how any such "gay genes" might be maintained.

Homosexual Genetics

In the early 1990s, Dean Hamer, a geneticist at the U.S. National Institutes of Health, led a study that reported the existence of a specific allele located on the X chromosome—Xq28—that predicted gay versus straight sexual orientation in men.[18] It generated a media firestorm.[iv] Subsequent research has been confusing, showing that at minimum, the situation is considerably more complicated than had been hoped by some (notably, most gay rights advocates) or feared by others (who insist that sexual orientation is entirely a "lifestyle choice"). Thus, some studies have failed to confirm any such role for Xq28,[19] while others have been supportive.[20]

It is also increasingly clear that whatever its impact on male homosexuality, this particular allele does not relate to lesbianism.[21] Moreover, other research strongly suggests that there are regions on the "autosomal" (nonsex) chromosomes that influence sexual orientation in people.[22] A reasonable summary statement at present is that when it comes to male homosexuality, there is almost certainly a direct influence—although probably not strict control—by one or more alleles. Ditto for female homosexuality, although it is increasingly clear that the genetic mechanism(s) and almost certainly the relevant genes themselves differ between the sexes.

Beyond the suggestive but inconclusive search for specific sex-orientation alleles, other genetic evidence has emerged. On average, approximately 3% of men and about 2% of women in the United States are gay, and yet, if we look at the sisters of homosexuals (gays and lesbians taken together), it turns out that more than 6% are lesbian. This is about three times what would be expected from a random sample. Similarly, 8% of the brothers of homosexuals turn out to be gay, which is significantly higher than the 3% that would be expected from chance alone.[23] To summarize: If one sibling is homosexual, this means that his or her sibling is significantly more than randomly likely to be homosexual as well. Although such a finding is *consistent* with genetics, by itself it doesn't prove a genetic connection, since a comparable result could arise if environmental factors alone were operating. After all, siblings don't only share half their genes; they are also likely to

---

iv. A decade later, he suggested the existence of a "God gene" (see this book, Chapter 7). Dr. Hamer hasn't yet announced that God is homosexual, nor—to my knowledge—has he reported thus far on the existence of a gene for finding genes.

share an environment. On the other hand, had the siblings of homosexuals turned out to be *no more likely* to be homosexual than would be expected by chance, then we would have to conclude that genetic factors (along with environmental ones) are unlikely to be involved. So a *prima facie* case exists, even without the independent gene sleuthing of Hamer and others.

Twin studies have yet more to contribute. Monozygotic (MZ) or "identical" twins share 100% of their genes, since they develop from a single egg that splits in two immediately after fertilization. Of course, MZ twins have also shared the same prenatal environment. Dizygotic (DZ) or "fraternal/sororal" twins shared the same prenatal environment as well, and since they have the same mother and father, they share 50% of their genes, which makes them no more similar genetically than full siblings born separately. Half-sibs (the same mother or father, but not both) share 25% of their genes. By comparing different kinds of twins, it is possible to learn quite a lot about the general degree of genetic influence for any trait, although precise alleles cannot be identified.

Numerous comparisons can be made, not only between MZ twins, DZ twins, half DZ sibs, and unrelated individuals, but also by introducing another distinguishing variable: whether such pairs were reared together or apart. For example, comparing MZ twins reared apart with MZ twins reared together helps tease out the impact of genotype: More precisely, it helps control for the role of shared environment, since such individuals will have the same genes while experiencing different environments. A key dependent measure here is "concordance rate," essentially the probability that both members of a pair possess a particular trait given that one of them has it—or, alternatively, the probability that both lack the trait given that one of them doesn't have it. To conduct such analyses is to confront a rapidly multiplying subuniverse of logical and statistical complexity, but the bottom line strongly supports genetic influence . . . although stopping short of genetic determinism.[24]

For example, the concordance of homosexuality among MZ twins is about 50%, showing that the role of genes is real, since the concordance among DZ twins is considerably lower.[25] But the fact that the MZ concordance rate isn't 100% shows a definite role for their environment, including gene–environment interactions.

(Since MZ twins share 100% of their genes, if genes totally determined sexual orientation, their concordance for homosexuality and heterosexuality should also be 100%.) Other comparisons are also important: MZ twins reared together share the same genes as well as the same environment (although the environments for two different individuals can never be precisely the same!); MZ twins reared apart share the same genes but very different environments; DZ twins reared together share 50% of their genes and somewhat the same environment; DZ twins reared apart share 50% of their genes and very different environments; adopted siblings have altogether different genes and somewhat the same environment; random pairs from the population at large have different genes and different environments.

It is impossible to summarize in detail the welter of twin-based findings without devoting an entire book to the effort. Among some of the interesting conclusions that can be drawn, however, is that the concordance of homosexuality for adoptive siblings, for example, is lower than for biological siblings, which in turn is lower than that for DZ twins, which is lower than that for MZ twins. This is precisely what would be expected if genes exert a nonzero effect. In addition, concordance rates among female MZ lesbians is higher than that among gay male MZ twins, and similarly, the concordance rate among female DZ lesbians is higher than among their male DZ counterparts—suggesting that the genetic influence on homosexuality may be higher among women than among men, while further supporting the idea that the genetic influence upon homosexuality differs somewhat, somehow between women and men.[26] Other studies confirm the fact that the tendency to be lesbian or gay has a substantial heritability—which means that a significant proportion of the variation in sexual preference correlates with variation in underlying genotype.[27]

Prior to recent times and the prospect of *in vitro* fertilization or do-it-yourself "turkey baster babies," the likelihood was that people who were exclusively homosexual did not reproduce at all; they, too, had to have descended from heterosexual ancestors, which by itself suggests a complex heredity for the trait.

Finally, perhaps the most cogent argument for a substantial genetic component to sexual orientation comes from a single qualitative, nonexperimental, nontechnical observation, but one that is so widespread as to be unarguable and highly revealing, namely, the stunning fact that around the world, huge numbers of people struggle against their sexual orientation, often desperately seeking to become heterosexual so as to avoid social ostracism and/or conform to their religious expectation of what constitutes appropriate sexual behavior. If sexual orientation were simply a personal "lifestyle" choice, it is inconceivable that so many people would voluntarily subject themselves to so much misery.

It is also notable that intrapsychic battles of this sort are overwhelmingly lost, despite the typically earnest—even desperate—desire of the participants to change, and (at least in the United States) notwithstanding a small army of ideologically committed therapists. Even those relatively few cases of "successful" conversion therapy typically last less than a year, and, moreover, they involve a disproportionate number of subjects who were initially bisexual rather than exclusively homosexual in the first place.[28]

Unlike certain traits that are under strict genetic control (eye color, blood type, etc.) and others that are entirely determined by the environment (e.g., what language someone speaks), most behavioral traits—including but not limited to sexual orientation—are influenced by both genes and environment. Accordingly, isn't it likely that individuals with an inclination toward homosexuality would have been more prone to behave homosexually in a more gay-tolerant social environment, and vice versa? If so, then in societies that did not welcome sexual diversity, homosexual-prone people might well have historically been more inclined to marry and even have children, all the better to fit in. This would have contributed to the maintenance of same-sex preference, but as we have already seen, it couldn't have done the job by itself.

We must conclude that even though the route from genotype to sexual orientation is winding and not yet entirely revealed, it unquestionably exists. Given, furthermore, that homosexuality is a cross-cultural universal, with the proportion remaining roughly the same around the globe and throughout human history, we are left with an undeniable evolutionary puzzle. In the pages to come, we will not unravel this puzzle; however, we shall attempt to identify and evaluate some of the key ingredients in what promises to be a very complex situation.

A Possible Role for Kin Selection

At first glance, homosexuality and altruism seem no more connected than apples and oranges. But of course, apples and oranges aren't altogether dissimilar (both are fruit). And homosexuality and altruism are similar as well, in that each poses a comparable theoretical dilemma, namely, the fact that alleles promoting either tendency necessarily promise—or threaten—to act against their own propagation. Altruism *means* an action that promotes the success of people other than oneself, and so basic definitional logic says that it should be replaced by alternative genes that promote one's own success, that is, genes for selfishness. Homosexuality *means* same-sex erotic preference, which also appears logic-bound to diminish the reproductive success of any genes that promote such activity. Like genes for altruism, genes for homosexuality should therefore be replaced by alternative genes, with selfishness succeeding altruism and homosexuality giving way to heterosexuality. But, like altruism, homosexuality does not merely exist; it flourishes in significant numbers.

As it happens, an especially satisfying scientific explanation for altruism has been proposed and is strongly supported by the evidence. It also offers some promise for explaining homosexuality. Known as "inclusive fitness theory" or "kin selection," it essentially argues that once evolution is seen to operate at the level of genes rather than organisms, the paradox of altruism melts away insofar as individuals are selected to act on behalf of their constituent genes. This is because beneficence toward others, at the level of behaving organisms, although appearing to be altruistic, can constitute unacknowledged selfishness at the level of genes, if "altruists" are actually benefiting identical copies of their own altruism-promoting genes, contained in other bodies. And in fact, humans, like other animals, typically dispense altruism toward genetic relatives—hence the phrase "kin selection."

This insight, due largely to the genius of theorist William D. Hamilton, has literally revolutionized evolutionary biology in recent decades.[29] It has been used to solve such mysteries as food sharing, alarm calling, and willingness to run risks defending others from predators. It is strongly implied in the "grandmother hypothesis" for the evolution of menopause, which we have already considered. It also stimulated biologists to look for a possible kin-selected basis for human homosexuality, since the reason food sharing, alarm calling, and predator repelling (in addition to other seemingly altruistic acts) are evolutionary mysteries is that when push comes to shove, they involve foregoing reproductive opportunities for oneself while conveying a compensatory benefit to others. And the answer, of course, is that at the genetic level, those "others" are really "oneself."[v]

Sharing food, giving alarms, and repelling predators—along with many other forms of social cooperation—were evolutionary conundrums because they translated into reproductive restraint.[vi] And in fact, the most satisfying application of inclusive fitness theory to a prior evolutionary mystery had to do with explaining the presence of sterile worker castes among social bees, wasps, and ants. It's a long story, basically revolving around the fact that because of their peculiar genetic architecture, worker bees, wasps, and ants share more genes with the offspring of the queen than they would with their own children, were they to reproduce. Not surprisingly, once kin selection became established within the intellectual repertoire of evolutionary biologists, there ensued a flurry of efforts to ascertain whether it could do for homosexuality what it has done for altruism. How neat it would be if homosexual humans were even a little bit like worker bees, producing on average fewer children than heterosexuals, but compensating genetically via their own inclusive fitness, that is, conveying a reproductive lift to their relatives, and thereby, to their own distinctive alleles.

It seems that the hypothesis was first explicitly proposed by noted evolutionary biologist Edward O. Wilson,[30] who suggested

---

v. The phrase "inclusive fitness theory" derives from Hamilton's insight that an accurate account of fitness must be more inclusive than simple reproductive success; it must be expanded to include the effect of a given behavior on identical copies of the genes in question that are carried in the bodies of those benefiting from the seemingly altruistic act.

vi. There is no particular evolutionary mystery attendant upon getting one's own food, defending self or family from predators, and so forth. It is only when behavior results in a kind of self-denial that it becomes problematic.

that because homosexuals were freed from the obligation of invest-ing time and energy on their own reproduction, perhaps they were then able to assist their siblings and other relatives to rear *their* offspring, to the ultimate evolutionary benefit of any homosexual-ity-promoting genes present in those additional children thereby produced.

Unfortunately, the data suggested otherwise.

For starters, available evidence did not show that homosexuals spent an especially large amount of time helping their relatives, or even interacting with them. Moreover, when homosexuals did provide notable amounts of assistance to others, it did not appear that this helping behavior was especially directed toward genetic relatives.[31] Another study, comparing 60 heterosexual with 60 homosexual English men, found "no significant differences between heterosexual and homosexual men in general familial affinity, generous feelings (willingness to provide financial and emotional resources), and benevolent tendencies (such as willing-ness to baby-sit)."[32] These results were based on surveys; accord-ingly, they revealed opinions and attitudes rather than actual behavior. Moreover, they involved modern industrialized societ-ies, which presumably are not especially representative of human-ity's ancestral situations. Nonetheless, it was reasonably concluded that if assisting one's relatives were a robust feature associated with same-sex preference, it should have been revealed.

Another hypothesis was promptly floated, namely, that since there is some anthropological evidence that homosexual men were more than randomly likely to become priests or shamans, perhaps the additional social prestige conveyed to their heterosexual rela-tives might have given a reproductive boost to those relatives—and thereby, to any shared genes that predisposed toward homosexuality.[33] An appealing idea, but once again, sadly lacking in empirical support.

Further discouraging to the kin selection hypothesis is that—especially in modern, Western societies—parents do not generally react with delight when they learn that a child is gay or lesbian, whereas if homosexual children were analogous to the "helpers at the nest" phenomenon among birds, we might expect if not out-right enthusiasm at least a consistent level of tolerant acceptance on the part of those older, breeding adults who can expect to be helped.[vii] One might also anticipate that if kin selection were involved, homosexuality would be more frequent if there are other siblings to be assisted and vice versa. But in fact, singleton children are no less likely to be homosexual than are those with siblings.

Another problem with attributing homosexuality to kin selection is that it isn't clear why individuals who enhance their fitness by helping relatives should *also* engage in same-sex erotic and bonding behavior at all. Why aren't people with an above-average predilection for aiding their relatives also inclined, say, to hop on one leg instead, or to experience olfactory hallucinations, or to talk in tongues? Why should their sexual predisposition be at issue in the first place, and given that it is, why aren't they inclined to have sex with plants, or to masturbate obsessively? After all, as already noted, same-sex copulations are not in themselves reproductive, and—like any sexual interactions—they also require lots of time and energy, which might otherwise be expended directly on behalf of reproducing relatives or somehow used to obtain other proximate rewards.

But on the other hand, it is possible that—as Mark Twain famously responded to the announcement of his own demise—the death of kin selection as an evolutionary explanation for homosexuality has been greatly exaggerated. Thus, as already noted, the less-than-impressive levels of intrafamily benevolence reported for homosexuals were based on technologized, 20th-century populations, which might not reflect the long period of small-scale, nontechnological hunter-gatherer living in which such tendencies would presumably have evolved. And in fact, some interesting and suggestive research has recently emerged, focusing on male homosexuals among a more traditional population on the island of Samoa.

Known as *fa'afafine*, these individuals do not reproduce. They are, however, fully accepted into Samoan society in general,

---

vii. In many bird species, young adults who are physiologically capable of reproducing do not do so; instead, they remain as "helpers at the nest" of their relatives—typically their own parents—assisting in the rearing of sibs and half-sibs. In the process, genes for altruistic helping and reproductive restraint can be promoted even if the individuals doing the helping do not breed at all, so long as they are present in those additional kin whose success they enable.

and into their kin-based families in particular. Of particular note is that *fa'afafine* are significantly more prone to behave in a positive avuncular manner than are heterosexual uncles. Thus, they are more likely to purchase toys for their nieces and nephews, babysit, contribute money for the children's education, and generally provide high levels of indulgence and emotional support, in addition to their material assistance. These men are not simply fond of all children; rather, they lavish their attention upon their nieces and nephews (with whom they share, on average, 25% of their genes). This supportive role of *fa'afafine* even exceeds the contributions of heterosexual women as supportive aunts.[34]

It has recently been argued, most cogently by anthropologist Sarah Hrdy, that for much of human evolutionary history, child-rearing was not the province of parents (especially mothers) alone; rather, our ancestors engaged in a great deal of "allo-mothering," whereby nonparents—other genetic relatives in particular—pitched in.[35] It makes sense that such a system would have been derived by *Homo sapiens*, of all primate species the one whose infants are born the most helpless and that require the largest amount of postbirth investment. Insofar as it genuinely does "take a village to rear a child," no one should be surprised if some of the most engaged assistants turn out to have been the child's gay relatives.

One effect of modernization has been a reduction in infant mortality and a parallel decrease in average family size, the so-called "demographic transition." A consequence of this, in turn, might be that with fewer children per family, the industrialized world offers less opportunity for homosexual offspring to convey benefits to their heterosexual siblings, simply because there are fewer of the latter. Add to this the fact that with enhanced mobility, it is increasingly common for children, regardless of their sexual orientation, to leave their nuclear family to attend school and eventually start their own domestic lives. Hence, it is possible that kin selection was involved in the initial evolution of human homosexuality, but with little or no fitness payoff currently detectable, except in traditional societies. It may also be significant, therefore, that unlike the experience of gays and lesbians in much of the industrialized world, *fa'afafine* are fully integrated into Samoan society and are not discriminated against.

The implications are potentially large, and not only for a deeper scientific understanding of how and why homosexuality may have evolved. Thus, if—as may well be the case—homosexuals are only able to display their kin-selected inclinations to assist their heterosexual relatives when homosexuality is tolerated, then what is maladaptive is discrimination against homosexuals rather than homosexuality itself. Let's be more optimistic: If current trends persist and homosexual rights continue their current trajectory toward greater acceptance, this might generate a return not only to a more "natural" human condition but also to a higher inclusive fitness payoff experienced by gays and lesbians as well as—no less—by their relatives.

Resources, Groups, and Reciprocity

There is yet another route whereby kin selection could have led to the evolution of homosexuality without requiring that gays and lesbians were doting brothers and sisters, uncles and aunts. If some human ancestors with a same-sex preference merely reproduced less (or not at all), this in itself could have freed up resources for their straight relatives, without necessarily requiring that the former were especially collaborative or directly altruistic to their breeding heterosexual relatives. The argument is similar to one that helps explain the widespread within-family social support for individuals who enter monasteries, nunneries, or the priesthood, substituting homosexual orientation for vows of chastity: Such actions can, in theory, reduce the pressure of scarcity on those left "outside."

It's worth emphasizing here that there is currently no evidence for a genetic propensity in favor of taking vows of chastity, whereas there is for homosexual orientation. Also, the "more resources for everyone else" hypothesis has more than a whiff of "group selection" about it, since it posits that by foregoing or diminishing their own reproduction, homosexuals would have conveyed a benefit to the remaining group members. The problem is that these beneficiaries are liable to have included nonrelatives as well as those sharing part of the homosexuals' genotype. As a result, this hypothesis is vulnerable to selfish exploitation by unrelated group members who might gain by homosexuals' reproductive restraint, without having to give up anything.[viii]

But the payoff needn't have been all or nothing. Freeing up of resources could conceivably have been at least a contributing factor, especially if while diminishing their own reproduction, homosexually inclined individuals were able to enhance the amount of food, living space, adult attention, and so forth that remained "all in the family," instead of conveying benefit unselectively, to everyone in the group.

There is also a case to be made for homosexuality having evolved via strict group selection, independent of any inclusive fitness benefits, as follows: If groups containing large numbers of homosexuals reproduced less rapidly, they would be less likely to overexploit their resource base.[36] Other models have also been proposed, focusing on social interaction rather than resource exploitation. For example, if homosexuality correlates with greater sociality and social cooperation, then groups composed of proportionately more homosexuals might function more smoothly, and also occupy better habitats, which in turn would contribute to greater reproductive success for their genes.[37]

Of course, this presupposes that a society containing significant numbers of homosexuals would be less fraught and conflict ridden than one with fewer, which would seem to necessitate far more tolerance and acceptance of same-sex preference than is true today, at least in the industrialized West. The theory, at least, is intriguing and consistent: Given that male–male competition for access to females is a frequent cause of violence—among animals as well as humans—a case could be made that the larger the number of gay males, the less competition among heterosexual males for access to females, since gay males, once they self-identify, are no longer reproductive threats to their heterosexual colleagues.

On the other hand, there might be a corresponding increase in competition among gay males themselves! This could, however, be expected to be less intense than among straight males, since the latter compete for females, a "resource" that lends itself to being reproductively monopolized—at least for 9 months at a time—whereas

---

viii. We'll look at the fraught question of group selection later, in Chapter 8, when we consider one of the chief hypotheses for the adaptive significance of religion.

male physiology makes it more possible, at least in biological terms, for gay lovers to "share."

There is another generalized explanation for the evolution of altruistic behavior, disconnected from group selection and which, unlike kin selection, makes no assumptions about genetic related-ness between altruist and beneficiary. Technically but incorrectly known as reciprocal altruism,[ix] it is simply a biological version of "you scratch my back, I'll scratch yours" or "one good turn deserves another." The basic idea, first elaborated by sociobiologist Robert L. Trivers in 1971, is that individual 1 could be selected to do something that benefits individual 2 if there is sufficient likelihood that some time in the future, the tables will be turned whereupon individual 2 repays the debt.[38] As Trivers demonstrated, a system of this sort could evolve so long as the cost to individual 1 for her initial action is relatively low, and the benefit to individual 2 is high. The biggest fly in the reciprocating ointment, however, is the temptation to cheat, that is, for individual 2 to accept aid when in need, but then decline to reciprocate when the situation reverses and it is time for individual 2 to repay the favor.

For all its appeal—emotional as well as intellectual—it has proven difficult to identify clear-cut examples of reciprocity among animals. (The sole uncontested case involves vampire bats, who indulge in a heartwarming practice whereby those individuals who have successfully flown and fed by night regurgitate part of their blood meal to others less fortunate. Grateful recipients are then likely to reciprocate when they are successful and their earlier benefactors would otherwise go hungry.[39]) Human beings, on other hand, are the reciprocators par excellence. We share all sorts of things, often exchanging favors when not trading actual objects.

The connection of all this to homosexuality may seem obscure. Indeed, it may well *be* obscure! But here is the idea. Reciprocity doubtless plays a role in cementing mateships, as it does with friendships. The fact that gays and lesbians are every bit as prone to invest in their same-sex partners as are heterosexuals may seem

---

ix. Incorrectly because as we'll see, it doesn't really imply altruism at all, but rather, selfish benefit for the supposed "altruist." Hence, I prefer to call it simply "reciprocity."

to be an evolutionary anomaly, insofar as the latter are far more likely to reproduce. Two considerations are relevant here: For one, as already noted, many homosexuals are actually bisexual, or otherwise capable or inclined to reproduce, so that mutual aid within a same-sex partnership can contribute at least somewhat toward the fitness of each. For another, let's assume that there is a kin-selected payoff to homosexuality, via assistance rendered to one's genetic relatives: This could lead to a generalized inclination to be helpful and thus for homosexual partners to express such inclinations as well. It also would not preclude taking care of oneself via reciprocity with a partner, especially when "altruistic" assistance to genetic relatives is not immediately necessary or feasible.

In addition, it has been suggested—although not as yet clearly demonstrated—that homosexuals tend to be especially talented at social skills such as caregiving. If so, then they could conceivably be especially prone to mutually fitness-enhancing reciprocity. If not, then we must look elsewhere. But where? Aside from kin selection, reciprocity, and group selection, are there other promising hypotheses for the genetically based evolution of homosexuality? The answer is yes.

Balanced Polymorphisms and Other Genetic Phenomena

A range of possibilities revolve around what geneticists call "heterosis," resulting in "balanced polymorphisms." Consider a well-known illness, sickle cell anemia, for which there are two relevant alleles: Call them Sn for normal red blood cells and Ss for sickle cell.[x] Ss generates a biochemical anomaly as a result of which the sufferer's red blood cells collapse into an erratic sickle shape, causing them to stick together and clog blood vessels. In double-dose ("homozygous") form—that is, when individuals are SsSs—the sickling allele is often lethal. One would therefore expect that it would quickly disappear from the human gene pool. Indeed, it is largely absent from most populations, except for certain regions

---

x. Please note: This is not to suggest that homosexuality is a pathology! Rather, the example of sickle cell disease simply provides a well-known model for how any trait can in theory be maintained over evolutionary time.

that have a long history of malaria. It turns out that for complex reasons, heterozygous individuals—who are SnSs and therefore carry a single dose of the sickling gene—are more malaria resistant than are homozygous normals (SnSn). As a consequence, the otherwise deleterious sickling gene has been retained in the human gene pool, even though it is strongly selected against in double-dose form.

For our purposes, the idea would be that perhaps a genetic predisposition for homosexuality, even if a fitness liability when homozygous, could have been retained over evolutionary time if it somehow conveys a compensating benefit when combined with one or more other alleles.[40] No precise candidate genes have yet been identified, but for now, the possibility cannot be excluded.[41] Moreover, several suggestive qualitative arguments can in fact be made. Here goes.

Geneticists recognize something called "linkage disequilibrium," which is simply a fancy way of saying what should be obvious to anyone who has taken a high school biology course: Genes aren't piled up randomly and independent of each other, like beans in a bottle. Rather, they are arranged, in a line, on chromosomes. And this physical *linkage* is bound to create a degree of *disequilibrium*, if we compare the frequency of genes as they actually exist with what would be expected based simply on the fitness value of each one taken separately. Even if a particular gene has an unhelpful effect on fitness, it could still be maintained in substantial numbers if it is physically linked—on the same chromosome—to some other gene conveying a benefit that more than compensates for the first one's disadvantage.

Even such linkage should eventually become less effective, however, since chromosomes (the X and Y sex chromosomes excepted) regularly break and then reattach, occasionally crossing over with their matching "homolog." This enforced separation of genes along a chromosome provides an opportunity—at least in theory—for every gene to be evaluated independent of those to which it had at one time been linked. But this sorting-out process takes time and depends on many other factors. Crossing over does not reliably set the stage for a lower fitness trait to be selected against.

There is also another, parallel process that could result in a lower fitness genetic tendency being retained over evolutionary time.

Known as "pleiotropy" (*pleio* = "many," *tropy* = "turn" or "influence"), it speaks to the rather common situation in which a single gene has multiple effects, which sometimes seem quite disconnected. Thus, genes "for" eye color in fruit flies often also influence the details of how the affected animals court—which means, of course, that the genes could just as well be identified as "for" courtship, with a pleiotropic side effect upon eye color! Something comparable could be going on with respect to sexual preference, if genes "for" same-sex preference also generated, let's say, more efficient kidneys or better eyesight. The result would then be the maintenance of homosexuality, not because it is adaptive in itself but in spite of the fact that it might be maladaptive, so long as its genetic underpinning were wedded to some positive aspect of anatomy, physiology, or behavior that more than compensates.

Sadly, for those of us who like our explanations simple, this idea, too, is still awaiting empirical support.

For yet another plausible idea whose only drawback is a lack of evidence, there is always the prospect that homosexuality-promoting genes simply arise unusually often, via mutation. There is mathematically solid theory showing that "mutation-selection equilibrium" could maintain even a trait as dramatic as exclusive homosexuality if the mutation rate were high enough and selection against such a trait were sufficiently low.[42] But there is a problem here, too, in that selection should, over time, work against such a mutational tendency, if alternative allele forms that are more stable convey higher fitness. (And an even greater problem is that such mutations have yet to be discovered![xi])

Male homosexuality is more frequent than its female counterpart, at least among human beings. Of an anthropological sample of 21 different societies, 11 (52%) had male-only homosexuality, 9 (43%) had both male and female homosexuality, and only 1 (5%) had female-only homosexuality.[43] Moreover, it appears that in every human society, the frequency of male homosexuality (around 3%) is half again higher than female (around 2%). This pattern is suggestive biologically no less than sociologically and could be due to any number of reasons, ranging from greater male vulnerability

---

xi. This difficulty, although seemingly insuperable at present, could conceivably be overturned by a research announcement tomorrow.

to in utero stress to a presumed lower threshold for male sexuality in general.

Developmental processes are often described as being relatively "plastic," if they are subject to substantial variation depending on environmental conditions, or "canalized," if they aren't. Of course, such terminology is simply descriptive; it doesn't explain why this difference exists. (We might call it the Rumpelstiltskin effect, whereby people are prone to think that a phenomenon has been effectively dealt with and will obligingly disappear—like that annoying, magical dwarf in the famous fairy tale—once it has been named.)

It appears that homosexuality is more plastic in women and more canalized in men, and in this case, at least, such greater plasticity among women is consistent with expectation based on evolution. For one thing, we can anticipate that compared to men, women would be more inclined to switch from heterosexuality to homosexuality with age, since women experience menopause, after which any preexisting heterosexuality ceases to convey a direct reproductive payoff, and which in turn would give greater scope for "sexual fluidity." This is what happens.[44] By the same token, biologists would predict that since men retain the capacity to reproduce into old age, they should be less predisposed to switch from heterosexuality to homosexuality as they get older, and this, too, is the case.[45]

There is growing evidence that much sexual preference is fluid, among both sexes, but especially women. Considerable debate and uncertainty swirl around how to describe and classify human sexual preferences, as well as how to explain them. Finnish researchers, for example, have data suggesting that nearly 33% of men and 66% of women have the potential for genetically influenced homosexuality.[46] It appears that on balance, more women than men are capable of adopting either same- or opposite-sex preference, with the "decision" for women especially likely to be influenced by the particular characteristics of any potential partner. Men, by contrast, are more prone to have a given sexual orientation first—either homosexual or heterosexual—and then secondarily to find suitable partners who match their existing preference.

Prominent among the defining genetic differences between men and women is the fact that males are XY and females XX. A sex-linked gene present on the X chromosome would therefore be effectively unpaired (since the Y chromosome carries very few genes, and those it possesses lack partner alleles on the X). Accordingly, any such X-carried trait is more likely to be expressed in males. A recessive allele present in a woman's X chromosome, by contrast, stands a chance of being overridden by an alternative allele on the other X. In this regard, it is interesting that among birds, in which females are the "heterogametic sex,"[xii] female homosexuality is more frequent than its male counterpart—the opposite of what occurs in mammals.[47]

Going further, let's note that a new mutation (or any already-present homosexuality-promoting allele) on a Y chromosome would likely be expressed in all of a man's sons, whereas a similar gene on a father's X chromosome may or may not be expressed among his daughters, since unlike a Y-chromosome gene, one carried on a paternal X chromosome would have to contend with the corresponding alleles on the other X chromosome contributed by the mother. It might later, of course, be expressed in his grandsons, but as the generations proceed the analysis becomes harder to make and any relationship is more likely to be missed.

Alternatively, if such a genetic factor exists on the Y chromosome, it could only be expressed in males—but then, what about female homosexuality? (Since women are XX and lack a Y chromosome, a genetic factor for lesbianism couldn't reside on the Y chromosome.)

For all the excitement about identifying a "gay gene"—and all the reality that to a significant extent, homosexuality clearly is mediated at least partly by genetics—it must be emphasized that genes don't tell the whole story. For one thing, it is possible to explain any trait, and especially to *explain away* any finding that appears to disconfirm a genetic hypothesis, by arguing that the trait in question shows "incomplete penetrance and variable expressivity" . . . which is to say, sometimes the trait shows itself (whether or not the underlying genes are there), and even when it does, its actual manifestation will vary greatly.

Let's conclude this section by emphasizing that no trait derives from genes alone or from the environment alone. To be more affirming: Every trait derives from the interaction of the two. That said,

---

xii. Among birds, males are designated ZZ and females WZ.

Homo Mysterious: Evolutionary Puzzles of Human Nature

we'll continue to examine the role of genetics in particular, simply because DNA is the substrate upon which natural selection acts.

Other Social Payoffs

Time, now, for a reasonable historical assumption about how we got to be the way we are: During our long Pleistocene adolescence as a species, men were probably evolutionarily fit in proportion as they were good with projectile weapons, at anticipating the habits of game and of potential enemies and competitors, and at attracting and keeping mates, of course . . . with much of the latter two occurring in proportion as men succeeded at the former four. With the development of agriculture and early civilization, however, it is likely that the optimally adapted person—of either sex—tilted more than previously toward social skills, verbal ability, etc.[48] The likelihood is that these traits had always been favored to some degree, but perhaps especially so once people occupied large settled communities. And so, the argument goes, natural and sexual selection came to favor social and communicative skills—at which homosexuals tend to exceed heterosexuals.[49]

What does this have to do with genetics? Just this. Maybe in evolutionary time, exclusive homosexuality has been a fitness catastrophe, like sickle cell disease, but just as sickle cell disease persists because in single dose its underlying allele conveys a benefit with respect to malaria, perhaps one or more homosexuality-promoting alleles were retained because they also conveyed a particular payoff. That fitness-supporting homosexual benefit could have derived from the verbal facility and/or social and communicative skills just described. The outcome might then be a stable frequency of exclusive same-sex preference, just as heterosis produces a steady frequency of people with sickle cell disease.

C. R. Dewar, who first developed this line of reasoning, argues that if selection has favored an intermediate degree of "gayness," perhaps because of verbal facility and related assets, this would lead to exclusive homosexuality cropping up persistently at one tail of the distribution, even though homosexuality itself would not have been selected for directly. He turns to head size of human embryos for an example. Thus, selection favors the production of babies whose heads are pretty much as large as possible, so as to accommodate maximum brain development. Sometimes, however, this selective pressure results in babies whose heads are simply too big to be accommodated by the mother's birth canal: The resulting cephalopelvic disproportion is a significant cause of mortality during childbirth, especially in societies without access to modern obstetrical procedures.

Nevertheless, Dewar argues, such genes aren't edited out of the population because they are advantageous when present at intermediate levels:

> It might be safer at birth to have a small head with a small brain and to be born with the ease of a puppy, but it is just too massive a disadvantage throughout the remainder of life. In reproductive terms it's better to take the risk associated with a large head. Similarly it might be too big a disadvantage in a post-hunter–gatherer society to be aggressive with poor communication and social skills (as a result of being highly responsive to available androgens) even if the alternative means there is a 5% chance of being exclusively homosexual. This also parallels the observation that homosexual children are born to heterosexual parents. Parents with large heads who have survived childbirth may themselves conceive children who do not. Indeed it is invariably the case that parents of children who die during childbirth survived their own birth.[50]

Bear in mind that in traditional societies, homosexuality often served a social role, beyond possible assistance in rearing the offspring of genetic relatives.[51] Perhaps the social payoff associated with same-sex preference—quite aside from any kin-selected payoff—was sufficient to keep same-sex alleles around, even though some proportion of regularly produced exclusive homosexuality (analogous to having a too-large head) was the price to be paid. Not quite heterosis as with sickle cell disease, but close.

Different Effects in Different Sexes?

A final gene-based hypothesis goes by the unfortunate name of "sexually antagonistic selection." It sounds complicated but is actually quite straightforward. What if one or more alleles that predispose toward homosexuality (and with it, reduced reproductive output) in one sex actually work in the opposite manner in the other sex? I prefer the phrase "sexually complementary selection," since the hypothesis does not so much imply antagonism between the genetic effect in males *versus* females as complementarity in outcome: A fitness decrement experienced when the relevant genes exist within, say, males is more than compensated—for the genes in question—by a fitness enhancement within females. And vice versa.

There is some supportive evidence. In one study, it was found that the fecundity of mothers of heterosexuals averages 2.07, whereas mothers of homosexuals, from the same population, average 2.73 offspring.[52] It turns out that numerous other relatives from the mother's line also showed higher fecundity.[53] In general, sexually complementary selection is suggested any time it can be shown that the female relatives of male homosexuals have a higher fitness than do the female relatives of heterosexual males. The result would be that in the process of selecting for greater female reproductive success, enhanced numbers of male homosexuals have also been produced, as a side effect.

To my knowledge, there is as yet no evidence for a reciprocal influence, whereby the male relatives of female homosexuals have a higher fitness than do male relatives of heterosexual females. And perhaps there never will be, given the accumulating evidence that female homosexuality and male homosexuality may be genetically underwritten in different ways.

Different Kinds of Social Glue

We turn now from focused genetic hypotheses to social ones—but in doing so, we are not moving away from evolutionary considerations. In fact, we aren't really stepping away from genetic matters, either. This is because if it turns out, for example, that homosexuality conveys a social benefit upon its practitioners—say, by providing a kind of social glue that enhances adult bonds—any long-term positive impact must depend on the "social benefit" translating into a genetic benefit and thus an evolutionary consequence . . . or else such a benefit would likely be short-lived. Behind the social payoffs hypothesized below there lurks presumed genetic and evolutionary payoffs as well.

Let's start with social hypothesis number one: practice. In might not make perfect, but let's face it, "doing what comes naturally"—that is, sex—is often surprisingly difficult without practice! After all, unlike eating, sleeping, keeping yourself warm, or scratching when you itch, courtship and copulation involve interaction with another individual, which introduces complexity into any occasion, especially one so inherently fraught as sex. In many cases, this is not simply a matter of becoming a "great lover," or even a good one, but simply meeting the basic requirements for biological success.

Homosexual behavior could especially lend itself as an adaptive opportunity for sexual practice if, compared to heterosexual encounters, homosexual activity is less liable to serious social repercussions if done clumsily. One might predict that insofar as it provides practice and learning, homoerotic behavior should be particularly frequent among juveniles, and less so among adults. This is the case. Many free-living animal species show same-sex mounting, nearly always among juveniles and nearly always diminishing rapidly with adulthood. On the other hand, the existence of exclusive homosexuality—and in relatively high numbers, as among *Homo sapiens*—goes against the expectations of the practice hypothesis. It's one thing for evolution to favor a behavior pattern that generates useful practice, quite another if the "practice" replaces the presumed goal. In addition, although some degree of homoeroticism occasionally accompanies human childhood and adolescence, there is no evidence that people who experiment sexually in this manner eventually function more successfully as heterosexuals. The "practice hypothesis" may thus apply more to animals than to people.

On to social hypothesis number two: sexual selection. The basic argument here is that evolutionary success isn't merely determined by ability to survive ("ecological" or "survival" selection), but also by an individual's success in attracting and keeping a mate. It is possible that a genetic tendency for homosexuality could be retained, even if it would otherwise seem to result in diminished breeding success, so long as such individuals were preferentially chosen by members of the opposite sex. This seems unlikely but is not impossible if, for example, some proportion of women have been favorably disposed toward homosexually inclined men who may also be especially caring and helpful, thus offering the promise of enhanced parental care.[54] Related to this is the observation, confirmed by many women, that they often find gay men appealing because they are less threatening than their heterosexual counterparts, whose overt female-directed sexuality can verge on the predatory. It remains to be demonstrated, however, that under such circumstances, gay men actually end up fathering a significant number of children. It is also unclear whether a reciprocal situation occurs, whereby at least some heterosexual men are especially attracted to women with tomboy traits, and if so, whether there is any connection between "boyishness" among adult women and same-sex preference.

The third social hypothesis revolves around the notion of homosexuality as social glue. Most research studies along these lines involve animal examples. Perhaps this is because homosexuality is more likely to have a social bonding effect among nonhuman creatures, or maybe biologists for some reason have simply been more intrigued than sociologists by this possibility. In any event, the thrust—pardon the expression—of many of these observations is captured in the title of one such research account: "Establishing Trust: Socio-sexual Behaviour and the Development of Male-Male Bonds Among Indian Ocean Bottlenose Dolphins."[55] Approximately one half of all observed homosexual copulations among these miniature whales are male–male. (Because male and female dolphins both possess genital slits, males can achieve intromission with other males.) Bonobos—"pygmy chimps"—are justly renowned for being hypersexual; what, then, are we to conclude about bottlenose dolphins, whose sexual "event rates"—for males— average more than 2 per hour, which is nearly 40 times higher than the frequencies reported for female bonobos in the wild?

Not coincidentally, bottlenose dolphins are highly social, and their breeding system is such that the reproductive success of males appears to hinge not merely on their heterosexual encounters but also on the extent of male–male cooperation in bringing such sexual liaisons about:

> Of particular interest in bottlenose dolphin research is the relationship, if any, between male homosexual behaviour and alliance formation, a crucial part of male mating strategies. Males form first-order alliances (pairs and trios) that cooperate to sequester and maintain exclusive access to a single female for up to six weeks . . . an event known as a

consortship. Some first-order alliances appear to remain highly stable for 15–20 years. They typically pair with one or two other alliances to form second-order alliances. Second-order alliances cooperate by helping each alliance keep their respective females during consortships. Although popular accounts occasionally infer that males coerce copulations on the female, such behaviour has never been observed. Males may also form a super-alliance of up to 14 individuals. Pairings and trios within the super-alliance are labile, with no more than three males consorting with a female at any time. However, if the pair or trio is challenged by an outside alliance, the entire super-alliance may help the pair or trio defend the female . . . a pattern otherwise seen only in humans.

The bottom line is that bottlenose dolphins form unusually intense male–male bonds, albeit in the service of heterosexual breeding success, and they also engage in an unusually high frequency of male–male sexual interactions, especially as juveniles. It seems reasonable—maybe even likely—that the latter takes place in furtherance of the former. But no one knows for sure. It is tempting to extrapolate to humans, who also form intense male–male bonds, although usually not with an eye toward cooperative defense of a breeding female. It is interesting, though, that human male–male bonds are probably most intense among combat soldiers, and that positive sexual relationships among warriors has a long and honored history.[xiii] (This might also suggest a new perspective on the controversy surrounding "gays in the military" within the United States.)

There are several other hypotheses that speak to the potential of homosexual activity generating a positive social outcome. In fact, from the perspective of "classical ethology"—in the tradition of Konrad Lorenz and Niko Tinbergen—same-sex behavior has long been seen as serving an important social function, quite independent of any sexual motivation.[56] Seemingly sexual acts, including genital rubbing, mounting, and even intromission, have thus been interpreted as simply part of a species' communicative

---

xiii. It could also be argued that defense of women, and all that this implies reproductively, is among the deeper evolutionary underpinnings of war fighting itself—in which regard people might not be all that different from bottlenose dolphins.

repertoire, an automatic means of nonerotic signaling, and not necessarily sexual at all.

It has been suggested, accordingly, that homoerotic interactions can contribute to reconciliation after a conflict. It certainly seems to do so among bonobos, at least: Female bonobos engage in significantly more genital–genital rubbing immediately after an aggressive interaction.[57] But things are quite different in other species. Among Japanese macaque monkeys, for example, female–female sexual encounters are less frequent, rather than more, following a conflict. In this case at least, aggressive behaviors *inhibit* subsequent homoerotic actions rather than facilitate them.[58] And here is an interesting side note, with possible wider implications: When a female Japanese macaque monkey is confronted with a desirable male who is not sexually interested in her, she will often react by mounting him! Suitably stimulated, the male will then frequently reverse positions and copulate with the sexually aggressive female.[59]

What about the possibility, accordingly, that female–female mounting is a similar tactic, used to inspire otherwise sluggish or distracted males? (One cannot help thinking of the widespread phenomenon whereby men typically find it sexually arousing to see images of lesbian sex.) Sadly for this intriguing hypothesis, the data suggest just the opposite: When male Japanese macaques attempt to mount females who are engaging in female–female mountings, the males are either ignored or sometimes even attacked and driven away![60]

Next, some other pro-social roles for homosexuality among certain animals at least and possibly offering models for the initial evolution and/or maintenance of homoerotic behavior among human beings. Just above, we looked briefly at the prospect that same-sex mounting facilitates reconciliation after conflict. In some species, such as acorn woodpeckers, it reduces tension and makes it less likely that conflict will occur in the first place.[61] In others, such as American bison, dominant individuals mount subordinates, with essentially no reversals.[62] A reasonable interpretation is that in such cases, homosexual behavior functions to diminish the frequency of conflict, just as it does among acorn woodpeckers, but by a more aggressive route: by reinforcing the existing dominance hierarchy, and thereby keeping everyone in line, rather than by directly fostering positive relationships as such.

Here are some more animal examples, also emphasizing competition, but without any discernible human implications. Consider a species of dung fly (doesn't everyone?). In one particular case, males mount females when they encounter them, and females typically accept the first male to do so. Males also mount other males who resist vigorously, jumping about and kicking while the mounter seeks—usually quite successfully—to remain on their backs, resembling a rodeo cowboy astride a bucking bronco.[63] This appears to be an outright male–male competitive strategy, since when a female appears, the male on top—the one who initiated the mounting—has given himself an advantage: He can jump off and immediately mount the female, while the male on the bottom is too encumbered to do so. In this case, although the behavior clearly involves same-sex mounting, it evidently occurs solely in the service of heterosexual mating success.

A similar situation has been described for a species of parasitic acorn worm.[64] When engaging in heterosexual copulation, male acorn worms first transfer sperm, followed by a secretion from a specialized cement gland, which seals the female's vaginal opening and serves as a kind of biological chastity belt that prevents the female from copulating with any other males. Not uncommonly, however, male acorn worms encounter other males, whereupon the aggressor maneuvers so as to transfer his cement gland substance, thereby plugging up the victim's genital opening and preventing him from copulating with any females. As a result, a possible heterosexual competitor is literally put out of commission. We can be confident, incidentally, that this behavior is not a case of mistaken identity, since in such cases, the aggressor transfers his sexual cement only, and no sperm.

The authors of this particular research report may have been overreaching when they described this phenomenon as "homosexual rape," since there is no evidence for homoerotic inclination on the part of the aggressor males. But whatever the proximate motivation, it is a behavioral strategy whose evolution can readily be discerned, involving as it does a straightforward competitive strategy that ultimately enhances the "perpetrators'" fitness the old-fashioned way: by making it more likely that such individuals will be able to reproduce heterosexually.

Returning to the general prospect that in at least some cases, enhanced breeding success arrives via competitive aspects of same-sex behavior, here is yet another intriguing animal example. Once again, this one does not offer direct parallels to the human condition but is worth contemplating nonetheless, if only for its "gee whiz" value. I am thinking of reproduction by proxy, as occurs among certain invertebrates, notably flour beetles. Here, males force copulations with other males, who then transfer the "lover's" sperm when he eventually mates.[65]

For an example of a more cooperative animal sexual style, consider the following, a case of adjustable sexuality that once again seems unlikely to teach us anything about human homosexuality but is worth pondering nonetheless, perhaps just for its own sake: In the marine snail, *Crepidula fornicata*,[66] all individuals begin life as male, after which they can change to female depending on the sex of their immediate partner. If a male *C. fornicata* has hooked up with another male, then one or the other will simply switch sexes. It's a sexual tactic delightfully reminiscent of the science fiction fantasy novel *The Left Hand of Darkness*, by Ursula LeGuin, in which inhabitants of the planet Gethen are neither male nor female, but bipotent. Periodically, they enter a state known as "kemmer," in which they experience a mating urge along with short-term anatomic differentiation. Depending on the chemistry within each duo, an individual may temporarily transform into either male or female, after which his or her partner develops into the opposite sex. Nothing is preset, however, so in LeGuin's made-up world, an individual may have been a mother to one child as well as a father to another, depending on how the sexual spirit operated at any given time.

Reproductive Skew

One of the more important recent ideas in evolutionary ecology concerns yet another aspect of social behavior: "reproductive skew" theory, a concept that has possible implications for many aspects of animal and human reproductive behavior, the evolution of homosexuality included.[67] The "skew" in reproductive skew refers to the disparity in reproductive success among members of a social group; typically, of course, dominant individuals are more successful than are subordinates. They are more fit, which is presumably the reason that individuals compete for dominance in the first place. Essentially, subordinates must "decide" whether or not to stay in the group, just as dominants must decide whether or not to let them do so. The currency is breeding success. Subordinates may leave if they are not permitted to breed at all, but this could be disadvantageous to the dominants, if having a group of at least a certain size contributes to their own breeding success (e.g., if it makes the group more successful when deterring predators or competing successfully with other groups). On the other hand, dominants are likely to be unenthusiastic about ceding too much success to the subordinates, that is, to anyone but themselves.[68]

Reproductive skew is likely to be greater the greater the difference in status between dominant and subordinate individuals, and vice versa: When those on top socially aren't very dominant over the subordinates, we wouldn't expect them to experience substantially higher fitness. Also, skew would be higher in proportion as subordinates have less prospect of breeding successfully if they were to set out on their own; this is because as their prospects diminish, subordinates are less able to drive a hard bargain, and dominants are correspondingly more empowered to push them around.

Counterintuitively, perhaps, skew is expected to be greater when dominants and subordinates are closely related, because in such a case, the success of dominant individuals carries within itself a degree of success for subordinates. Hence, the latter are not so greatly disadvantaged if their personal reproductive success is relatively lower, since they succeed genetically, by proxy, so long as the dominants do so. At the same time, dominants need to avoid demanding too much sacrifice from subordinates, who in turn need to restrain themselves so as to keep the dominants from retaliating against them. In short, there's a need for negotiations.

The relevant point for our purposes is that to some degree, homosexuality might ultimately be found to be imposed upon certain individuals by others within the local community, most likely by stress effects mediated by neurohormones and analogous—in consequence, if not physiological mechanism—to subordinates being kept from breeding.

It should be clear at this point that when it comes to underwriting gay versus straight sexuality, social interactions may be no less important than direct genetic predispositions. Moreover, it is not obvious whether—and if so, in which cases—animal homosexuality can usefully illuminate the case of *Homo sapiens*. Here is one possibility, suggested to me by the observation that among several different species of nonhuman primates, dominant males accept the homoerotic advances of subordinates, who are often juvenile as well. These subordinates receive physical protection and sometimes status advancement in the social hierarchy. Here is the idea: What if homosexuality among human beings has—at least in the past—served as a means of social advancement, especially on the part of otherwise younger and/or subordinate individuals?

It is known that in classical Greece, for example, boys provided sexual gratification to older and supposedly heterosexual men. If they profited by this, in terms of social advancement and even possibly sexual access to women as well, selection could have favored a degree of bisexuality. This notion, like most of those presented in this chapter, does not exclude any of the many other possible hypotheses already discussed, and it has the added advantage of explaining why homosexuality is more common in men than in women: Insofar as men generally have a more insistent and less discriminating sex drive, they are more likely to desire and appreciate immediate sexual gratification. This would be especially the case in harem-forming societies, in which a comparatively small number of men monopolize a relatively large proportion of the women, thereby leaving many men sexually unsatisfied.

There are other examples of same-sex behavior among animals ultimately serving to convey benefits via competition. Among a number of species—notably fish—males engage in "alternative sexual strategies," whereby in addition to "traditional" males who are typically large, dark colored, and inclined to vigorously defend mating territories, some males develop into "female mimics," who are mistaken as such by the traditional males and courted heterosexually. As a result, these female mimics are often able to gain access to females, with whom they attempt to mate. It does not seem likely that cases of this sort carry much direct relevance for human beings, although they add to our appreciation of the diversity of ways in which seemingly homoerotic behavior may be strictly heterosexual after all, not involving anything approaching the subjective dynamics of what people generally mean by "homosexual."

Here is another circumstance, well described among animals, that may or may not have any relevance for human beings. I suspect that it does not, although it's intriguing enough to be worth describing. The phenomenon is known as female mimicry, whereby males increase their (heterosexual) mating success by resembling females. We already considered such tactics among fish. Something similar—known to biologists as "delayed plumage maturation"—also occurs among birds. In many species, male plumage is brighter and more colorful and eye-catching than its female counterpart, so as to attract female attention as well as display the male's physical qualities. At the same time, such display plumage often invites aggression by other males, so in some cases, not surprisingly, young adult males delay their full-fledged male looks. Since they typically resemble females as a result, such discreet males are often courted by other, traditionally showy males. In such cases, however, there is no reason to think that these recipients of homoerotic attention are actually homosexual in the human sense; rather, they employ female mimicry to buy themselves surcease from male–male competition, as well as increasing the probability that they will be able to obtain sneak copulations from females.[69]

I don't know any cases of the inverse, in which females increase their fitness by mimicking males.

Neoteny, Birth Order, and Some Other Proximate Factors

Given the high frequency of apparently homosexual play among juvenile mammals in particular, as well as the phenomenon of delayed plumage maturation among birds, another question arises: Is there any sense in which human homosexuality is an example of neoteny, the retention of juvenile characteristics among adults of a species? More specifically, if for whatever reason some individuals retain a more "juvenile" brain into adulthood, couldn't this predispose toward homosexuality? It is well known that we all lose neurons with age, and so, what if in some people, those neurons associated with same-sex interactions are simply lost at a lower rate? It has already been proposed that at the subcellular level, modifications in programmed cell death, "apoptosis," could make male brains more feminine and female brains more masculine.[70]

Several other proximate causes have been proposed and deserve mention. For example, there appears to be a birth-order effect: One factor that evidently predisposes toward a male being homosexual is if he has older brothers. This association appears somewhat robust, which in itself is notable, given that even correlations—never mind causation—have been so elusive.[71] The "fraternal birth-order effect" might be due to the impact of the uterine environment on a developing fetus, since it seems likely that when a woman repeatedly bears a male fetus, she accumulates antimale antibodies, which could modify the developing brain of subsequent children.[72] But no one knows if this really happens.

It has long been suspected that hormonal factors are also implicated, but their actual role, if any, remains unproven. It does seem clear, however, that among male homosexuals, sexually relevant brain regions respond to a derivative of testosterone in a manner not found among male heterosexuals.[73] Significantly, perhaps, a comparable estrogen derivative activates parallel brain regions of lesbian but not heterosexual women.[74]

There have also been numerous reports—many of them conflicting—regarding brain differences between straight and gay people,[75] notably the claim of differences in structure of the hypothalamus.[76] In addition, it is well established that hormones—especially steroids such as estrogen and testosterone—are typically important in potentiating sexual behavior, including same-sex mounting. This is especially true for females, while the impact of testosterone and its various chemical relatives seems to be more complex.

One problem with these and other such findings is that even if there are consistent neuroanatomic and/or hormonal distinctions between gays and straights, and even controlling for likely questions as to whether a subject was[xiv] "really" homosexual (as opposed to bisexual, for example), it isn't possible to conclude with confi-

---

xiv. The past tense is appropriate here, since these detailed studies of brain anatomy necessarily have to be conducted as autopsies.

dence that such differences are the cause of homosexuality, as opposed to being a result of many years of homosexual practice. In addition, let's imagine that gay men are that way because of a difference in their hypothalami, or some other brain region such as their superchiasmatic nuclei. This would still beg the evolutionary question: Why has natural selection favored the existence of such mechanisms in the first place?

Or, stated slightly differently: Why do such differences persist in the human population, given the fitness decrements we have already discussed?

Making the Best of Things

We also need to consider a possibility we shall shortly examine with regard to the evolution of religious belief and of the arts, namely, that homosexual behavior might be not so much *mal*adaptive as simply *non*adaptive. That is, it might not have been selected for, but persists instead as an incidental by-product of other traits that presumably have been directly favored.

One of these traits could have been the simple (actually, not so simple) yearning to form a pair bond, seeking emotional or physical gratification. As to why such an inclination would exist at all—that is, why human connections are perceived as pleasurable—the answer may well be that historically (and prehistorically) it has often been in the context of an ongoing pair bond that individuals were most likely to reproduce successfully. And this, in turn, would be due to the fact that in a species such as *Homo sapiens*, which gives birth to helpless young that require substantial parental investment over many years, evolution would have equipped people with a tendency to form such bonds. If a suitable heterosexual partner isn't available—as we have already considered in the case of prison populations—it is imaginable that a same-sex relationship will be consummated instead.

Carrying this a step farther, it is now well established that same-sex pairings are relatively common among animals, especially many bird species. The typical situation in such cases is that female–female couples form when there is a shortage of males. These avian "lesbian" couples often reproduce, so clearly their "homosexuality" is not exclusive; given the well-known proclivity for males to take advantage of opportunities to copulate outside their pair bond as well as within it, no one should be surprised that females paired with females also get fertilized.[77] It is noteworthy that such females don't reproduce as successfully as do male–female pairs, but they always do better than solitary individuals, since—especially among birds, with their high metabolic rates, and hence, their need for constant provisioning of nestlings—two adults have a definite advantage over "single parents" when it comes to rearing a brood.[78]

An interesting example comes from a colony of Laysan albatrosses, on Hawaii, where 31% of all couples consisted of two females. In this case, such pairings were remarkably long term: several female–female couples staying together for at least 8 years, with one pair remaining "a unit" for 19 years! These animals face an interesting dilemma, since they normally lay just one egg per year, and that is all that an albatross nest can accommodate. When two females cohabit, they continue to make a one-egg-sized nest even though each female commonly lays her own egg. The extra one typically rolls out, isn't incubated, and doesn't hatch. It may be that the long duration of Laysan albatross female–female mateships is itself a prerequisite for such a social system to exist at all, since it provides an opportunity for a female whose egg was excluded one year to recoup and be successful during the next.[79]

It could be argued that female–female pairing removes "excess" females from the group, thereby reducing the group's overall reproductive rate to the advantage of all, just as male–male pairings removes "excess" males. The problem, once again, is how (aside from, say, kin selection) natural selection could favor any voluntary reproductive self-restraint on the part of same-sex paired individuals. It seems more parsimonious to attribute such pairing to the individuals in question having been unable to establish a heterosexual mateship.

This situation, although intriguing, seems to offer little or no insight into the human situation, which often involves individuals who seem to be no less attractive than their heterosexual counterparts. In the case of human beings, moreover, sexual orientation is almost entirely a function of personal proclivity (whether generated by genes, environment, or an ineffable combination of the two) rather than because opposite-sex options aren't available.

In some cases, same-sex behavior can even result from simple mistaken identity, something strongly implicated in animals, from invertebrates to vertebrates.[80] Walk through a marsh in the American South during early spring: You might well find the toe of your boot (maybe even both boots!) clasped by a male bullfrog, eager to mate. In fact, these fellows are so undiscriminating when it comes to copulation that they have even evolved a particular identifiable croak that essentially says, "Get off, you dummy, I'm a male!" Such occurrences speak to a very low threshold for sexual stimulation on the part of certain individuals (most commonly males) of certain species. They do not, however, seem to qualify as homosexual behavior, but are simply mistakes—which have not been strongly selected against, because the potential payoff is large and the cost of an error is relatively low. There is little reason to believe, however, that gays or lesbians are "that way" because they cannot tell men from women. Rather, they prefer individuals of one sex or the other as sexual partners and it is that preference— an important part of the proximate causation of homosexual behavior—that we are seeking to explain in terms of its ultimate or evolutionary causation.

Maybe it is neither preference nor mistaken identity, but rather simply a consequence of heterosexual deprivation. The so-called "prison effect" is well known: When deprived of suitable heterosexual partners, some individuals act sexually toward whoever is available. Frequently, in such cases, the more active partner in particular denies being homosexual, and it is at least conceivable that the behavior is more an example of dominance signaling than sexuality (recall the American bison described earlier). Nonetheless, sexual arousal is typically involved.

Closely related to deprivation resulting from strict sexual segregation and isolation is a kind of "overflow" hypothesis, by which homosexual behavior might result from the combination of a high sex drive and an inability—for a variety of possible reasons—to obtain heterosexual satisfaction.[81]

There is yet another perspective on high sex drive, namely, the possibility that homosexual acts are driven primarily (and proximally) by the simple prospect of obtaining sexual pleasure, using any willing individual. Think back to those female Japanese macaque monkeys who commonly mount males in an effort to stimulate them to return the favor. In pursuit of the likely adaptive significance of this behavior (getting themselves fertilized by desirable heterosexual partners), female macaques may well have been proximally induced to mount certain males by obtaining immediate pleasurable sensations—possibly including orgasm—via physical stimulation, presumably of their clitoris. Once female macaques had biologically discovered the potential for sexual satisfaction via genital stimulation, they might also have found that it was available from other females as readily as from males.[82] Males, too, could have made a comparable discovery. And there is no reason, of course, for all these revelations to have been limited to nonhuman animals.

By contrast, at least one peculiar mechanism, found in some animals, has not (yet?) been found to operate in human beings: the strange case of host manipulation by a parasite or pathogen. Numerous examples are known, for example, of pathogens essentially hijacking the behavior of their host victims, causing them to behave in ways that benefit the pathogens rather than the hosts. For example, the life cycle of a parasitic flatworm known as *Dicrocoelium dentriticum* involves doing time inside an ant, followed by a sheep. Getting from its insect host to its mammalian one isn't easy, but the resourceful worm has found a way: Ensconced within an ant, some of the worms migrate to its brain, whereupon they manage to rewire their host's neurons and hijack its behavior. The manipulated ant, acting with zombielike fidelity to *Dicrocoelium*'s demands, climbs to the top of a blade of grass and clamps down with its jaws, whereupon it waits patiently and conspicuously until it is consumed by a grazing sheep. Thus transported to its happy breeding ground deep inside sheep bowels, the worm turns, or rather, releases its eggs, which depart with a healthy helping of sheep poop, only to be consumed once more by ants.

A remarkable story, and one that has many other parallels in the annals of host–parasite interactions. Take cholera. The terrible, watery diarrhea for which this disease is known probably isn't just a symptom, but a manipulation of the human gastrointestinal tract whereby the cholera bacillus, *Vibrio cholerae*, gets to infect new hosts. It is currently unclear what, if anything, such cases have to do with sexual behavior, among human beings or other animals, although one might wonder whether STDs are able, in any way, to manipulate the behavior of their victims so as to facilitate their own transmission.

Certainly, concern about AIDS has greatly enhanced awareness of male–male transmission of this particular disease, but such traditionally heterosexual STDs as syphilis and gonorrhea should not be overlooked. When the role of pathogens is considered, nearly always the question is how sexual behavior influences pathogen transmission. But there is at least the possibility that the connection occasionally goes in the other direction, with pathogens influencing sexual behavior. There is a fungus, *Entomophthora muscae*, that kills domestic flies that it infects. Dead victims develop a notably swollen abdomen, which strongly resembles the body of a healthy female, loaded with eggs and, hence, sexually desirable. Uninfected males are then drawn to copulate with these corpses, a behavior that transmits the fungus yet further.[83] This raises the striking prospect that to a degree not often realized, pathogens may actually manipulate the sexual behavior of their hosts, although it must be emphasized that no such connections to human homosexuality have ever been identified, or even seriously proposed.

By contrast, as we have seen, there are lots of hypotheses for the evolution of homosexuality. Although we can state with complete confidence that same-sex preference is definitely not a simple "lifestyle choice"—instead, it is clearly founded on biology of some sort—we must also conclude that it remains a tantalizing evolutionary mystery. Unlike the US military's ill-conceived and now defunct "don't ask, don't tell" policy, however, many reputable investigators are asking not *who* is homosexual, but *why* are there homosexuals, and we can be quite confident that eventually, nature is going to tell.

Notes

1. Haldane, J. B. S. (1927). A mathematical theory of natural and artificial selection. Part v: Selection and mutation. *Proceedings of the Cambridge Philosophical Society, 23*, 838–844.

2. Bell, A. P., & Weinberg, M. (1978). *Homosexualities: A study of diversity among men and women.* New York: Simon & Schuster; Saghir, M. T., & Robins, E. (1973). *Male and female homosexuality: A comprehensive investigation.* Baltimore, MD: Williams & Wilkins.

3. Kinsey, A. C., Pomeroy, W. B., & Martin, C. E. (1948). *Sexual behavior in the human male.* Philadelphia: W. B. Saunders Co.

4. For example, Rahman, Q., & Hull, M. S. (2005). An empirical test of the kin selection hypothesis for male homosexuality. *Archives of Sexual Behavior, 34,* 461–467.

5. Williams, G. C. (1975). *Sex and evolution.* Princeton, NJ: Princeton University Press.

6. Stokes, J. P., Damon, W., & McKirnan, D. J. (1997). Predictors of movement toward homosexuality: A longitudinal study of bisexual men. *Journal of Sex Research, 34,* 304–312; Worthington, R. L., & Reynolds, A. L. (2009). Within-group differences in sexual orientation and identity. *Journal of Counseling Psychology, 56,* 44–55.

7. Whitam, F. L. (1983). Culturally invariable properties of male homosexuality: Tentative conclusions from cross-cultural research. *Archives of Sexual Behavior, 12,* 207–226.

8. Quoted by Kennedy, H. (1997). Karl Heinrich Ulrichs: First theorist of homosexuality. In V. Rosario (Ed.), *Science and homosexualities.* New York: Routledge.

9. Friedman, R. C., & Downey, J. I. (1998). Psychoanalysis and the model of homosexuality as psychopathology: A historical overview. *American Journal of Psychoanalysis, 58,* 249–270.

10. Freud, S. (1915). Addendum to *Three Essays on Sexuality* (1905). *Standard Edition, 7,* 123–246.

11. Zenchak, J. J., Anderson, G. C., & Schein, M. (1981). Sexual partner preference of adult rams (*Ovis aries*) as affected by social experiences during rearing. *Applied Animal Ethology, 7,* 157–167.

12. Poiani, A. (2010). *Animal homosexuality: A biosocial perspective.* Cambridge, UK: Cambridge University Press.

13. Friedman, R. C. (1988). *Male homosexuality.* New Haven and London: Yale University Press.

14. Wolfe, L. (1979). Behavioral patterns of estrous females of the Arashiyama West troop of Japanese macaques (*Macaca fuscata*). *Primates, 20*(4), 525–534.

15. Bagemihl, B. (2000). *Biological exuberance: Animal homosexuality and natural diversity.* New York: Stonewall Inn Editions (St. Martin's Press).

16. Zuk, M. (2006). Family values in black and white. *Nature, 439,* 917.

17. For example, Grosjean, Y., Grillet, M., Augustin, H., Ferveur, J. F., & Featherstone, D. E. (2008). A glial amino-acid transporter controls synapse strength and courtship in Drosophila. *Nature and Neuroscience, 11,* 54–61; Liu, T., Dartevelle, L., Chunyan, Y., Homgping, W., Wang, Y., Ferveur, J-F., & Guo, A. (2008). Increased dopamine level enhances male–male courtship in Drosophila. *Journal of Neuroscience, 28,* 5539–5546; Kurtovic, A., Widmer, A., & Dickson, B. J. (2007). A single class of olfactory neurons mediates behavioural responses to a Drosophila sex pheromone. *Nature, 446,* 542–546.

18. Hamer, D. H., Hu, S., Magnuson, V. L., Hu, N., & Pattatucci, A. M. L. (1993). A linkage between DNA markers on the X chromosome and male sexual orientation. *Science, 261,* 321–327.

19. Rice, G., et al. (1999). Male homosexuality: Absence of linkage to microsatellite markers at Xq28. *Science, 284,* 665–667.

20. Bocklandt, S., et al. (2006). Extreme skewing of X chromosome inactivation in mothers of homosexual men. *Human Genetics, 118,* 691–694.

21. Hu, S., Pattatucci, A. M., Patterson, C., et al. (1995). Linkage between sexual orientation and chromosome Xq28 in males but not in females. *Nature Genetics, 11,* 248–256.

22. Mustanski, B. S., Dupree, M. G., Nievergelt, C. M., Bocklandt, S., Schork, N. J., & Hamer, D. H. (2005). A genomewide scan of male sexual orientation. *Human Genetics, 116,* 272–278.

23. Poiani, A. (2010). *Animal homosexuality: A biosocial perspective.* Cambridge, UK: Cambridge University Press.

24. Eckert, E. D., Bouchard, T. J., Bohlen, J., & Heston, L. L. (1986). Homosexuality in monozygotic twins reared apart. *British Journal of Psychiatry, 148,* 421–425.

25. Whitam, F. L., Diamond, M., & Martin, J. (1993). Homosexual orientation in twins: A report on 61 pairs and three triplet sets. *Archives of Sexual Behavior, 22,* 187–206; Bailey, J. M., Pillard, R. C., Neale, M. C., & Agyei, U. (1993). Heritable factors influence sexual orientation in women. *Archives of General Psychiatry, 50,* 217–223.

26. Bearman, P. S., & Brückner, J. (2002). Opposite-sex twins and adolescent same-sex attraction. *American Journal of Sociology, 107,* 1179–1205.

27. Pillard, R. C., & Bailey, J. M. (1998). Human sexual orientation has a heritable component. *Human Biology, 70,* 347–365.

28. For example, Throckmorton, W. (1998). Attempts to modify sexual orientation: A review of outcome literature and ethical issues. *Journal of Mental Health Counseling, 20,* 283–304.

29. Barash, D. P. (2003). *Revolutionary biology: The new, gene-centered view of life.* New Brunswick, NJ: Transaction Publishers.

30. Wilson, E. O. (1975). *Sociobiology, the modern synthesis.* Cambridge, MA: Belknap Press; Wilson, E. O. (1978). *On human nature.* Cambridge, MA: Harvard University Press.

31. Bobrow, D., & Bailey, J. M. (2001). Is male homosexuality maintained via kin selection? *Evolution and Human Behavior, 22,* 361–368.

32. Rahman, Q., & Hull, M. S. (2005). An empirical test of the kin selection hypothesis for male homosexuality. *Archives of Sexual Behavior, 34,* 461–467.

33. Ruse, M. (1982). Are there gay genes? Sociobiology and homosexuality. *Journal of Homosexuality, 6,* 5–34.

34. Vasey, P. L., Pocock, D. S., & VanderLaan, D. P. (2007). Kin selection and male androphilia in Samoan fla'afaline. *Evolution and Human Behavior, 28,* 159–167; Vasey, P. L., & VanderLaan, D. P. (2009). Materteral and avuncular tendencies in Samoa: A comparative study of women, men and *fa'afafine.* *Human Nature, 20,* 269–281.

35. Hrdy, S. B. (2009). *Mothers and others.* Cambridge, MA: Belknap Press.

36. Cook, M. (1996). A role for homosexuality in population genetics. *Evolutionary Theory, 11,* 135–151.

37. Kirby, J. (2003). A new group selection model for the evolution of homosexuality. *Biology and Philosophy, 18,* 683–694.

38. Trivers, R. L. (1971). The evolution of reciprocal altruism. *Quarterly Review of Biology, 46,* 35–57.

39. Wilkinson, G. S. (1984). Reciprocal food sharing in the vampire bat. *Nature, 308,* 181–184.

40. I believe that the first proposal along these lines was by the renowned ecologist Hutchinson, G. E. (1959). Homage to Santa Rosalia, or, why are there so many kinds of animals? *The American Naturalist, 93,* 145–156.

41. Gavrilets, S., & Rice, W. R. (2006). Genetic models of homosexuality: generating testable predictions. *Proceedings of the Royal Society of London Series B Biological Sciences, 273,* 3031–3038.

42. Zhang, X.-S., & Hill, W. G. (2005). Genetic variability under mutation selection balance. *Trends in Ecology and Evolution, 20,* 468–470.

43. Kirkpatrick, R. C. (2000). The evolution of human homosexual behavior. *Current Anthropology, 41,* 385–413.

44. Diamond, M. (2008). *Sexual fluidity: Understanding women's love and desire.* Cambridge, MA: Harvard University Press.

45. Kinnish, K. K., Strassberg, D. S., & Turner, C. W. (2005). Sex differences in the flexibility of sexual orientation: A multidimensional retrospective assessment. *Archives of Sexual Behavior, 34,* 173–183.

46. Santila, P., Sandnabba, N. K., & Harlaar, N. (2008). Potential for homosexual response is prevalent and genetic. *Biological Psychology, 77,* 102–105.

47. Numerous references in Poiani, A. (2010). *Animal homosexuality: A biosocial perspective.* Cambridge, UK: Cambridge University Press.

48. Dewar, C. S. (2003). An association between male homosexuality and reproductive success. *Medical Hypotheses, 60,* 225–232.

49. Willmott, M., & Brierley, H. (1984). Cognitive characteristics and homosexuality. *Archives of Sexual Behavior, 13*(4), 311–319; Wegesin, D. J. (1998). A neuropsychologic profile of homosexual and heterosexual men and women. *Archives of Sexual Behavior, 27*(1), 91–108; Sanders G. (1997). Sexual orientation differences in cerebral asymmetry and in the performance of sexually dimorphic cognitive and motor tasks. *Archives of Sexual Behavior, 26*(5), 663–680.

50. Dewar, C. S. (2003). An association between male homosexuality and reproductive success. *Medical Hypotheses, 60,* 225–232.

51. Baldwin, J. D., & Baldwin, J. I. (1989). The socialisation of homosexuality and heterosexuality in a non-Western society. *Archives of Sexual Behavior, 18*(1), 13–29; Callender, C., & Kochems, L. M. (1985). Men and not-men: Gender-mixing statuses and homosexuality. *Journal of Homosexuality, 11*(3–4), 165–178.

52. Iemmola, F., & Camperio-Ciani, A. (2009). New evidence of genetic factors influencing orientation in men: Female fecundity increase in the maternal line. *Archives of Sexual Behavior, 38,* 393–399.

53. Zietsch, B. P., Morley, K., & Shekar, S. N. (2008). Genetic factors predisposing to homosexuality may increase mating success in heterosexuals. *Evolution and Human Behavior, 29,* 424–433; Camperio-Ciani, F., Corna, & Capiluppi, C. (2004). Evidence for maternally inherited factors favouring male homosexuality and promoting female fecundity. *Proceedings of the Royal Society of London Series B, 271,* 2217–2221.

54. Muscarella, F., Fink, B., Grammer, K., & Kirk-Smith, M. (2001). Homosexual orientation in males: Evolutionary and ethological aspects. *Neuroendocrinology Letters, 22,* 393–400.

55. Mann, J. (2006). Establishing trust: Socio-sexual behaviour and the development of male-male bonds among Indian Ocean bottlenose dolphins. In V. Sommer & P. L. Vasey (Eds.), *Homosexual behaviour in animals.* Cambridge, MA: Cambridge University Press.

56. Wickler, W. (1967). Socio-sexual signals and their intraspecific imitation among primates. In D. Morris (Ed.), *Primate ethology.* Chicago: Aldine.

57. De Waal, F. B. M. (1997). *Bonobo: The forgotten ape.* Berkeley, CA: University of California Press; Hohmann, G., & Fruth, B. (2003). Intra- and inter-sexual aggression by bonobos in the context of mating. *Behaviour, 140,* 1389–1413.

58. Vasey, P. L. (2004). Pre- and postconflict interactions between female Japanese macaques during homosexual consortships. *International Journal of Comparative Psychology, 17,* 351–359.

59. Vasey, P. L. (2002). Same-sex partner preference in hormonally and neurologically unmanipulated animals. *Annual Review of Sex Research, 13,* 141–179.

60. Vasey, P. L., & Gauthier, C. (2000). Skewed sex ratios and female homosexual activity in Japanese macaque: An experimental analysis. *Primates, 41,* 17–25.

61. MacRoberts, M. H., & MacRoberts, B. R. (1976). Social organization and behavior of the acorn woodpecker in central coastal California. *Ornithology Monographs (American Ornithologists' Union), 21*

62. Vervaecke, H., & Roden, C. (2006). Going with the herd: Same-sex interaction and competition in American bison. In V. Sommer & P. L. Vasey (Eds.), *Homosexual behaviour in animals.* New York: Cambridge University Press.

63. Preston-Mafham, K. (2006). Post-mounting courtship and the neutralizing of male competitors through "homosexual" mountings in the fly *Hydromyza livens* F. (Diptera: Scatophagidae). *Journal of Natural History, 40,* 101–105.

64. Abele, L. G., & Gilchrist, S. (1977). Homosexual rape and sexual selection in acanthocephalan worms. *Science, 197,* 81–83.

65. Levan, K. E., et al. (2008). Testing multiple hypotheses for the maintenance of male homosexual copulatory behaviour in flour beetles. *Journal of Evolutionary Biology, 22,* 60–70.

66. Ambrogio, O. V., & Pechenik, J. A. (2008). When is a male not a male? Sex recognition and choice in two sex-changing species. *Behavioral Ecology and Sociobiology, 62*, 1779–1786.

67. I believe this idea was first broached by Poiani, A. (2010). *Animal homosexuality: A biosocial perspective*. Cambridge, UK: Cambridge University Press.

68. Vehrencamp, S. L. (1983). Optimal degree of skew in cooperative societies. *American Zoologist, 23*, 327–335; Vehrencamp, S. L. (1983). A model for the evolution of despotic versus egalitarian societies. *Animal Behaviour, 31*, 667–682.

69. Saetre, G. P., & Slagsvold, T. (1996). The significance of female mimicry in male contests. *American Naturalist, 147*, 981–995.

70. Finlay, B. L., Wikler, K. C., & Sengelaub, D. R. (1987). Regressive events in brain development and scenarios for vertebrate brain evolution. *Brain, Behavior and Evolution, 30*, 477–488.

71. Blanchard, R., & Bogaert, A. F. (2004). Proportion of homosexual men who owe their sexual orientation to fraternal birth order: An estimate based on two national probability samples. *American Journal of Human Biology, 16*, 151–157.

72. Blanchard, R. (2004). Quantitative and theoretical analyses of the relation between older brothers and homosexuality in men. *Journal of Theoretical Biology, 230*, 173–187.

73. Savic, I., Berglund, H., & Lindström, P. (2005). Brain response to putative pheromones in homosexual men. *Proceedings of the National Academy of Sciences of the United States of America, 102*, 7356–7361.

74. Berglund, H., Lindstrom, P., & Savic, I. (2006). Brain response to putative pheromones in lesbian women. *Proceedings of the National Academy of Sciences of the United States of America, 103*, 8269–8827.

75. For example, Swaab, D. F., & Hofman, M. A. (1990). An enlarged superchiasmatic nucleus in homosexual men. *Brain Research, 537*, 141–148.

76. LeVay, S. (1991). A difference in hypothalamic structure between heterosexual and homosexual men. *Science, 253*, 1034–1037.

77. Barash, D. P., & Lipton, J. E. (2002). *The myth of monogamy: Fidelity and infidelity in animals and people*. New York: Henry Holt & Co.

78. Hunt, G. L., & Hunt, M. W. (1977). Female-female pairing in Western Gulls (*Larus occidentalis*) in Southern California. *Science, 196*, 1466–1467.

79. Young, L. C., Zaun, B. J., & VanderWerf, E. A. (2008). Successful same-sex pairing in Laysan albatross. *Biology Letters, 4*, 323–325.

80. Barlow, G. W. (2000). *The cichlid fishes: Nature's grand experiment in evolution*. New York: Perseus; Harari, A. R., et al. (2000). Intrasexual mounting in the beetle *Diaprepes abbreviatus* (L.). *Proceedings of the Royal Society of London Series B Biological Sciences, 267*, 2071–2079.

81. Vasey, P. L., et al. (2008). Courtship behaviour in Japanese macaques during heterosexual and homosexual consortships. *Behavioral Processes, 78*, 401–407.

82. Vasey, P. L., & Duckworth, N. (2008). Female-male mounting in Japanese macaques: The proximate role of sexual reward. *Behavioral Processes, 77,* 405–407.

83. Møller, A. (1993). A fungus infecting domestic flies manipulates sexual behaviour of its host. *Behavioral Ecology and Sociobiology, 33,* 403–407.

CHAPTER FIVE

Art I: Cheesecake, By-Products, and Groups

POOR ALFRED RUSSEL WALLACE! Virtually unknown these days compared to Darwin, Wallace was one of the 19th century's greatest biologists and perhaps the preeminent field naturalist of all time. Those who have heard of Wallace know him primarily as the codiscoverer, with Darwin, of natural selection. But whereas Darwin had laboriously worked out the details, with copious examples from the living world, over a period of decades, Wallace literally came upon the principle of natural selection in a kind of brainstorm, a moment of epiphany while he lay in a malarial fever at a remote island campsite in what is today Indonesia.

The story has oft been told: Barely recovered from his illness, Wallace sent Darwin a brief manuscript setting out "his" theory, which in turn nudged Darwin to speed up publication of the much lengthier book—*On the Origin of Species*—that Darwin had been perfecting, more or less in private, over many years. Less well known is the fact that Wallace parted intellectual company with Darwin when it came to explaining one particular aspect of one particular species: the mental capacities of *Homo sapiens*. At issue here were the "loftier" functions, those associated with music, poetry, dance, literature, painting, and sculpture—those activities that we loosely gather together as "higher culture" or, more simply, art.

A Dispute Among Giants

Both Wallace and Darwin had argued that natural selection doesn't create adaptations that exceed their demand; in other words, evolution doesn't make animals or plants any better—that is, any faster, stronger, prettier, or smarter—than they need to be. Natural selection is a rigorous and relentless pruner, eliminating any expenditure of energy or time that doesn't provide a fitness payoff (which is to say, enhanced reproductive success) that makes up for its cost. In short, there are no free lunches. Evolution does not produce frills, fanciness, or finery for its own sake—rather, only if such traits give their possessors some sort of reproductive advantage. Anything that is gratuitously fancy and expensive, that doesn't in a sense "pay for itself" in terms of fitness, will not occur; or, if it arises via mutation and random genetic recombination, it will be strenuously selected against.

Using this principle of adaptive parsimony, Wallace felt that the human brain was far more advanced, more capable of feats of gratuitous complexity, than our ancestors could have required. He was struck by the fact, for example, that individuals of the "barbarian races," exposed to the intellectual extravagances of European civilization, quickly rose to the occasion, becoming fluent in new languages, capable of absorbing the accoutrements of high society and the elaborate refinements of Victorian art, music, literature, and the like.

In 1869, Wallace wrote that "natural selection could only have endowed the savage with a brain a little superior to that of an ape, whereas he actually possesses one but very little inferior to that of the average member of our learned societies." The problem, as Wallace saw it, was that the human brain appears to be "an instrument . . . developed in advance of the needs of its possessor." His evidence was the fact that "savages"—given the opportunity—could learn to grasp European music, art, literature, and philosophy, and yet, they didn't employ these subtleties in their own, natural state.

Clearly, according to Wallace, the capacity to engage in painting, poetry, opera, and so forth, activities that go beyond the necessities of brute survival and reproduction, had arisen without being needed, and therefore, without being selected for. The answer, as Wallace saw it, must be divine intervention. Only a beneficent God could have endowed human beings with such excessive, biologically irrelevant capacities. "The inference I would draw from this class of phenomena," Wallace concluded, "is that a superior intelligence has guided the development of man in a definite direction, and for a special purpose."

Darwin was dismayed, and then some. "I hope you have not murdered too completely your own and my child," he wrote to Wallace in 1869, concerned that his comrade in science had dropped the ball when it came to explaining human nature. Actually, for all his accomplishments, Wallace strayed from science in other respects as well, becoming an ardent believer in spiritualism, séances, and the prospect of communicating, via mediums, with the dead. But, even allowing for the predictable racism of his time, Wallace had put his finger on a genuine conundrum. Of course, he was not alone, nor was he the first.

"Is it not strange," asks Benedick, in Shakespeare's *Much Ado About Nothing*, "that sheep's guts should hale souls out of men's bodies?" Strange indeed . . . not that an animal's intestines can make interesting sounds, but that people are so entranced by particular patterns of vibrations, whether of a string, a membrane, a column of air, or whatever. Although Darwin rejected Wallace's recourse to divine intervention, he fully acknowledged the puzzle posed by the arts in general and by music (the most abstract art) in particular. As Darwin wrote in *The Descent of Man*, "Since neither the enjoyment nor the capacity of producing musical notes are faculties of the least use to man in reference to his daily habits of life, they must be ranked amongst the most mysterious with which he is endowed."

Similarly mysterious is the fact that we pay rapt attention to stories that we know to be untrue and spend lifetimes and fortunes in possessing and contemplating visual representations of reality or—stranger yet—patterns that clearly don't look like anything at all, combinations of words or images or structures that serve no obvious purpose whatsoever.

Readers not steeped in evolutionary thinking may be perplexed at this point, not seeing what all the fuss is about. "The arts, for instance, are commonly thought to be good for us in any number of ways," writes philosopher Denis Dutton,

> giving us a sense of well-being or feelings of comfort. Art may help us to see deeper into the human psyche, aid convalescents in hospitals to recover more quickly, or give us a better appreciation of the natural world. It may bind communities together, or alternatively show us the virtues of cultivating our individuality. Art may offer consolation in moments of life crisis, it may soothe the nerves, or it may produce a beneficial psychological catharsis, a purging of emotions that clears the mind or edifies the soul. Even if all of these claims were true, they could not by themselves validate a Darwinian explanation of the arts, unless they could somehow be connected with survival and reproduction. The problem here is a temptation to bask in warm feelings about the arts and then to trip over a stock fallacy of classical logic: "Evolved adaptations are advantageous for our species. The arts are advantageous for our species. Therefore, arts are evolved adaptations."[1]

In addition to the fact that evolution simply does not oper ate via the "good of the species," the problem is that any purported explanation for the arts, if it is to explain how and why the arts evolved, has to be based on a firm biological foundation—which is to say, it must show how the arts contributed, not to happiness, consolation, self-realization, or the greater glory of God, but to fitness. In short, it would have to show how people who create, produce, and enjoy the arts experience higher reproductive success than our more practical-minded Philistine ancestors who kept their spears sharp, their mates faithful, and their offspring well fed, and who didn't waste time admiring the sunset, never mind laboring to reproduce a simulacrum of it on a cave wall.

How can we explain the evolution of such seemingly irrelevant, unadaptive, yet time- and energy-consuming activities as the arts?

The Search for Artistic Cranes

There are several possibilities. Let's begin with Wallace's answer: divine intervention. All right, now let's go on to the next. I don't mean to be snide (well, maybe I do), but the reality is that a theological "explanation" of this sort would apply to each of the evolutionary mysteries considered in this book—and indeed, to all phenomena—rendering irrelevant any efforts to uncover natural-istic bases for anything. In his book, *Darwin's Dangerous Idea*, phi-losopher Daniel Dennett introduced two alternative metaphors for explaining the natural world: sky-hooks and cranes. Sky-hooks are anchored—or rather, unanchored—in the clouds. They pur-port to hold up conceptual structures but are themselves neither stable nor secure.[i] Cranes, by contrast, rest on hard, empirical, scientific ground, comparatively mundane but supporting their loads via direct connection to solid reality. The present book is a search for cranes.

Maybe the evolutionary origins of art are a moot question, because there simply is no such thing as "art" as a unitary phenom-enon. The whole concept of art as a cross-cultural human univer-sal could conceivably be bogus, if the very notion of "the arts" is a Western creation, one that simply does not translate to other societies, whose standards and traditions are vastly different. Clearly, what we call the arts occur in many manifestations—painting, music, poetry, dance, etc.—just as it is obvious that there are superficial differences in the actual forms of art practiced in different cultures.

Indeed, the human enterprise is so diverse that efforts to identify common patterns across different cultures are bound to evoke what is sometimes called the "Pago-Pago problem," as fol-lows: An anthropology symposium has just heard a detailed account of, say, marriage practices in nearly a hundred different and unre-lated societies, with the suggestion that the activity in question qualifies as a cross-cultural universal, whereupon someone stands up in the back of the auditorium and announces triumphantly, "That's not the way they do things in Pago-Pago . . .."

In fact, there are more than enough commonalities—use of color for decoration, of sound to constitute music, of stories to hold the attention and feed the imagination of listeners, and so

---

i. By coincidence, a climbing equipment store used to market a device they called a Skyhook. It was a piece of steel, roughly S-shaped; the accompanying instructions called for hooking the topmost curve on overhanging rock and connecting the lower part to one's person, after which, "thinking only pure thoughts," you step out.

forth—across cultures for us to be justified in calling all of them "art," differing in detail but not in overall pattern. In fact, the very argument that Balinese art is different from Inuit art, from ancient Grecian pot ornamentation or the latest electronic installation at New York's MoMA, itself presupposes that there is something that in all these cases fits under the rubric of art!

Although I argued earlier that an evolutionary look at religion need not necessarily diminish the latter's claim to legitimacy or "truth," in fact, we all know that to some extent it does just this. What about an evolutionary look at art? The likelihood is that it will have a similar effect, but less intensely, since religion makes claims as to existential truth, whereas art always presupposes that beauty is in the eye of the beholder. It's just that to a remarkable degree—and one that cultural relativists have a hard time accepting—even the most diverse human eyes evince similar inclinations.

Moreover, there is enough commonality among the different manifestations of art to justify combining them in a single chapter. One potential way to approach this vast canvas would be to divide the subject along traditional disciplinary lines and to separately consider music, visual art, sculpture, dance, literature and stories, etc., examining in turn various hypotheses for the evolution of each. But there is sufficient overlap when it comes to explanatory hypotheses to justify a more conceptual approach and to examine the possible adaptive significance of the arts by focusing on each hypothesis in turn, slicing the pie in this way rather than by artistic category.

Granted, next, that art exists—that, like Supreme Court Justice Potter Stewart's celebrated account of pornography ("I may not be able to define it, but I know it when I see it"), art is a genuine and identifiable phenomenon, even if somewhat ineffable—another way to discount the intent of this chapter would be to argue for strict cultural determinism, the possibility that we needn't concern ourselves with evolutionary hypotheses for the arts because such activities aren't, strictly speaking, "biological" at all. Rather, maybe asking why people engage in art is like asking why they speak French versus Chinese. The answer, of course, is that some people speak French and others speak Chinese depending on the language they are exposed to, which in turn depends on the culture in which they are raised.

Much the same is true of the arts. Take music. American teenagers are likely to listen to rap, or acid rock, or country 'n western, or blues, or Gregorian chants, or Bach chorales, or Broadway show tunes, or just about anything, depending on who they are, where they grow up, who their friends and parents are, and so forth. Ditto for Sudanese teenagers, Greenlanders, etc. Culture is determinative, just as someone's cultural experiences determine whether she speaks French or Chinese.

But it's not quite so simple. After all, whether a French or Chinese speaker, or something else, everyone who is biologically normal speaks one language or another. We clearly have a species-wide predisposition for language, something for which our shared biology is doubtless responsible, although the specifics of which language—or even, which dialect—are determined by local, culturally bound experiences. "Why French?" and "Why Chinese?" are therefore not interesting evolutionary questions, since the answer is obviously a function of individual learning and culture, not biology. "Why language?" however, is another matter.

By the same token, we can discount the claim that because the arts are culture bound, and in that sense culturally determined, they are not also part of human biology. The *details* of music, visual representation, dance, storytelling, and so forth are without question culture bound and thus culturally determined, but it is a notable fact that even people who argue that what constitutes "art" in New York differs from "art" in New Guinea agree that something we can call "art" exists in both places. Standards of beauty vary, but around the world, people find things they consider beautiful, and these things aren't limited to practical matters, such as a "beautifully" sharp knife or a nice, warm hat.

Art has a number of features that indicate its deep biological roots. There is, for example, no human society that does not have some form of art, and, moreover, it assumes the same major forms (music, dance, and creation of visual designs, story, and verse) in all of them. Everywhere, art evokes deep feelings, just as it develops early and reliably in all normal individuals, although the quality of creation or performance generally improves with practice and training. If the arts were literally "culture bound," we would expect them to vary much more dramatically than they do from one culture to another, and also to be absent from some societies.

"The evolution of *Homo sapiens* in the past million years," writes one noted authority,

> is not just a history of how we came to have acute color vision, a taste for sweets, and an upright gait. It is also a story of how we became a species obsessed with creating artistic experiences with which to amuse, shock, titillate, and enrapture ourselves, from children's games to the quartets of Beethoven, from firelit caves to the continuous worldwide glow of television screens.[2]

Worldwide, people create, admire, and value things and even concepts (songs, stories, poems, etc.) that are of no immediate practical import. That is to say, they make art. And they started doing so very long ago: The earliest cave art—from Chauvet in France—is believed to date from about 30,000 BC.

"There are good reasons to suspect that we may need biology as well as culture to explain art," according to Brian Boyd, professor of English at the University of Auckland:

> (1) it is universal in human societies; (2) it has persisted over several thousand generations; (3) despite the vast number of actual and possible combinations of behavior in all known human societies, art has the same major forms (music and dance, the manual creation of visual design, story and verse) in all; (4) it often involves high costs in time, energy and resources; (5) it stirs strong emotions, which are evolved indicators that something matters to an organism; (6) it develops reliably in all normal humans without special training, unlike purely cultural products such as reading, writing, or science. The fact that it emerges early in individual development – that young infants respond with special pleasure to lullabies and spontaneously play with colors, shapes, rhythms, sounds, words, and stories – particularly supports evolutionary against nonevolutionary explanations.[3]

At the same time there are good reasons to suspect that the biological explanation for art will not be obvious, or easy. Why is this? Simply put, although it is no mystery *that* biology underpins art, it is not at all obvious *why* it does so. Thus, there is no question, for example, that we need biology to understand the universal, cross-cultural human penchant for eating, or for sex. Even though the details of meal preparation and of sexual mores vary widely across cultures, the very existence of eating and of sex are hardly mysteries: The former is necessary for physical sustenance, and the latter, for reproduction. Not so for art.

"Poetry," as W. H. Auden once noted, "makes nothing happen." Eating and copulating make lots of things happen, things that obviously contribute to fitness. But poetry, painting, music, dance, literature, sculpture, and the like? They seem to be gratuitous add-ons, indulgences that are as rococo and baroque as, well, rococo architecture or baroque music.

Such things seem irrelevant to biological success and, indeed, downright silly and frivolous. Worse yet, a case can be made that they are actually *disadvantageous*, liabilities to a creature that presumably has been honed and pruned by natural selection to do only things that contribute to its reproductive success—or at least, not to do things that get in the way. Yet around the world, people not only dance, sing, write poetry, tell stories, and so forth, but they also typically invest in such activities with great consequence; their artistic achievements are among the things about which human beings are most proud.

"Why do we pursue the trivial and futile," asks evolutionary psychologist Steven Pinker, "and experience them as sublime?" Even if we experienced them as neutral or barely noticed them, the real question is, *Why do we engage in such activities at all?* Wouldn't natural selection favor the Philistines, who, being indifferent or even antagonistic to the arts, spent their time and energy on more obviously productive pursuits? Assuming that Wallace was wrong, and the arts do not owe their existence to divine patronage, the evolutionarily obvious answer is that somehow the arts are biologically productive. But how?

Cheesecake?

One possibility is that although the arts derive from natural causes—that is, evolution—they have not been directly selected for as such.

After all, there is much in the natural world that people admire, in ways comparable to their admiration for art: a lovely sunset, for example, or the play of moonlight on water, or the perfect symmetry of a spider's web. But, as Dutton points out, "The spider's web that glistens in the morning dew was dictated by a genetic code in the spider's tiny brain. The web may be a lovely sight to our eyes, but its beauty is a mere by-product of a spider's way of enjoying breakfast." The web-spinning spider is a masterpiece of evolution, but to count as art, a thing must be generated out of intent and not be the result of sheer instinct, which just happens to have produced—to an observing human—a coincidentally pleasing outcome. Early in the 20th century, Marcel Duchamp took things a step further and introduced a new wrinkle into conceptions of art when he developed the concept of *objets trouvés* ("found objects"), which aren't created by the artist, but rather, simply discovered and designated "art." Most famous, or infamous, is Duchamp's "Fountain," a urinal that he called art and that art lovers and art scholars have wrestled with, unsuccessfully, for nearly a century.

Another equally controversial take on the role of intention in art suggests that the arts—even when produced with more foresight and conscious creativity than is presumably mustered by the artiest arachnid—are nonetheless an accidental result of selection acting with a distinctly nonartistic goal.

Thus, for Steven Pinker, as for most evolutionary biologists, the human mind is not biologically driven to make art any more than is a web-spinning spider. Rather, the mind is an organ designed by natural selection for "causal and probabilistic reasoning about plants, animals, objects, and people. It is driven by goal states that served biological fitness in ancestral environments, such as food, sex, safety, parenthood, friendship, status, and knowledge." We have accordingly been outfitted with a mental toolbox that accomplishes these goals. And here is Pinker's key point: "That toolbox, however, can be used to assemble Sunday afternoon projects of dubious adaptive value"—like music, painting, etc.

Among those things the brain does is (1) bring about conditions and situations that enhance our fitness (or rather, that have done so in the environments we experienced in the past) and also (2) register pleasure and satisfaction when these conditions and situations are achieved, as a way of getting us to do those things. For example: The structure of our mind and its connection with the rest of the body facilitates our obtaining food, not least by generating the sensation we call "hunger," which motivates us to eat and, if necessary, to hunt, gather, cook, and so forth, and which then cause us to feel good after we've eaten. But things can get tricky. We can find ways to achieve number 2 without any connection to number 1.

Pinker's favorite example is strawberry cheesecake, which provides the sensation of sweetness (indicative of ripe fruit), plus a creamy texture (characteristic of fats). It isn't good for us—that is, it isn't adaptive—but many people are drawn to it nonetheless, because it mimics sensations that were adaptive for most of our evolutionary past. For Pinker, the arts are "cheesecake for the mind." Applied to music in particular, the "cheesecake hypothesis" states that music is "a pure pleasure technology, a cocktail of recreational drugs that we ingest through the ear to stimulate a mass of pleasure circuits at once." During our long Pleistocene childhood, these were fitness-enhancing experiences, and so, we have evolved to respond favorably to them.

Accordingly, the widespread fondness for strawberry cheesecake derives not from direct selection for such a preference, but rather because selection has favored the existence of genes that predispose us to generate central nervous system receptors that respond with

> trickles of enjoyment from the sweet taste of ripe fruit, the creamy mouth feel of fats and oils from nuts and meat, and the coolness of fresh water. Cheesecake packs a sensual wallop unlike anything in the natural world because it is a brew of megadoses of agreeable stimuli which we concocted for the express purpose of pressing our pleasure buttons.[4]

The problem, of course, is that strawberry cheesecake does not enhance our fitness—but we like it anyhow, because it unconsciously reminds us of things that do.

Pinker also espouses another explanation for maladaptive human enterprises, not so much the arts alone as philosophy and, to some extent, religion. Begin once again with the assumption that the mind evolved for one reason and one reason only: to promote the evolutionary success of the body—and thus the genes—that produced it. Doing so would have required the ability to ask and answer questions, nearly all of them practical: where to get food, how to avoid enemies, how to impress a mate, how to care for your children, what to do when a hyena growls, etc.

But having provided us with a questing organ, namely, our brain, evolution may have outfitted us with more horsepower than we really need. More accurately, it may have provided us with a device that sometimes turns its attention to things that evolution didn't have—in a sense—"in mind." And so, we worry about the meaning of meaning, we ask questions in the realm of metaphysics, and we spend time and energy calculating pi to a gazillion decimal places. This is somewhat like the famous answer to the question, "Why climb Mt. Everest?"—"Because it is there." Because our brains are there, we sometimes use them in ways that sometimes are a sheer waste of time. But because we have such large brains—for perfectly good biological reasons—we are bound not only to assemble those "Sunday afternoon projects of dubious adaptive value" but also to enjoy doing so.

Devotees of the arts (and not merely those with an evolutionary sweet tooth) have long had their hands full explaining "what good" are opera, poetry, ballet, and so forth. How dispiriting to be told that—at least in terms of their evolutionary pedigree—such activities have no function at all! And so, not surprisingly, Pinker's cheesecake hypothesis has not generated much enthusiasm from those who create art for a living, and even less so from critics and scholars who devote themselves to understanding and evaluating music, poetry, literature, and the like. It may well be hard on the ego to spend one's professional life interpreting the creative work of others, and harder yet to be told that the whole enterprise is fundamentally derivative and irrelevant to what is "real." (Interestingly, however, it doesn't seem to be the case that pastry and dessert chefs feel themselves inferior to those who cook the main course.)

Perhaps the cheesecake hypothesis works best when it comes to cheesecake, but not necessarily for art.

On the other hand, cheesecake for the mind may offer the benefit that it is comparatively risk-free—which is hardly the case for such a high-cholesterol confection as, well, cheesecake! As Pinker sees it, engagement with the arts might well be "a way of figuring out how to get at the pleasure circuits of the brain and deliver little jolts of pleasure without the inconvenience of wringing bona fide fitness increments from a harsh world."—like pornography, which, after all, is safer sex than the real thing. Maybe the arts are similarly derivative substitutes for "the real thing," which—like pornography—evidently does the job sufficiently well for enough people to be commercially successful. Less dramatically, but perhaps more accurately: Although we often think of them as expensive, sometimes ridiculously so, maybe the arts are actually an evolutionary bargain, providing cheap and low-risk thrills in place of the real thing.

From Cracked Kettles to Spandrels

It is undoubtedly easier and less risky to experience a love affair via Jane Austen or Hollywood—that is to say, vicariously—than to experience reality, with all its tribulations.[ii] Literature, painting, sculpture, theater, and movies offer a simulacrum, an opportunity to enter into what appear to be genuine experiences but are actually removed from the real thing. Via the arts we can go through all sorts of exciting or instructive events but in the safety and security of our own home, theater seat, and so forth.

Anthropologist and scholar of aesthetics Eckart Voland proposes that we consider the situation of a moth circling a lantern at night. Presumably, the moth is enjoying herself, or at least, meeting certain deep-seated needs for visual stimulation of a particular type. Voland's analogy leads him to propose a variant on Pinker's cheesecake: that we, too, are moths, who "succeeded in inventing a lantern in order to have fun circling it."[5]

Maybe so, but almost certainly, there's more to it.

At one point, for example, in Flaubert's *Madame Bovary*, Emma has just expressed her infatuation with Rodolphe (one of her extramarital lovers), using a series of amorous clichés. There follows a brief journey inside Rodophe's head, in which he devalues Emma's expressions of love as "exaggerated speeches that concealed mediocre affections" and the "emptiest of metaphors." Rodolphe, it turns out, is as intellectually shallow as Emma, and, as Flaubert points out, he therefore fails to appreciate that "none of us can

---

ii. Presumably it is less rewarding as well, but that's another question.

ever express the exact measure of our needs, or our ideas, or our sorrows, and human speech is like a cracked kettle on which we beat out tunes for bears to dance to, when we long to move the stars to pity."[6]

In this beautiful and oft-quoted passage, Flaubert may have hit on something biologically profound. Language is a marvelous attribute, but for most of us, most of the time, it is indeed a "cracked kettle," inadequate to express our needs, ideas, or sorrows. Perhaps this is one reason that human beings have invented the arts, as a way of going beyond the mundane, quotidian expressions and achievements of daily, functional life and attempting to satisfy our need, on occasion, "to move the stars to pity." We achieve this via poetry, song, painting, and dance, the various human expressions that—when done especially well—have the power to literally take one's breath away. Bequeathed a large brain and questing mind (likely for relatively mundane, fitness-enhancing adaptive reasons), it is entirely possible that we find ourselves frustrated by glimpsing the contrast between the depth of what we can detect within ourselves and the "cracked kettle" of our limited capacities.

If so, then it is delightfully incongruous that Flaubert's celebrated description of the inadequacy of language is itself a notable example of language transcending itself, that is to say, of becoming art.[iii]

Here is yet another way of saying nearly the same thing, but a bit less highfalutin: If not cheesecake, or candlelight, or an effort to get something extra out of our demanding but cracked kettles, perhaps the arts are spandrels. A spandrel is an obscure architectural term that has achieved currency among evolutionary biologists thanks to a now-classic article by Stephen Jay Gould and Richard Lewontin titled "The Spandrels of San Marco and the Panglossian Paradigm: A Critique of the Adaptationist Paradigm."[7] A spandrel is a roughly triangular space necessarily created when a rectangular structure is superimposed on an arch. Spandrels aren't especially interesting or important in their own right, but they have taken on particular meaning in the evolutionary literature

---

iii. Or maybe it's not surprising after all, since Flaubert was renowned for laboring intensely over a single phrase, trying to capture—via his art—the precise expression of his own yearnings.

ever since Gould and Lewontin used them as metaphors by which to criticize what they saw as excessive "adaptationism" among their biologist colleagues.

The cathedral of San Marco contains many spandrels, all of them beautifully decorated. Gould and Lewontin pointed out that these spandrels were not produced to provide a venue for artistic display; rather, they are simply necessitated by structural geometry. Once there, however, they provided an opportunity for elaborate decoration. For Gould and Lewontin, if the interior of San Marco cathedral were an organism, it would not be legitimate to consider its spandrels to be adaptations "designed" by natural selection as ways of displaying visual art. Rather, they exist for other, purely structural reasons. By the same token, the arts could be spandrels, and nothing more, bearing the same relationship to the large human brain and its questing, restless mind that the spandrels of San Marcos bear to architectural necessity.

Maybe so. Bear in mind, however, that cheesecake, once invented and enjoying popularity—even if "unadaptive" and thus somehow biologically illegitimate—lends itself to various adaptive variations and modifications. There is good cheesecake and, well, cheesy cheesecake, rich and creamy, mouthwatering confections and dry, crummy, poorly made junk food. Undoubtedly, our appreciation for art is much more complex (involving much more nuance) than simple enjoyment of cheesecake, but then, gourmets in general and cheesecake mavens in particular would probably argue that there is lots of nuance in a discerning evaluation of cheesecake, too!

Once spandrels exist, they are almost literally blank canvases upon which human ingenuity and creative imagination can work. And from this point on, they can be subject to the pulls and pushes, the shaping and configuring of selection, no less than if they had been originally evolved for a particular purpose.

In his book *The Art Instinct*, Denis Dutton deploys a helpful and nonartsy automotive metaphor, beginning with the uncontroversial observation that cars aren't designed to produce heat. Heat is generally unwanted, occurring as an unavoidable ("nonadaptive") spandrel-like by-product of internal combustion engines. Moreover, the presence of so much internally generated heat actually threatens to be *mal*adaptive, necessitating an elaborate cooling system of radiators, hoses, water pumps, etc. At the same time, all that unwanted heat can actually turn out to be useful after all, in running a car's heater on a cold day. The cooling system of a car is thus an adaptation, designed to make the best of a bad situation (too much heat), and the car's heater is also an adaptation, making the best of a problem by incorporating a design that provides warmth for the car's occupants.

Analogously, it is altogether possible that the arts are not an adaptation in themselves, but are incidental by-products of big brains or, as we'll see, perhaps deriving from the need for social cooperation, mother–infant coordination, and so forth—but once they exist, like the heat in an auto engine, the next step could well have been to employ them, adaptively, to serve additional useful ends. If so, then we shouldn't necessarily expect the arts to have just one adaptive role (more on this later).

Another way of looking at this is to distinguish between evolutionary origins of a trait and those pressures responsible for maintaining and shaping it. The cheesecake and spandrel hypotheses suggest that the arts may have originated as a kind of evolutionary afterthought, a necessity analogous to the fact that heavy objects sink and light ones float, and not a product of direct selection at all. Nonetheless, it should be emphasized that this does not render the arts—once they appeared—any less subject to selective pressures than baroque cathedral decorators were indifferent to the use they made of spandrels. If the arts emerged simply because we have big brains, just as spandrels emerged simply because that's what happens when you impose a straight ceiling above a rounded arch, they still must have experienced some sort of evolutionary momentum to become so widespread and elaborately developed.

A similar explanation applies to what might be dubbed the "boredom hypothesis," which goes like this. Evidence from modern hunter-gatherers suggests quite strongly that rather than their lives being a grim concatenation of desperate efforts to stay alive (and reproduce), the "primitive" lifestyle actually may have been the "original affluent society."[8] Thus, the Kung people of the Kalahari average only about 20 hours of obvious work per week. Maybe what we call the arts developed as a means whereby our ancient ancestors whiled away the hours when they had nothing more pressing to do—essentially relieving the boredom by singing, dancing, telling stories, and so forth. The payoff would be amplified insofar as people who did this were less likely to endanger themselves by doing something potentially dangerous, like wandering aimlessly about and possibly blundering into a hungry sabre tooth.

I find this notion less than persuasive, however, simply because it doesn't explain why the arts as we know them, for all their diversity, nonetheless exist in discrete forms (music, dance, painting, sculpture, stories) in all cultures, and—more specifically—why people find these activities suitable and satisfying alternatives to boredom. In a sense, it posits spandrels but on a different canvas: of unobligated time rather than architectural space. It doesn't come to grips with the question of why the arts as such have evidently achieved such significant evolutionary momentum.

Let's look at some possible sources of that "momentum."

A Social Payoff?

One likely prospect involves the social role of the arts. True, the solitary, struggling artist is something of a cultural icon, but one that is pretty much limited to Western society, and to the last century or so at that. Although it is notoriously difficult to compose, or to write, paint, sculpt, or otherwise spin creative gold out of cerebral straw with an audience literally breathing down one's neck, the reality is that overwhelmingly, even if art is typically *made* in solitary splendor, it is *performed* and *experienced* with others.

But why?

For some intriguing research that speaks to this question, consider work by evolutionary psychologists Sebastian Kirschner and Michael Tomasello.[9] Their report, titled "Joint Music Making Promotes Prosocial Behavior in 4-Year-Old Children," strongly suggests that music fosters social bonding and group cohesion. Four-year-old children were induced to make music together—dancing and singing—and were then matched with other 4-year-olds who had been given similar levels of physical activity and linguistic interaction, but without the shared music making. Members of the two groups were then exposed to identical opportunities to help each other in a staged event in which the children had been trying to transfer marbles from one location to another, but in all cases the devices were rigged so that one child literally lost her marbles.

The results were clear: Children who had previously made music together were significantly more likely to spontaneously help each other. Even in those rare cases when assistance was *not* forthcoming, the music makers were more likely to spontaneously explain why they weren't helping, implying that they felt a greater obligation or inclination to do so. The researchers suggest that the key is shared involvement in a coordinated task:

> We propose that music making, including joint singing and dancing, encourages the participants to keep a constant audiovisual representation of the collective intention and shared goal of vocalizing and moving together in time – thereby effectively satisfying the intrinsic human desire to share emotions, experiences and activities with others.

Music goes far back in human antiquity, including the recent discovery, in southwestern Germany, of ancient flutes from at least 40,000 years ago.[10] No one can doubt that music has powerful effects on mood and emotion. It is important to distinguish between music as an innate and universal human penchant—what anthropologists identify as a "cross-cultural universal"—and the societally generated specificity of musical forms, from Gregorian chants to rap, from simple lullabies to Beethoven's Ninth Symphony. Music, in short, is everywhere, although its details vary greatly.

The same is true of the arts generally, and although a group-focusing, coordination-generating function may well be especially intense when it comes to music, it is at least possible that a similar adaptive payoff is associated, to varying degrees, with all of the arts. If cooperation is good for society, then maybe music in particular and the arts in general have been selected for as a way of achieving it.

Another cluster of hypotheses looks at music and the other arts as having evolved as a means of achieving coordination and collaboration within that most intimate social "group," consisting of mother and infant.[11] The prime mover in this interpretive enterprise is Ellen Dissanayake, who makes a compelling case that the key driving force has been the mother–infant bond, which in turn facilitates early learning, as well as basic coordination between young child and its primary caretaker, enabling this biologically crucial dyad to maintain "contact" even when not literally touching.

Although the mutual rituals of mother and infant do not occur with the conscious intention of generating cohesion, this universal dyadic dance could be the source—both developmental and evolutionary—of much human artistry. Dissanayake points out that we use a simple word, "ceremony," to encompass much that is complex and artistic, but as she sees it, this is actually "a one-word term for what is really a collection or assembly of elaborations of words, voices, actions, movements, bodies, surroundings, and paraphernalia" that ultimately ramifies into songs, chants, dance, drama, mime, and so forth. Dissanayake's important ideas in this regard are cogently presented in her book, *Art and Intimacy: How the Arts Began.*[12]

When it comes to mother–infant interaction, the details of *what* is communicated are probably less important than the fact of communication itself, more accurately, maintaining lines of communication. To be sure, not only are lullabies universal, but there is a predictable pulse, rhythm, and pitch employed by adults worldwide when interacting with infants. Perhaps, as one researcher has put it, "the melody is the message."[13] Once established in the mother–infant dyad, it could have ramified to the rest of society.

For Kirschner and Tomasello, the most important proximate mechanism promoting the evolution of music is what they call "shared intentionality," which operates via a collective sense of having moved and created together. Note that the resulting "creation" need not be a physical object; making music together can do quite nicely. Kirschner and Tomasello argue that music-making children "made the intuitive decision to help the other child because they felt immediate empathic concern with the peer's misfortune" when she began to lose her marbles. Absent the "shared intentionality" of singing and dancing, such empathic concern was diminished.

Music has long been highly functional in work situations, where it enables greater coordination among the participants, hence the proliferation of songs in which people aren't just subtly encouraged to cooperate—the kind of unconscious motivated altruism revealed among children by Kirschner and Tomasello—but also encouraged to be directly functional in adult work situations. Chain-gang songs from the American South motivate participants to pull, push, pound with a hammer, and so forth, and ethnomusicologists have documented similar coordinative singing around the globe when it comes to threshing wheat, pounding cassava, grinding corn, etc. Any doubters might want to listen (on YouTube, for example) to a Russian classic, *The Song of the Volga Boatmen* ("Yo-ho, *heave*-ho; Yo-ho, *heave*-ho . . ."). It is almost impossible to refrain from pulling an imaginary rope at the powerful intonation of "heave."

A similar process may well have helped coordinate and motivate our ancestors preparing for a hunt or for combat. Think about marching songs and chants and of the little-known Dutchman, Maurice of Nassau, prince of Orange (1567–1625). Maurice, one of the most important innovators in military science, originated the close-order drill. More than 400 years after he introduced this technique, it still permeates basic training, worldwide. The sight of soldiers marching—and sometimes singing and chanting—in unison may seem an almost comical anachronism given today's high-tech military technology, but as Maurice first codified it (and before him, innumerable tribal war leaders may well have intuited), shared rhythmic sound and movement generates the kind of de-individuated coordination that evidently pays dividends. "When a group of men move their arm and leg muscles in unison for prolonged periods of time," writes the noted historian William McNeill,

> a primitive and very powerful social bond wells up among them. This probably results from the fact that movement of the big muscles in unison rouses echoes of the most primitive level of sociality known to humankind. . . . Military drill, as developed by Maurice of Nassau and thousands of European drillmasters after him, tapped into this primitive reservoir of sociality directly. Drill, dull and repetitious though it may seem, readily welded a miscellaneous collection of men, recruited often from the dregs of civil society, into a coherent community, obedient to orders even in extreme situations when life and limb were in obvious and immediate jeopardy.[14]

In a subsequent treatise, *Keeping Together in Time: Dance and Drill in Human History*, McNeill expanded on this theme, albeit without explicitly noting its evolutionary dimension.[15] McNeill pointed out, as well, how "dance and drill" help to achieve and emphasize group identity, a phenomenon that also predominates in nonmilitary contexts as well. Consider the extent to which teenagers and young adults in particular identify themselves by their particular musical preferences.

It probably isn't coincidental that on September 12, 2001, the politically diverse and ideologically disunited membership of the US Congress—wishing to show solidarity in the face of a national tragedy—gathered on the steps of the US Capitol and sang *God Bless America*. Together.

Interestingly, there is considerable evidence from research in social psychology that music making itself may be less important than cooperation in *any* shared enterprise. Eating together, for example, also creates a bond, which is one reason why "breaking bread" with a stranger is often considered an especially important ritual among many cultures. We might expect a similar effect from digging a ditch, building a wall, and so forth. One of the most renowned demonstrations in social psychology, the so-called robber's cave experiment, artificially generated an alarmingly high degree of animosity among 12-year-old boys at a summer camp by designating them as members of different, competing groups, the "Eagles" and the "Rattlers." At one point, mutual antagonism became so great that it was nearly decided to terminate the experiment prematurely.

The researchers found, however, that they could essentially eliminate the between-group conflict by introducing a superordinate goal that could only be achieved by Eagles and Rattlers working together: specifically, pushing a tanker truck up a hill (without which, it was claimed, the camp would have no water). The social atmosphere was so changed after this intervention that the boys unanimously voted to return home in the same bus.[16]

There have been other, related suggestions, such as the possibility that music in particular emerged as a display signal, by which individuals chorused together and thereby advertised the strength of their coalition, indicating not only their numbers but also the degree of their commitment.[17] Another hypothesis, similar although not identical, is that music making was less important as a means of achieving internal cohesion within a group than as a way of displaying their unity to competing groups.[18]

Among other potential proximate contributors to the appeal of the arts in general—and perhaps of music in particular—a notable one is the so-called chameleon effect, based on the widespread power of unconscious mimicry.[19] Consider, for example, how often people find themselves unintentionally mimicking each other's physical postures while talking.

These hypotheses, with their various versions of cohesion/coordination/commitment, all imply a degree of group benefit, and therefore, each is subject to the same concerns described earlier with regard to possible group-beneficial aspects of religion. As we have seen, for example, group benefits are vulnerable to cheating (e.g., someone might sing lustily, but not actually participate in dangerous intergroup competition if push came to shove). If so, then the signal itself wouldn't be entirely reliable and might not be taken seriously by the intended audience: "Sure, these guys can sing up a storm, but maybe their bark is worse than their bite." Nonetheless, it is hard—even downright foolish—to deny the role of art in generating social solidarity.

Any such hypothesis faces the same problem as the social hypothesis described earlier for homosexuality, namely, the difficulty of group selection. But once again, even though group selection has a deservedly bad reputation when it comes to animals, it just might apply to the human case with respect to the arts and—as we'll soon see—perhaps also to religion.

Toward Greater Foxiness

One of the most renowned essays by British philosopher Isaiah Berlin was titled "The Hedgehog and the Fox." It was an elaboration of the following fragment attributed to Archilochus, an ancient Greek poet: "The fox knows many little things, but the hedgehog knows one big thing." Archilochus, in turn, was writing about the difference between multifaceted, culturally sophisticated Athens (the fox) and Sparta, a single-minded, military power. It should not be lost on those of us seeking to understand the evolutionary origin of the arts that Sparta, not Athens, won the Peloponnesian War, largely because of its hedgehoglike, single-minded focus on military success. Hence, we ought not denigrate the potential value of anything that contributes to social cohesion and coordination.

On the other hand, it is Athens—not Sparta—that comes to mind when we consider artistic creativity, which seems not to augur well for the arts as generating hedgehoggy social coordination. Moreover, at least in modern societies, the arts in general and music in particular serve many functions other than competition and facilitation of war. But this doesn't negate the prospect that they might have initially evolved in a group-oriented and possibly competitive context or, at least, by virtue of their ability to convey benefits to society as a whole.

Since the hypothesis of group coordination came up when considering religion, just as it has now emerged for art, it is reasonable to ask which came first, art or religion? This may well be a foolish question, since it can be answered, with equal plausibility, either way. Brian Boyd argues that art came first, but this may well simply reflect the bias of a scholar who has devoted himself to the study of art (in Boyd's case, fiction). A scholar of religion would likely see her special research interest as having been primary, arguing perhaps that in the grip of religious ecstasy, or motivated by feelings of divine awe and righteous enthusiasm, people proceeded to create great art.

Boyd maintains that "religion needs art as a precursor." Not necessarily. Maybe art needs religion as a precursor, via group identification. "Religion," writes Boyd, "depends on the power of story." Indeed it does. But maybe storytelling, along with visual art, music, dance, etc., began as an effort to give voice to "spiritual" feelings!

At the same time, a possible payoff via coordination and collaboration blurs the distinction between the evolutionary origin of religion and of the arts in general, and of music as well. Not that this is necessarily a bad thing: Maybe religion and the arts do in fact share an adaptive payoff in precisely this regard. After all, religions worldwide are suffused with artistic creation: notably music, dance, poetry, and often architecture, sculpture, and painting. Defenders of religion often point, in fact, to their glorious artistic productions, from the music of Bach to the dome of the Sistine Chapel or the Hagia Sophia.

The social coordination hypothesis—whether narrowly interpreted to derive only from mother–infant interaction or seen more broadly, associated with social coordination among adults—does not preclude the possibility that music and dance in particular could have developed initially as an incidental, nonadaptive byproduct of the human mind (whether cheesecake or spandrel) but was then subsequently taken over for other, more explicitly adaptive functions. Here is a metaphor: Throughout the United States, and especially since the passage of the Americans with Disabilities Act, there has been a proliferation of street-corner ramps, intended to permit wheelchairs to navigate smoothly between sidewalk and road surface. These sidewalk cuts are also used by skateboarders and bicyclists, probably more often than by people in wheelchairs, although this was not the original "adaptive" purpose of these ramps. Maybe the arts are sidewalk cuts of the human mind, originally produced for one purpose but then co-opted for another.

There are many manifestations of the social coordination hypothesis. But at least one humanist, Denis Dutton, is having none of it. Dutton is one of a small but increasingly influential group of academics: humanists who have been enthralled by evolution and have bucked their peers in making a case for the role of biology in understanding the arts. In his book *The Art Instinct*, Dutton makes the curious claim that the arts are primarily solitary rather than social. In support, he cites Leo Tolstoy's essay "What Is Art?" a very funny account of the arguments and competition deriving from an opera rehearsal. To be sure, the arts can generate controversy and competition, but so can just about anything. Tolstoy's hilarious description hardly counts as significant evidence that the arts are somehow antisocial. Similarly, the fact that many of the arts are enjoyed in solitude—reading literature alone at home, listening to a CD of the Missa Solemnis—doesn't mean that stories and chorales originally evolved to be experienced this way.

These days people often listen to their iPods when no one else is around, and presumably they have long hummed to themselves as well. But most of us rarely sing when alone, just as we don't typically laugh when by ourselves. From songs to symphonies, music may be created—in the sense of first originated—in private, but music *making*, in terms of its performance and enjoyment, is nearly always a public, social event. Even when people listen to music alone, the likelihood is that they are engaging in a kind of substitute sociality, whether or not they sing along (which, significantly, they often do). It is hard to imagine our prehistoric ancestors plugging in their iPods or MP3 players and luxuriating to Stone Age music in solitary Pleistocene splendor . . . and not just because there were no such gizmos then. Moreover, although people admittedly experience most of the arts in solitude, their experience is nearly always more intense when they sway, clap, stamp, cry, laugh, or simply watch and listen *together*.

Reading and writing, those most solitary of artistic experiences, are also exceedingly recent, and even after their invention perhaps 8,000 years ago, the great majority of people were illiterate, consuming their "literature" by listening to bards and storytellers. Modern museum-goers, walking by themselves, privately plugged into their informational guided cassettes, individually keyed to particular paintings or sculpture, are similarly novel in the human evolutionary experience; for millennia, visual art, like theater or dance, was a collaborative enterprise, experienced in public, not private. Contrary to Professor Dutton's confident assertion, the arts have long been and currently *are* essentially social.

But as we are about to see, this doesn't necessarily mean that the arts evolved in the service of group coordination. There are other possibilities.

Notes

1. Dutton, D. (2009). *The art instinct.* New York: Bloomsbury.
2. Dutton, D. (2009). *The art instinct.* New York: Bloomsbury.
3. Boyd, B. (2009). *On the origin of stories: Evolution, cognition, and fiction.* Cambridge, MA: Harvard University Press.
4. Pinker, S. (2002). *The blank slate: The modern denial of human nature.* New York: Viking.
5. Voland, E. (2003). Aesthetic preferences in the world of artifacts: Adaptations for the evaluation of honest signals? In E. Voland & K. Grammer (Eds.), *Evolutionary aesthetics.* Berlin: Springer-Verlag.
6. Flaubert, G. (2010). *Madame Bovary.* (L. Davis, Transl.). New York: Viking.
7. Gould, S. J., & Lewontin, R. (1979). The spandrels of San Marco and the Panglossian paradigm: A critique of the adaptationist paradigm. *Proceedings of the Royal Society of London B, 205,* 581–598.
8. Sahlins, M. (1972). *Stone age economics.* Piscataway, NJ: Aldine Transaction.

9. Kirschner, S., & Tomasello, M. (2010). Joint music making promotes prosocial behavior in 4-year-old children. *Evolution and Human Behavior, 31*, 354–364.

10. Conard, N. J., Malina, M., & Munzel, S. C. (2009). New flutes document the earliest musical tradition in southwestern Germany. *Nature, 460*, 737–740.

11. Dissanayake, E. (2000). Antecedents of the temporal arts in early mother-infant interaction. In N. Wallin, B. Merker, & S. Brown (Eds.), *The origins of music*. Cambridge, MA: MIT Press.

12. Dissanayake, E. (2000). *Art and intimacy: How the arts began*. Seattle: University of Washington Press.

13. Fernald, A. (1989). Intonation and communicative intent in mothers' speech to infants: Is the melody the message? *Child Development, 60*, 1497–1510.

14. McNeill, W. H. (1982). *The pursuit of power*. Chicago: University of Chicago Press.

15. McNeill, W. (1995). *Keeping together in time: Dance and drill in human history*. Cambridge, MA: Harvard University Press.

16. Sherif, M., Harvey, O. J., White, B. J., Hood, W. R., & Sherif, C. W. (1961). *Intergroup conflict and cooperation: The robbers cave experiment*. Norman, OK: University of Oklahoma Book Exchange.

17. Merker, B. (2000). Synchronous chorusing and human origins. In N. L. Wallin, B. Merker, & S. Brown (Eds.), *The origins of music*. Cambridge, MA: MIT Press.

18. Hagen, E., & Bryant, G. (2003). Music and dance as a coalition signaling system. *Human Nature, 14*, 21–51.

19. Lakin, J. L., Jeffries, V. E., Cheng, C. M., & Chartrand, T. L. (2003). The chameleon effect as social glue: Evidence for the evolutionary significance of nonconscious mimicry. *Journal of Nonverbal Behavior, 27*, 145–162.

CHAPTER SIX

Art II: Play, Practice, and Sex (Again)

PERHAPS ART EVOLVED BECAUSE it provided an adaptive payoff via learning, something that benefited individuals regardless of its impact on the larger social group. After all, the arts offer abundant opportunities for instruction. John Dryden maintained that theater in particular offers "a just and lively image of human nature, representing its passions and humours, and the changes of fortune to which it is subject, for the delight and instruction of mankind." Revisiting our earlier and perhaps overly negative discussion of art as providing vicarious, pornography-like opportunities for "cheap thrills," maybe the emphasis should be less on the arts as procurer of subjective pleasures and more on how they provide palatable opportunities for adaptive information gathering, whether boring or dangerous or in between.

Learning and Play

Art—particularly literature—can be useful in providing not just "teachable moments," but also "teachable narratives," stories that have genuine substance while offering prolonged connection as we work our way through them. Such instructive narratives aren't necessarily as simplistic and iconic as "What might happen if I kill my father and marry my mother?" or "What are my options if Uncle Claude kills Dad and then marries Mom?" Rather, things can be at least somewhat more subtle: how to navigate a boring marriage to an even more boring country doctor, and what is likely to transpire if you have an affair? Beyond narratives of personal drama or historical scope (such as Napoleon's invasion of Russia), imaginative stories—especially if they are not too imaginative, that is, if they retain the key quality of believability—can provide lessons that help us navigate the ordinary daily dramas that constitute a normal life.

Nor is the potential payoff of art limited to learning about our personal lives. It might help us explore the real world more generally. "Art opens up new dimensions of possibility space," according to Bryan Boyd, "and populates it with imaginative particulars." Or, as Lewis Mumford once suggested, "If man had not encountered dragons and hippogriffs in dreams, he might not have conceived of atoms." Maybe so, but isn't it equally likely that we have often been misled by our imagination, deluded into believing in dragons and hippogriffs, along with ogres, saints, demons, dragons, gods, gremlins, trolls, and fairies? When dealing with the real world, which is notably intransigent, a case can be made that the human imagination needs not so much wings as lead weights. We must be anchored in reality, if only because when it comes to the harsh truths of evolutionary success or failure, that's precisely where we find ourselves.

This, in turn, makes it all the more puzzling that when it comes to literature and its verbal companion, storytelling, people across the globe prefer fiction to nonfiction. One might expect, by contrast, that people would react with disdain and disgust to stories that are known to be untrue! After all, we have little use for dull knives, unpalatable food, ships that don't float, or houses that fall down—that is, things that don't meet the stern tests presented by reality. And yet, it's not quite true that we lower our standards when it comes to fiction, *so long as it is acknowledged for what it is.*

John Tooby and Leda Cosmides, two leaders in the new discipline of evolutionary psychology, note that "It appears as if humans have evolved specialized cognitive machinery that allows us to enter and participate in imagined worlds."[1] They call it "decoupled cognition," the quality—if not unique among *Homo sapiens*, then without doubt unusually developed in our species—of knowingly playing "make-believe." Children do it all the time; adults, too, in the guise of fiction in particular, and the arts in general.

Aristotle, in his *Poetics*, argued that people have an innate tendency to imitate, to create representations of the real world:

> For it is an instinct of human beings from childhood to engage in mimesis (indeed, this distinguishes them from other animals: man is the most mimetic of all, and it is through mimesis that he develops his earliest understanding), and equally natural that everyone enjoys mimetic objects. A common occurrence indicates this: we enjoy contemplating the most precise images of things whose actual sight is painful to us, such as forms of the vilest animals and of corpses.

But positing an "instinct" for mimesis no more explains its existence than does the claim that people engage in art simply because they have an art instinct.[i] In his book *Creative Evolution*, French philosopher Henri Bergson argued that the key to evolution—and to consciousness—was possession of an *élan vital*, to which biologist Julian Huxley responded that this helped explain the nature of life about as much as we illuminate the nature of a railway engine by pointing to its "*élan locomotif*." (A few centuries earlier, in Moliere's *The Imaginary Invalid*, we learned similarly, from a quack doctor, that opium causes sleep by virtue of its "soporific power.") The biologically relevant question is, "Why are people moved to imitate aspects of the real world?" Such imitation, even when undertaken seriously, has an unmistakably playful component.

Human beings are the most playful of animals, and in his book *On the Origin of Stories*, Brian Boyd argues for play as the keystone adaptive payoff of the arts. Art, he points out, inspires cognitive processing of complex information patterns and is therefore good for us; moreover, it does so in a context that—for all its

---

i. Not meaning to be too hard on Aristotle, it is nonetheless hard to refrain from noting that he also wrote that things accelerate while falling because they become increasingly "jubilant" as they approach the ground. Given the often disastrous consequences of the encounter, one might have expected falling objects to be ever-more apprehensive instead.

seriousness—is nonetheless one step removed from the real world, thereby allowing a greater margin for error while giving free rein to imagination and experimentation.

Dogs use their characteristic "play-bow" (head, shoulders, and front legs down, rear legs and back elevated) to indicate that what is to follow is "cognitively decoupled" from other, more serious acts. People use "once upon a time." Boyd points out that "in play we act as if within quotation marks," and that

> we can define art as cognitive play with pattern. Just as play refines behavioral options over time by being self-rewarding, so art increases cognitive skills, repertoires, and sensitivities. A work of art acts like a playground for the mind, a swing or a slide or a merry-go-round of visual or aural or social pattern. The more often and the more exuberantly animals play, the more they hone skills, widen repertoires, and sharpen sensitivities. Play therefore has evolved to be highly self-rewarding. Through the compulsiveness of play, animals incrementally alter muscle tone and neural wiring, strengthen and increase the processing speed of synaptic pathways, and improve their capacity and potential for performance in later, less forgiving circumstances.

According to Boyd, the adaptive value of the arts is indistinguishable from the adaptive value of play, just as, presumably, the arts themselves are essentially a form of play, a way of exploring the world without the stark reality test of reality itself. By contrast, science—although often best undertaken with a playful, exploratory mindset—necessarily collides with the empirical truths of physical and biological nature, stern task mistresses indeed. Although scientists are free to hypothesize to their hearts' content, eventually they must be constrained by the empirical truths of the actual world. As Daniel Patrick Moynihan famously pointed out, people are entitled to their own opinions, but not to their own facts. They are similarly entitled to their own arts, but not their own science.

If Newton or Einstein hadn't lived, we almost certainly would nonetheless have basic physics as well as relativity. If Lavoisier hadn't discovered oxygen, it is certain that someone else would have, just as somebody would have figured out that the heart pumped blood even if William Harvey had never been born. The double-helix structure of DNA was there for the unraveling; had it not been accomplished by Watson and Crick, others would have done so.[ii] And it doesn't diminish the stature of Darwin himself to be reminded—as noted early in the preceding chapter—that Alfred Russel Wallace glimpsed the same basic truth of nature, independently. But if Shakespeare or Bach had not been born, we can rest assured (or rather, bereft) that we wouldn't have Hamlet or the Goldberg Variations. This is not to argue that the arts are more valuable than the sciences; rather, because they result from the playful, free flow of imagination, unconstrained as science is by reality, the arts aren't just unique, but—at the risk of outraging language purists—in a sense, "more unique."

Even so, the arts are also anchored in reality, just less tightly bound. And although people doubtless learn about the world via music and the visual arts as well, Boyd argues that fiction and storytelling constitute the richest arena for playful learning via art:

> Because it entices us again and again to immerse ourselves in story, it helps us over time to rehearse and refine our apprehension of events. Fiction, I propose, does not *establish* but does *improve* our capacity to interpret events. It preselects information of relevance, prefocuses attention on what is strategically important, and thereby simplifies the cognitive task of comprehension. At the same time it keeps strategic information flowing at a much more rapid pace than normal in real life, and allows a comparatively disengaged attitude to the events unfolding. It trains us to make inferences quickly, to shift mentally to new characters, times, and perspectives. Fiction aids our rapid understanding of real-life social situations, activating and maintaining this capacity at high intensity and low cost.

Later, Boyd proposes that the most important function of fiction is that "By appealing to our fascination with agents and actions, fiction trains us to reflect freely beyond the immediate and to revolve things in our minds within a vast and vividly populated world of the possible." In an earlier book, *Madame Bovary's Ovaries: A Darwinian Look at Literature*, coauthored with my daughter, Nellie, I suggested that one of the most damning critiques of any work of literature is that it isn't believable, which means that it must deal with the world of the evolutionarily possible. To be vivid and enduring, literature must represent images

---

ii. Indeed, their discovery of the structure of DNA took place in the context of a vigorous race among several scientists, working competitively in different laboratories.

of human behavior that are consistent with the evolutionary constraints and inclinations that biology knows to exist, and that people intuit as being "realistic." And indeed, literature consistently depicts such patterns as male–male competition, female initiated mate selection, kin- and reciprocity-based altruism, parent–offspring conflict, and so forth.

But it is one thing to posit that literature—even when pre-Darwinian, or when written without regard to the insights of evolutionary biology—will nonetheless reflect certain biological truths about human nature. That is, it is one thing to predict *what* literature will depict, but quite another to understand, as we are now attempting, *why* it exists at all.

Returning to hypotheses for the existence of art more generally, Boyd makes the novel suggestion that, in concert with its playful functionality, artistic creativity has been selected for much for the same reason as sex has: as a way of increasing variation—whether genetic (sex) or ideational (art). In this regard, it is interesting that the adaptive significance of sex, too, like that of art, has long perplexed biologists. Like art, sexual reproduction seems wasteful (at least, compared with the alternative of asexual breeding, which, among several benefits, has the added payoff of ensuring that an asexually reproducing individual has 100% of its genetic material reflected in each of its offspring, compared to a mere 50% for parents who employ sex). And it may be more than coincidental that the currently favored hypothesis for the existence of sex is that despite its 50% genetic tariff, it pays for itself by producing genetic variability among one's offspring.

As a result, when the environment changes—which it inevitably does—or when new pathogens or parasites arrive, parents who breed sexually have a greater chance of achieving success via at least some of their genetically diverse offspring. By the same token, maybe "artistic license" benefits its producers and consumers, and pays for its seeming profligacy, by expanding the boundaries of the imaginable. If so, then when the social environment changes—and it, too, like the physical and biological environment, inevitably does—people who have experienced the potential diversity afforded by imaginative art may enjoy an advantage comparable to organisms that cushion their biological risk via sexually generated genetic diversity.

Encountering a dragon in a story can be thrilling; meeting one in a back alley would be terrifying. But if we really did encounter a genuine dragon, we might well respond more effectively if we had already encountered various scenarios in our imaginations, via the stories we heard. And of course, for dragons one can substitute human competitors, or collaborators, or collaborators turned competitors and vice versa, romantic partners, rivals, and so forth—the entire gamut of potential life experiences that are reflected (with various degrees of accuracy) in art generally and stories in particular.

Aspiring chess masters study famous matches, often memorizing classic openings, end games, and so forth. The game of life is no less complicated than chess, which makes it possible that much of the appeal of narrative art derives from an appeal similar to that of eating nourishing food: consuming certain things, like studying certain game plans, is good for us.

Returning to our earlier metaphor of the hedgehog and the fox, people who partake of artistic possibilities are foxy, armed with a diverse array of resources, whereas without the arts, one is left with a hedgehoglike mastery of one big thing—reality as it currently presents itself—but with a limited array of alternative moves.

The connection between art and reality is complex and intriguing, paralleling in some ways the connection between culture and biology. Thus, a strong case can be made that when it comes to preferences for visual art, humanity's long Pleistocene sojourn has left a discernible evolutionary imprint: Cross-culturally, people prefer scenes that include open grassland or prairie, as well as trees and/or rocky outcroppings.[2] This combination has given rise to "prospect/refuge theory," since the former offers the prospect of long-distance vision—all the better to spot enemies or prey, my dear—while the latter suggests opportunities to take refuge if need be.[3] Add water, shake gently, and the result—if not quite a Garden of Eden—strongly resembles the environment in which our species spent most of its early evolutionary childhood. Although prospect/refuge theory offers a possible explanation for why we prefer certain images, stories, etc., over others, it nonetheless fails to illuminate why we *create* these things. Perhaps they simply provide pleasure, because of the potential—albeit illusory—of satisfying a need that is nonetheless genuine.

To some extent, of course, the pleasure derived from art is no different from that evoked by "the real thing," such that one of the joys of, say, viewing a pleasant country scene may be the extent to which it re-creates the pleasure of actually experiencing the real thing. The likelihood, for example, is that both events induce a similar secretion of satisfaction-inducing neurosecretions. This might seem to be an evolutionary problem, insofar as it can be maladaptive to focus on a simulacrum rather than the genuine article (consider the downsides of drug addiction, or pornography). But it may also be an unavoidable consequence of having adaptively strong proclivities and predispositions; perhaps you can't have one—adaptive preferences for certain situations and thus a neuronal sensitivity to stimuli that reflect those situations—without the other, a vulnerability to being fooled. Perhaps, then, in the case of art, we should substitute "willingness" or "benevolent capacity" for "vulnerability."

"Art necessarily is illusion," writes psychologist Roger N. Shepard.

> In the immense history of life on earth, art is but a very recent development. Since its emergence with *Homo sapiens*, there has been insufficient time . . . for the evolution of extensive neural machinery adapted specifically to the interpretation of pictures. The implication is inescapable: Pictures most appeal to us, to the extent that they do, because they engage neural machinery that had previously evolved for other purposes.[4]

Gossip and "Theory of Mind"

Turning now from the visual to the narrative arts, another practical, teaching payoff may derive from its role as a vehicle for sharing social information, which is to say, a classy form of gossip. Evolutionary anthropologist Robin Dunbar has made the intriguing suggestion that one of the keys to sociality—especially among primates (which includes *Homo sapiens*)—is social grooming, which includes the iconic inclination of monkeys and apes to sit around and pick ectoparasites off their best friends. Dunbar points out that as proto-hominid group size increased, it became increasingly difficult to maintain cohesion via direct physical contact, at which time verbal communication—gossip—may well have replaced grooming.[5]

Insofar as he is correct, it isn't a huge step from gossip as grooming to stories as gossip. Indeed, much of the pleasure and delight modern readers derive from fiction may be very similar to what is gained from reading autobiographies, biographies, history, memoirs, and so forth, and which in turn differ only slightly from the payoff that comes from watching soap operas, reading confessional magazines, or sharing the latest news on friends, family, neighbors, and celebrities.

Gossip needn't have the negative connotation it is typically accorded. It doesn't have to be frivolous. After all, it has long been in our interest—highly social species that we are—to keep tabs on who's doing what, who's up and who's down, what's the latest dish on so-and-so or such-and-such. And stories provide a fine way of doing this, while also adding a dose of social glue.

In addition, fiction isn't altogether untrue. Mark Twain once quipped that the difference between fiction and nonfiction is that the former must be "more real." To be valued, a story must convey accurate truths about human nature: how people respond—and hence, how they can be expected to respond—under particular circumstances. Stories always incorporate insights into the behavior, and often the underlying mental processes, of other people. As such, they may well be useful in conveying information about what psychologists call Theory of Mind, which refers to the capacity of human beings to put themselves inside the heads of someone else, so as to anticipate their perceptions and behavior more accurately. There is much debate among specialists as to whether animals other than *Homo sapiens* possess an accurate Theory of Mind, but no doubt people do, just as there is no doubt that such information can be biologically as well as socially adaptive.

Whether functional as play or gossip, as a primer in Theory of Mind, or as something entirely different, stories are always about people, or animals, or—rarely—things. Never are they purely concerned with abstract concepts. This seemingly obvious conclusion hides a potentially important truth: the importance of stories as providing useful inroads into the lives of other people, animals, or things. For a lively example, consider this selection from *Sylvie and Bruno Concluded*, written by Lewis Carroll and published in

1893; it was the last novel written by the creator of the Alice books.[iii] At one point, a little girl named Sylvie implores the Professor to tell her and her brother Bruno a story:

> Bruno adopted the idea with enthusiasm. "Please do," he cried eagerly, "Sumfin about tigers—and bumble bees—and robin red-breasts, oo knows!"
>
> "Why should you always have live things in stories?" said the Professor. "Why don't you have events, or circumstances?"
>
> "Oh, please invent a story like that!" cried Bruno.
>
> The Professor began fluently enough. "Once a coincidence was taking a walk with a little accident, and they met an explanation—a very old explanation—so old that it was quite doubled up, and looked more like a conundrum—" He broke off suddenly.
>
> "Please go on!" both children exclaimed.
>
> The Professor made a candid confession. "It's a very difficult sort to invent, I find. Suppose Bruno tells one first."
>
> Bruno was only too happy to adopt the suggestion.
>
> "Once there were a Pig, and a Accordion, and two jars of Orange-marmalade . . .."

Portrait of the Artist as a Show-Off

When it comes to evolutionary hypotheses for the arts, this one has been vilified almost as much as Pinker's cheesecake—especially by humanists worried that their subject is getting insufficient deference, and who also, it must be said, don't understand evolutionary theory as well as they ought. In a nutshell, it involves what Darwin called "sexual selection." And it was given its clearest formulation by evolutionary psychologist Geoffrey Miller of the University of New Mexico.[iv]

---

iii. I thank Brian Boyd for pointing me to this selection. Like so many others, I had read *Alice in Wonderland* and *Through the Looking Glass*, but nothing else by Lewis Carroll.

iv. Personal note: After reading Miller's book on the subject, I inadvertently found myself muttering, "How stupid of me not to have thought of that," in unintentional mimicry of Thomas Huxley upon first reading *The Origin of Species*.

Miller's thesis is simple, yet profound. As he sees it, the human mind evolved as a result of sexual selection, essentially the equivalent of the peacock's tail, except that among peacocks, the key choosers are the females, whereas in our case, the choice generally works both ways: males choosing females as well as females choosing males.

In any sexually reproducing species, it is highly adaptive for would-be parents to select the best possible partner with whom to reproduce. Several factors converge in this regard. For one thing, mate-seeking individuals will be more fit (evolutionarily) in proportion as their breeding partner is healthy and fit (physically). For another, since sexual reproduction involves combining one's genes with someone else's, it is important that the chosen someone possess genes that are likely to contribute positively toward producing healthy and successful offspring. In addition, once individuals of either sex are attractive to members of the other, there arises a secondary, derivative benefit from mating with such individuals: They are likely to produce offspring who also possess these sexually attractive traits, and who therefore will be more likely to be successful themselves when they mature and enter the mating marketplace. Finally, these considerations are likely to be especially valid in species that are at least somewhat monogamous, that is, in which males and females make a substantial commitment to each other, which in turn italicizes the importance of making a reproductively advantageous mate choice.

In his book *The Mating Mind*, subtitled *How Sexual Selection Shaped the Evolution of Human Nature*, Miller gets abundant explanatory mileage out of sexual selection, and not simply as an explanation for the arts. In fact, he isn't directly concerned with explaining the arts as such, so much as spotlighting the role of sexual selection in producing the human mind, in all its remarkable complexity. He points out, for example, that the brain itself—an energetically expensive organ as well as one that is highly vulnerable to mutational damage—serves as an ideal fitness indicator, a kind of biological trophy displayed by members of one sex that serves to attract members of the other.

This is similar to the brain's products, and not just obviously useful behavior of the sort that contributes to individual survival.

Also relevant: those uniquely human characteristics that have so bedeviled generations of evolutionary biologists and are the subject of this chapter, namely, art, music, dance, poetry, and other manifestations of creativity that seem unlikely to contribute directly to fitness. Sexual selection promises to shed light even on certain human traits that might not otherwise appear to need special explaining . . . until we look at them through its uniquely illuminating lens.

Take language.

Miller makes a powerful case that human language exhibits a verbal luxuriance that is difficult to interpret in other than sexually selected terms. Bear in mind that Darwin originally conceived the concept of sexual selection in an effort to explain the existence of such exaggerated, highly elaborated, and seemingly useless traits as the lyrebird's feathers or—most famously—the peacock's tail. His argument—controversial in its day but increasingly supported now—was that although certain characteristics don't contribute to personal survival (and may even be deleterious), they ultimately pay their way in terms of reproductive success insofar as they contribute to an individual's ability to attract and keep a mate, hence the phrase "sexual selection."

At first glance, human language does not seem equivalent to the peacock's tail. After all, the peacock's tail is the iconic example of something that seems excessive, overbuilt—indeed, deleterious—and thus explicable only in terms of sexual selection rather than survival selection. By contrast, although the adaptive significance of human language may not be obvious, the problem isn't that language—like the peacock's tail—is difficult to explain, but rather that it is explicable in terms of numerous possible adaptive payoffs: social coordination, sharing of information, and so forth, such that the very fact of language does not seem to qualify as an evolutionary mystery. And yet, as Miller points out, human language may be more like a peacock's tail than is generally realized.

Like the peacock's tail, human language is more elaborate than simple survival would seem to require. One way to assess this would be to compare the minimum vocabulary needed to satisfy basic, quotidian tasks with the actual vocabulary most people possess. Miller points out that most of the words that most people know are used only rarely. Why, then, he asks, do we retain such a large stable of largely unused resources?

> The most frequent 100 words account for about 60 percent of all conversation; the most frequent 4,000 words account for about 98 percent of conversation. This sort of "power law" distribution is common: the 100 most successful movie actors probably account for 70 percent of all money paid to all actors; the 100 most popular Internet sites probably handle a similar proportion of Internet traffic; and so forth. It is not surprising that vocabulary use follows a power law, but it is surprising that our average vocabulary is so large, given how rarely we use most of the words that we know. It could easily have been that just 40 words account for 98 percent of speech (as it does for many two-year-olds), instead of 4,000 (as it does for most adults). As it is, any of the words we know is likely to be used on average about once in every million words we speak. When was the last time you actually spoke the word "cerulean"? Why do we bother to learn so many rare words that have practically the same meanings as common words, if language evolved to be practical?

The plot thickens when we consider that even English—which hosts an exceptionally large number of words, numbering more than 1 million—can still function effectively after being stripped down to a mere skeleton. Thus, something called Basic English was created in the 1920s, using just 850 words. One of its co-creators, Oxford philosopher I. A. Richards, noted that under his system and using, for example, just 18 verbs, "it is possible to say . . . anything needed for the general purposes of everyday existence—in business, trade, industry, science, medical work—and in all the arts of living, in all the exchanges of knowledge, desires, beliefs, opinions, and news which are the chief work of English."[6] Missing from this assessment is a likely "chief work" of any language: demonstrating one's intelligence, via verbal facility. As Miller notes, one would not expect to see a personal ad that said "looking for prospective mate who knows fifty thousand useless synonyms," and yet, it is entirely possible that people have evolved outsized vocabularies for exactly the same reason that peacocks have evolved outsized tails, because tale telling—and the ability to employ appealing words in the process—suffices for people like tail growing works for peacocks.

In the language of evolutionary biology, such traits are effective "fitness indicators," and as such, likely to be selected for because they contribute to sexual and thus reproductive success, no less than, say, the ability to ward off infection contributes to survival and thus reproductive success. This emphasizes a frequent misunderstanding of sexual selection, in which it is seen as somehow counter to survival (or natural) selection. There are, indeed, some interesting differences, notably the fact that whereas survival selection tends to be a minimalizing process, eliminating gewgaws and doodads, favoring biological design that is maximally efficient, sexual selection generates excessive, show-offy traits. But sexual selection is no less "natural" than is survival selection, and indeed, both operate via the same bottom line: differential reproduction.

There is one intriguing difference, however. Although both sexual selection and survival selection are equally natural and reproduction focused, the former is oddly recursive. When it comes to survival selection, the totality of the environment (physical as well as biological) operates upon organisms to favor certain characteristics over others. This has some impact upon environments as well—the dietary proclivities of elephants, for example, have had a definite impact on the nature of the African savannah—but by and large, environments select for organisms and not vice versa. With sexual selection, however, the organisms themselves are bestowing reproductive advantage upon members of their own species, favoring some of them over others. Insofar as sexual selection has been especially important among *Homo sapiens*, the result is that to an extent not often appreciated (by scientists as well as the lay public), human beings have literally created themselves.

Contrasting sexual selection with survival selection, Miller emphasizes the unique feedback component of the former, as he speculates playfully on what would happen if natural selection worked like its sexual counterpart:

> Organisms would select which environments exist, as well as environments selecting which organisms exist. Strange, unpredictable feedback loops would arise. Would the feedback loop between polar bears and Arctic tundra result in a tundra of Neptunian frigidity where bears have fur ten feet thick, or a tundra of Brazilian sultriness where bears run nude? Would migratory birds select for more convenient winds, lower gravity, and more intelligible constellations? Or just an

ever-full moon that pleasingly resembles an egg? Yet this is just what happens with sexual selection: species capriciously transform themselves into their own sexual amusements.

Courtship involves sexual choice, which, in turn, places a positive premium on "fitness indicators," characteristics that provide reliable information as to the adaptive quality of a prospective mate. As such, sexual choice itself served to stretch the capacities of the human mind, even as it rewarded those who indicated—via such mental gymnastics as verbal play, musical ability, and other manifestations of artistic creativity—that their brains were in especially good shape. As Miller puts it, sexual selection "asked not what a brain can do for its owner, but what fitness information about the owner a brain can reveal."

Miller points out, for example, that to a large extent, human courtship involves verbal interaction, and that baby making (one of the bottom lines when it comes to evolutionary success) requires about 3 months of unprotected sex, which, at roughly 2 hours of conversation per day in the early stages of an intimate relationship, and an average rate of 3 words spoken per second, results in roughly 1 million words spoken by each partner . . . per conception. Thus might sexual selection contribute directly to fitness, via such seemingly "useless" traits as verbal facility.

After all, there is nothing like talking to reveal not only what's on one's mind but also the nature and quality of that mind. And for human beings, ancestral no less than current, the mental status of a potential reproductive partner was likely to loom large indeed.

Cross-cultural surveys of mating preferences across a variety of cultures have shown a strong preference for, among other things, a sense of humor. Being able to tickle your partner's funny bone might be a useful indicator of something immediate and practical, such as the ability to withstand future difficulties and disappointments. But the reality is that a good sense of humor, like a powerful vocabulary, is no more likely to be of direct survival value than is—to choose some activities not entirely at random—the ability to tell a good story, sing a song, paint a picture, write a poem, sculpt a statue, and so forth. In short, the argument can be made (or, in more suitably florid linguistic terminology, the scientific hypothesis propounded) that verbal facility, like competence in music, visual art, dance, and the like, may have evolved in the service of sexual selection, a way in which the artist demonstrates his or her cerebral fitness and, insofar as the demonstration is successful, actually increases his or her evolutionary fitness as a result.

Here is another point. A narrow survival selection view of language would generate the prediction that listening should be more beneficial and thus more sought after than speaking since, after all, we learn (and thus stand to profit personally) via the former, rather than the latter. But in fact, people are more likely to compete to be the one broadcasting "information" than to be its recipients. This, in turn, is consistent with the notion that language itself may be largely a form of display (although it also conforms to the sociobiological view that communication is often manipulation[7]). At the same time, much sexual display is not simply "epigamic"—directed toward mate choice—but also effective when it comes to male–male or female–female competition.

The key to the sexual selection hypothesis is that many traits aren't fitness enhancing so long as we restrict our intellectual horizon to those that are strictly survival related. Widen the perspective, however, to include mate choice, and a whole new world opens up, with much of the human mind seen to be a sexual ornament. "The Darwinian revolution could capture the citadel of human nature," writes Miller, "only by becoming more of a sexual revolution—by giving more credit to sexual choice as a driving force in the mind's evolution. Evolutionary psychology," Miller urges, "must become less Puritan and more Dionysian." His project has therefore been to think less about the "survival problems our ancestors faced during the day" and more about "the courtship problems they faced at night"—or, more poetically, "whether the mind evolved by moonlight." Ditto for the arts.

Interestingly, a similar suggestion was made by Oscar Wilde, a master of aesthetics but a novice when it came to evolutionary biology. Wilde contrasted the practicality of ethics with the luxuriance of aesthetics: "Ethics, like natural selection, make existence possible. Aesthetics, like sexual selection, make life lovely and wonderful, fill it with new forms, and give it progress, variety and change."[8]

The mind's moonlight reveals unexpected patterns; for example, via language, our great-, great-grandmothers and -grandfathers were able to get, almost literally, into each other's minds—something that isn't an option for the nonlinguistic. As a result, and perhaps for the first and only time in biological evolution, thought itself—via sexual selection—became subject to direct adaptive pressure. It is often and correctly stated that the sexiest part of the human body is what resides between the ears. Via language in particular (and, perhaps, the arts in general), mental traits became as apparent to the sexual chooser as a partner's height, weight, body fat, breast size, or shoulder width. And as a result, we were selected to be simultaneously consumers as well as producers of mental accomplishment. If so, then we also literally created the mental capacities that led to such accomplishments, by selecting as sexual partners individuals with the capacity to accomplish; at the same time, sexual selection would also have been favoring the ability to be astute "art appreciators," insofar as our ancestors who made good choices would have been rewarded by leaving more descendants.

In addition to the prospect of illuminating the adaptive value of the arts, Miller's critique of much cognitive psychology is cogent, and perhaps even devastating:

> most experimental psychology views the human mind exclusively as a computer that learns to solve problems, not as an entertainment system that evolved to attract sexual partners. Also, psychology experiments usually test people's efficiency and consistency when interacting with a computer, not their wit and warmth when interacting with a potential spouse. . . . But evolution does not care about information processing as such: it cares about fitness.

Miller adroitly brings in Thorstein Veblen and the power of conspicuous consumption as sexual advertisement, asking, "How could mate choice favor a costly, useless ornament over a cheaper, more beneficial ornament?" to which he adds, puckishly, "Why should a man give a woman a useless diamond engagement ring when he could buy her a nice big potato, which she could at least eat?" In a sense, mental quality is also something of a "useless ornament," except insofar as it is profoundly useful as an indicator of mate quality. And one of the best ways to demonstrate such quality is via language in particular and the arts in general.

But the argument isn't limited to artistic use of language. In fact, in *Sexual Selection and the Descent of Man*, Darwin ventured a similar hypothesis for the evolution of music, emphasizing its connection to love via courtship:

> Music arouses in us various emotions. . . . It awakens the gentler feelings of tenderness and love, which readily pass into devotion. . . . All these facts with respect to music and impassioned speech become intelligible to a certain extent, if we may assume that musical tones and rhythm were used by our half-human ancestors, during the season of courtship, when animals of all kinds are excited not only by love, but by the strong passions of jealousy, rivalry, and triumph.

In addition to a possible connection between music and courtship vocalizations (e.g., bird songs), Darwin emphasized its possible relationship to language as well, notably emotion-laden oratory:

> The impassioned orator, bard or musician, when with his varied tones and cadences he excites the strongest emotions in his hearers, little suspects that he uses the same means by which his half-human ancestors long ago aroused each other's ardent passions, during their courtship and rivalry.

Among our ancestors, Miller writes, "If an individual made you laugh, sparked your interest, told good stories and made you feel well cared for, then you might have been more disposed to mate." And today? We take our dates to restaurants where we pay professional chefs to cook them great food, or to concerts or dance clubs where professional musicians excite their auditory systems, or to films where professional actors entertain them with vicarious adventures, or to museums where they admire the works of great painters, and so forth. The chefs, musicians, authors, painters, and actors do not actually get to have sex with our dates. They just get paid. We get the sex if the date goes well. Of course, modern courtship still requires talking, and we still have to look reasonably good, and it is crucially important to demonstrate at least a passing familiarity—ideally, full critical understanding and appreciation—of the performances and productions in question. But at least in the wealthy West, the market economy has shifted much courtship effort from the principals to professionals. To pay the professionals, we have to make money, which means getting a job. The better one's education, the better one's job, the more money one can make, and the better the vicarious courtship one can afford. Consumerism thus turns the tables on ancestral patterns of human courtship, making it a commodity that can be bought and sold.

Miller usefully distinguishes between "top-down" and "bottom-up" strategies, the former involving elite culture, created by those few possessing remarkable talent, the latter involving "folk aesthetics," made by normal people. Interestingly, his fitness display theory of aesthetics works better for folk aesthetics than for its elite counterpart. Folk aesthetics concerns what ordinary people find beautiful or otherwise appealing; elite aesthetics concerns the objects of art that upper crust opinion makers anoint as deserving time and attention. Folk aesthetics deals far more directly with the talent of the artist. Here is Miller's account:

> In response to a landscape painting, folks might say, "Well, it's a pretty good picture of a cow, but it's a little smudgy," while elites might say, "How lovely to see Constable's ardent brushwork challenging the anodyne banality of the pastoral genre." The first response seems a natural expression of typical human aesthetic tastes concerning other people's artistic displays, and the second seems more of a verbal display in its own right.

After pondering this, it is difficult not to sympathize with the "Philistine" assessment of, say, abstract expressionism that shrugs, "My dog could have made that," or "Looks more like an accident than like art." Miller touches an important biological chord, whereby works of art are evaluated specifically as indicators of the artist's talent and skill, rather than by what the work "says." His approach requires us to cease condescending and ask why most people are so resistant to forms of art that do not reveal, clearly, the competence of the artist. When someone viewing an exhibition of modern art—or better yet, a novel "installation"—responds something like, "This is art? My 3-year-old could do the same," the irked parent may be labeling himself or herself a Philistine, but is also reflecting a deep truth of human creativity: the degree to which it served to advertise something about the creator, notably his or her talent and skill.

The fact that we admire virtuosity in artistic creations—something often taken for granted—itself speaks to its origin in sexual selection. As much as some people value *objets trouvé*, or Marcel Duchamp's "ready-mades" such as his infamous "Fountain," the reality is that most people equate good art—and certainly great art—with good (and, when possible, great) talent. We admire a rainbow, but we don't consider it a work of art—of nature, yes, or of optics, moisture, meteorology, etc., but not of art. For that, human skill must be somewhere, somehow, on display.

Most artists, musicians, writers, etc., do not attribute their creative urges to natural selection in general or to sexual selection in particular. But this does not mean that sexual success has not fundamentally powered the creative, artistic imagination.

Perhaps, then, a more directly relevant animal model of artistic creation isn't so much the peacock as the bowerbird, a group of species in which, unlike peacocks, the males are relatively nondescript but make up for this by building elaborate structures (bowers), which in some cases are also carefully decorated with flowers, berries, shells, feathers, pieces of scrap metal and glass, etc., all for the purpose of charming females into mating with them. They produce something remarkably similar to human art, entirely as a result of sexual selection acting through female choice.

Satin bowerbirds are among the best-studied species, with a penchant for using their beaks to paint the walls of their bowers with regurgitated fruit glop, especially favoring the color blue. Geoffrey Miller suggests that if one could interview a male satin bowerbird, it might say something like this:

> I find this implacable urge for self-expression, for playing with color and form for their own sake, quite inexplicable. I cannot remember when I first developed this raging thirst to present richly saturated color-fields within a monumental yet minimalist stage-set, but I feel connected to something beyond myself when I indulge these passions. When I see a beautiful orchid high in a tree, I simply must have it for my own. When I see a single shell out of place in my creation, I must put it right. Birds-of-paradise may grow lovely feathers, but there is no aesthetic mind at work there, only a body's brute instinct. It is a happy coincidence that females sometimes come to my gallery openings and appreciate my work, but it would be an insult to suggest that I create in order to procreate. We live in a post-Freudian, postmodernist era in which crude sexual meta-narratives are no longer credible as explanations of our artistic impulses.

If art is created as a fitness indicator on the part of the artist, this might help explain why it is made, and also why the artist typically takes great pleasure in his or her achievement, often feeling compelled to struggle beyond the likelihood of immediate pecuniary rewards. But it doesn't answer the sibling question: Why do we find *someone else's* fitness indicators pleasurable? It is one thing to *produce* art, but why do nonartists enjoy *experiencing* it? Why isn't the world of art populated entirely by producers, with no consumers?[v]

Answer: Maybe for the same reason that a peahen presumably enjoys looking at a peacock's tail or the female satin bowerbird responds to the cerulean artistic accomplishments of the male. This is not to say that art is likely to be sexually arousing (although often enough, it is), but that "pleasure" in the experiencing of art needn't be any different from the pleasure associated with experiencing good food, or rest, or sex. It is an evolutionary mechanism that motivates continued experiencing of whatever is found pleasurable—and in nearly all cases, fitness-enhancing experiences are those that generate pleasure. If so, then it would be surprising if art didn't generate pleasure, and in fact, if it doesn't, one can legitimately question whether it qualifies as art.

Pleasures, Penchants, and Misunderstandings

As mentioned earlier, many scholars of art—even some who have otherwise shown themselves open to evolutionary interpretations—deride the sexual selection hypothesis, just as they resist any implication that the arts have arisen as an evolutionary by-product. In most cases, it appears that they do not fully understand the process of evolution. Thus, Brian Boyd errs in discarding the by-product hypothesis, claiming that if it were true, "if art offers only illusory benefits, people could live more successfully in cities, could cope better with the strains of urban life, *without* the pleasures

---

v. One could argue that this has already occurred, given the current state of the Internet, with nearly everyone, it seems, being a blogger and no one having the time to pay attention to each other's efforts.

of art: . . . without music, stories, parades, carnivals, concerts, shows. A bleak civic environment would outdo a vibrant one." To the contrary, this ignores the adaptive value of big brains and thus the argument that if the arts are a nonadaptive by-product of our having big brains (which might well have evolved to serve the more immediate and practical goals of social coordination, tool use, predicting the actions of others, etc.), then selection, having fostered big brains, would also foster the arts, as an unavoidable consequence. A small-brained human species might well experience a "bleak civic environment," but it would also have to cope with the various other maladaptive consequences of having small brains.

Surprisingly, Professor Boyd also misunderstands how evolution operates to generate pleasure as the handmaiden of adaptive behavior, erroneously dispensing with the sexual selection hypothesis as follows: "If art had no role to play in human survival, if it were useless in those terms . . . then we would engage in art overwhelmingly in our fertile years, and only so long as fertile individuals of the opposite sex were among their audience." Nonsense! This is equivalent to arguing that sex could not possibly be connected to reproduction, because people engage in it when they are not fertile, when postmenopausal, or when using birth control.

Evolution has outfitted our species with a penchant for sexual activity, largely because it contributes to reproductive success (but also for social, bonding reasons, too), and as a result, we derive pleasure and satisfaction from sex even when reproduction is not at issue. Ditto for art: Once evolution has endowed us with an appreciation for art as produced by others as well as a penchant for creating it ourselves, there is no more reason for this appreciation and penchant to disappear among people who are nonreproductive than for couples who have elected intentional childlessness to forgo sex.

Boyd goes on to suggest, with equal illogic, that if sexual selection is involved, "An infant's delight in hearing nursery rhymes or lullabies, a mother's in crooning them, a grandmother's pride in weaving designs . . . anyone's silent reading of fiction of keen interest in the work of long-dead artists would be impossible to explain."

To the contrary, images of movie stars retain their appeal, even if the people depicted are long dead, just as a peahen finds a peacock's tail attractive even if its owner might be temporarily unavailable. We can be seduced, similarly, by the music of Mozart or Beethoven, the poetry of Baudelaire or Rimbaud, or the paintings of Cezanne or Picasso without the literal prospect of combining any of their genes with our own.

Boyd acknowledges that artists are motivated not just by an inchoate need for self-expression, but also by the adaptive payoff that comes from enhanced status. And yet, he simultaneously denies a role for sexual selection. This is most curious, since sexual selection consists precisely of intersexual selection (so-called epigamic selection, in which members of one sex are chosen by members of the other), combined with intrasexual competition, whereby individuals of either sex compete among themselves. Status is not an end in itself, but rather, it is of biological value precisely because it leads to reproductive success via sexual selection. The fact that creative artists typically value the success and status they receive is not only consistent with the sexual selection hypothesis but also fundamental to it.

Achieving social status is not an alternative to sexual selection; rather, it is one of the main ways whereby sexual selection operates. "If there were no beautiful women," Aristotle Onassis is reputed to have said, "money would be meaningless." So, too, would being the center of attention as a creator of great stories, paintings, songs, etc. This leads, in turn, to a controversial issue: whether creative genius is sexually asymmetrical.

On the one hand, the fact that there are so many more "great masters" than "great mistresses" in every major artistic discipline is consistent with the sexual selection hypothesis, since males—sperm makers, and therefore capable of inseminating many females—would be more strongly selected to be sexual/artistic/creative show-offs than would females, who are egg makers and thus less able to transfer sociosexual success into a large Darwinian reproductive payoff. In addition, the evidence is overwhelming that *Homo sapiens* is primarily polygynous, and in such cases, males are favored who manage to attract more than their "fair share" of sexual attention, whether via head-to-head combat as with elk or by doing something that gets them selectively chosen by females, as with those "artistic" bowerbirds.

But on the other hand, it is clear that cultural biases and social norms have long restricted the creative outlets for women. Doubters should read Virginia Woolf's essay on a hypothetical "Judith Shakespeare," a meditation on how an equally or even more talented sister of William would have had her talents suppressed. Moreover, as the cultural prohibitions against women's artistic creativity have fallen, the ranks of women artists have swollen. This suggests that women's artistic capacity may well be at least as great as their manly counterparts, and not limited to being an appreciative—albeit discerning—audience.

There is yet another evolutionary argument for biologically based equality with respect to the arts: Unlike many mammal species, in which females choose among pushy, courting males, in the case of human beings, sexual choice works both ways. Men choose among women, just as women choose among men. This is presumably because *Homo sapiens* has such a long developmental trajectory, with infants born completely helpless and requiring substantial and prolonged investment long after birth. As a result, ancestral men have been selected to seek for something more than healthy DNA and a suitably packaged body[vi] with whom to combine their genes and in which to incubate their offspring. Cross-culturally, men as well as women identify kindness, intelligence, and a sense of humor among the primary traits sought for in a romantic partner.[9]

Earlier, we briefly considered the fox and the hedgehog as a metaphor for societies with (fox) and without (hedgehog) artistic diversity and for individuals with and without artistic capabilities. It can also be applied to intellectual styles, and indeed, this was Isaiah Berlin's intent in his now-classic essay. He contrasted foxes such as Shakespeare, Moliere, Goethe, and Joyce, who exemplified many different themes and perspectives, with hedgehogs such as Plato, Dante, Dostoyevsky, and Ibsen, each of whom focused on a particular defining idea or approach. Tolstoy, the ostensible

---

vi. In practical, proximate terms, this has meant a sexually attractive one.

subject of Berlin's essay, desperately wanted to be a religiously Christian hedgehog, but the depth and complexity of his characterizations showed that he couldn't help being a fox.

In any event, it is noteworthy that in developing evolutionary hypotheses for the arts, most scholars tend to be hedgehogs, promoting a unitary explanation: The arts are a by-product, or cheesecake, or a tactic for achieving group cohesion, or a product of sexual selection, and so forth. Such intellectual tunnel vision may itself be an adaptive academic strategy, since scholars are more likely to achieve renown by associating themselves with a single, memorable hypothesis rather than spreading their reputation across various shades of gray. It is also possible, of course, that the predominant scientific view is simply and honestly that a single grand idea will prove, in most cases, to be correct.

According to Aldous Huxley, "At present all too many scientists ... seem to think that theories based upon the notion of 'nothing-but' are somehow more scientific than theories consonant with actual experience, and based upon the principle of not-only-this-but-also-that."[10] And it may be that a single hedgehoggy hypothesis will ultimately prove to be correct. My guess, however, is that in this case—as in most others considered in the present book—foxiness wins.

The ancient Roman playwright Terence is particularly known these days for his comment, or boast, *Homo sum: humani nil a me alienum puto* ("I am a man: nothing human is alien to me"). When it comes to explaining that wholly human phenomenon, the arts, perhaps no evolutionary hypothesis should be considered entirely alien, either.

Notes

1. Tooby, J., & Cosmides, L. (2001). Does beauty build adapted minds? Toward an evolutionary theory of aesthetics, fiction and the arts. *SubStance, 94/95*, 6–27.
2. Orians, G. (In press). *Environmental aesthetics*. Chicago: University of Chicago Press.
3. Appleton, J. (1975). *The experience of landscape*. New York: Wiley.
4. Shepard, R. N. (1990). *Mind sights*. San Francisco: Freeman.
5. Dunbar, R. (1998). *Grooming, gossip, and the evolution of language*. Cambridge, MA: Harvard University Press.

6. Richards, I. A. (1943). *Basic English and its uses*. London: Kegan Paul.
7. Dawkins, R., & Krebs, J. R. (1978). Animal signals: Information or manipulation? In J. R. Krebs & N. B. Davies (Eds.), *Behavioural ecology*. Oxford, UK: Basil Blackwell Scientific Publications.
8. Wilde, O. (1891, 2007) *The critic as artist: With some remarks upon the importance of doing nothing and discussing everything*. New York: Mondial.
9. Buss, D. M. (1989). Sex differences in human mate preferences: Evolutionary hypotheses resting in 37 cultures. *Behavioral and Brain Sciences, 12*, 1–49.
10. Huxley, A. (1963). *Literature and science*. New Haven, CT: Leete's Island Books.

CHAPTER SEVEN

Religion I: Genes, Memes, Minds, and Motives

IT IS POSSIBLE THAT this chapter is a waste of time—yours as well as mine. Maybe religion isn't an evolved human trait after all, but instead, entirely a product of culture, learning, and social tradition. After all, the religions of humankind are extraordinarily diverse, and, moreover, they are clearly passed on from person to person, nearly always from parents to children . . . but via transmission that is cultural, not genetic.

The Greek historian Herodotus, writing about 2,500 years ago, tells the following story. Darius, king of Persia, was intrigued to learn that east of his empire, in India, the Callatians ostensibly cannibalized their dead. He was also told that to the West, the Greeks cremated theirs. Darius sent emissaries to each, asking what it would take for them to switch practices. The Callatians responded indignantly that nothing could ever induce them to do something so barbaric as to bury their dead, while at the same time, the Greeks were equally adamant that they would never eat theirs. Darius concluded ruefully that not he, but custom, was king.

We might call it Darius's Dictum, and indeed, the presumed primacy of custom over biology has long been the reigning ideology of social science. Doesn't it apply not merely to funeral practices—which, after all, are closely tied to religion—but to religion itself?

Probably not. (So you can rest easy: This chapter likely isn't a waste of time after all.)

For one thing, even though there is tremendous worldwide diversity in the precise nature of religious practices, the fact remains that every human society engages in some form of religion[i]; they are an example of what anthropologists call a "cross-cultural universal." And when something is consistent across all human groups, despite the enormous cultural differences between them, this in itself is *prima facie* evidence for some sort of biological underpinning. Human beings are a vast planet-wide experiment in which one thing—our biological essence as members of *Homo sapiens*—is held constant, while other things, namely, customs, are permitted to vary. When, in a scientific experiment, one thing is held steady while others are permitted to vary, after which something else stays unchanged, it is reasonable to think that the persistent outcome is due to whatever has also been held constant. In our case, this is the human genome. When it comes to the precise details of religion, Darius's Dictum holds: Custom is indeed king.

Considering just the world's major religions, there is immense diversity, even if we disregard the specifics of ritual and focus on underlying concepts. Thus, Judaism and Hinduism emphasize the narrative dimension; for Islam, the key is submission to the will of God; for Confucianism, the key appears to be social ethics; for Christianity, it's primarily doctrine; and for Jews, it's how to be a *mensch*. Today's religions differ, as well, in their conception of the fundamental problems: For Confucians the primary evil is disorder; for Christians, sin; for Buddhists, suffering; for Hindus, the eternally recurring cycle of birth and death. And there is every reason to think that the earliest manifestations of religion were at least as diverse.

But as for religion itself—as distinct from religions themselves—the details of concern and custom bow to biology, since underneath the huge superficial diversity, there appears to be a biological

---

i. This is not the same as claiming that all people within every society engage in religion. By the same token, all human societies have some means of solemnizing marriage, but this does not mean that all people are married.

underpinning that enables us to talk about "religion" as something that acknowledges its universality and underlying common denominators.

God Genes?

In that case, what about going to the other extreme? If the key isn't culture, but biology, then what about the prospect that people have a "God gene"? Wouldn't that explain everything? No again, and for several reasons. First, as we'll see, there is no "God gene." And second, even if there were, the question would remain: Why is there such a gene (or such a God-seeking brain region, or God-seeking hormone, etc.)? An evolutionary mystery isn't solved by pointing to a particular gene, brain region, or hormone, just as a murder mystery isn't solved by pointing to a particular weapon, even if it turns out to be the "correct" one. The detective wants to know who wielded it, and why.[ii]

"The human mind evolved to believe in the gods," according to Edward O. Wilson.[1] "It did not evolve to believe in biology. . . . Thus it is in sharp contrast to biology, which was developed as a product of the modern age and is not underwritten by genetic algorithms." I hesitate to disagree with a great biologist (and one who has been something of a mentor to me), but in this regard, I think Professor Wilson is mistaken. The human mind may or may not have evolved to believe in the gods; that's the subject of this chapter. But it seems evident that we definitely evolved to believe in biology, or at least, to readily accept and respond to biology's basic truths: the difference between animals and plants and between predators and prey, the significance of genetic relatives—even without necessarily knowing anything about genes or DNA.

---

ii. This brings up an important distinction, between proximate causation (the immediate cause of something) and ultimate causation (the evolutionary reason for the proximate mechanism existing at all). Thus, people typically eat "because" they are hungry, with hunger produced by stomach contractions, blood sugar changes, certain hormone levels, etc. These are all proximate mechanisms. At the level of ultimate, or evolutionary, causation, hunger occurs as a way of inducing individuals to nourish themselves when such nourishment is biologically adaptive.

We evolved to "believe" in biology in the same way that we evolved to believe in physics: an intuitive understanding of Newtonian mechanics, including force, friction and momentum, acceleration, and, yes, gravity, even if our ancestors knew nothing about gravitons or differential calculus.[iii] They didn't know anything about quantum mechanics or relativity, any more than they evolved to believe in the Krebs cycle (the process whereby cells extract energy from food), although they certainly evolved to take advantage of the ATP produced via the Krebs cycle. Perhaps a belief in the supernatural is somehow privileged because of our biology, but no more so than a belief in biology itself.

At the same time, it seems likely that religious belief is strongly influenced by our own preferences, and not simply by an objective assessment of validity. Francis Bacon, considered by many to be the conceptual founder of science as an organized enterprise, suggested that "Man prefers to believe what he prefers to be true," which is not entirely different from other beliefs (e.g., in the honesty of one's relatives and friends, in our own basic goodness, etc.). So maybe the issue is preference rather than actual truth—what Stephen Colbert calls "truthiness." This raises the additional question: Regardless of whether religions are "true" (and whatever true means in this context), why do so many people find them "truthy"? What is there in human nature combined with the nature of religion that makes the latter so appealing to the former? According to Karen Armstrong in her book *A History of God*, religion is "something that we have always done. It was not tacked on to a primordially secular nature by manipulative kings and priests but was natural to humanity."[2]

This appears to be true, but doesn't explain very much. More specifically, from whence commeth this naturalness?

At the outset, let's dispense with a seemingly obvious answer that upon inspection turns out to be no answer at all: Religion has evolved because it provides comfort. This merely substitutes "comfort" for a purported explanation. To say that people find religion comforting is the same as saying that it makes them feel good or contributes to their sense of well-being (and perhaps, of

---

iii. The mathematical procedure used to determine rates of change, including the acceleration due to gravity.

course, to their genuine well-being, too). But it begs the question. Sleep provides comfort when we're tired, food provides comfort when we're hungry, and sex provides comfort when we're erotically needy. The human psyche has evolved to find these experiences, and numerous others, pleasurable and comforting because they contribute ultimately to our biological success. What about religion?

In most cases, when we closely observe an animal—or even a plant, for that matter—we find that its nature, including its behavior no less than its structure, is likely to "make sense." This means that we can generally determine how a particular behavior or structure contributes to the organism's success. The fins of a fish help it swim; the feathers of a bird enable it to fly; the eyes of a horse or of a human being allow it to see. In such cases, one needn't be an expert to intuit what evolutionary scientists call the "adaptive significance" of the characteristic in question. What especially repays further attention are those cases when the practical, success-promoting effects of a structure or behavior isn't clear. A notable example is altruism, which had long been an evolutionary puzzle since it seems to defy bio-logic for individuals to behave in a way that reduces their own fitness while enhancing that of others. Such altruism—although admirable by ethical standards—should be eliminated by natural selection and replaced by genetic tendencies to maximize, not reduce, the success of any predisposing genes.

In the case of altruism, such a paradox led to the crucial insight that what appears to be altruism at the level of bodies is actually selfishness at the level of the genes themselves, something that is particularly evident when biologists looked for—and found—close correspondence between genetic relatedness and the predisposition toward "altruism." In most cases, if we see an animal—or a person—expending calories or running risks to get food, or a mate, or defending its offspring, we typically know what's going on. But if we see said animal—or person—doing something that appears silly, wasteful, or downright hurtful, then the antennae of evolutionary scientists are likely to twitch.

If a physicist from Alpha Centauri were to examine the body shape of fish, especially their fins and tails, he/she/it would be able to deduce a great deal about the nature of water. Similarly, close attention to the structure of feathers and of birds' wings would provide huge insight into what constitutes "air." The list could easily be expanded, the basic point being that because of the way natural selection works, there is a very close correspondence between the nature of living things and the nature of the real world. This poses a fascinating problem for students of religion: Even if we are prepared to agree with Gandhi that "all religions are true,"[iv] we need to ask why religion is a cross-cultural universal. After all, people need air to live—also food, water, sleep, and so forth. But these truths have not resulted in cross-cultural belief systems that worship air, pray to water, or offer sacrifices to sleep.

On Costs and Benefits

Religion poses an interesting evolutionary mystery for yet another reason: It is costly.

Attending church, synagogue, or mosque takes time and energy that could be spent otherwise. Thus, simply showing up for religious observances imposes what economists call an "opportunity cost" (the simple fact that doing anything—so long as it requires time, energy, or resources—occurs at the cost of reduced opportunity to do something else). Religions nearly always levy some sort of explicit tax as well, ranging from voluntary donations to strict tithing. Not uncommonly, the faithful must submit, in addition, to extensive training, sometimes including difficult and painful initiation procedures, or if nothing else, sponsoring and supporting the existence of a special class of what seem to be social parasites known as priests, ministers, monks, deacons, rabbis, shamans, and so forth. Most important, however, is the disconnect between faith—defined as "belief without evidence"—and quotidian life itself, grounded as the latter is in day-to-day evidentiary reality.

"The most common of all foibles," wrote H. L. Mencken, "is to believe passionately in the palpably not true."[3] There is much to be said for optimism, but the fact remains that many of the beliefs encouraged by religion are not only palpably untrue but also

---

iv. To be honest, I am more likely to agree with the inverse: All religions are false.

downright lethal: The Lord's Resistance Army, for example, a rebel group in Uganda, has convinced many of its juvenile followers that they are impervious to enemy bullets. One would think that such palpably untrue and overtly fitness-diminishing beliefs would not persist for long. As Steven Pinker puts it, "A freezing person finds no comfort in believing he is warm; a person face-to-face with a lion is not put at ease by the conviction that it is a rabbit."[4] In fact, maybe delusions of these sorts are comforting, or at-ease putting . . . but if so, not for long. And therein lies the evolutionary mystery. Even when the demands of faith are less than lethal, and even if they are somewhat more defensible—not necessarily provably true but at least not patently absurd and readily disprovable—they nonetheless tend to go directly against the evidence of daily experience as well as common sense: for example, someone is born to a virgin who is eventually killed but later ascends bodily to heaven, or worship of a god with the body of a man and the head of an elephant.

"It is undesirable," wrote philosopher and mathematician Bertrand Russell, "to believe a proposition when there is no ground whatever for supposing it to be true."[5] There is a big issue here: Insofar as the human brain and mind are fine-tuned to maximize fitness, what's the payoff for being so downright wrong when it comes to how the world works? As we shall see, maybe such belief is desirable to evolution (which is to say, favored by natural selection), even if unappealing to rationality minded thinkers such as Bertrand Russell.[v]

Whether its teachings are factually wrong or right, "Religion is a human universal," notes anthropologist Jonathan Benthall, "and those who think they can eliminate it by scientific argument or ridicule are no more likely to succeed than those who would eliminate sexuality or playfulness or violence."[6] I don't think I could eliminate religion by scientific argument or ridicule (although frankly, I would do so if I could). What I am seeking to accomplish in this chapter is to try to understand, scientifically, why religion is a human universal, why—as Benthall indicates in the subtitle of his book—"a secular age is haunted by faith."

---

v. And, to be honest, the author of this book.

In his book *On Human Nature*, Edward O. Wilson[7] noted that

> Skeptics continue to nourish the belief that science and learning will banish religion, which they consider to be no more than a tissue of illusions. Today, scientists and other scholars, organized into learned groups such as the American Humanist Society and Institute on Religion in an Age of Science, support little magazines distributed by subscription and organize campaigns to discredit Christian fundamentalism, astrology, and Immanuel Velikovsky. Their crisply logical salvos, endorsed by whole arrogances of Nobel Laureates, pass like steel-jacketed bullets through fog.

In Lewis Carroll's *Through the Looking Glass*, Alice tells the White Queen that she cannot believe things that are impossible. "I dare say you haven't had much practice," replies the Queen. "When I was your age, I always did it for half an hour a day. Why, sometimes, I've believed as many as six impossible things before breakfast." It is widely noted that much of religious faith involves believing in the impossible—not in spite of the impossibility, but because of it. This is fine as poetry, but just as natural selection ruthlessly weeds out maladaptive traits (a tendency to approach predators as though they are one's friends, or to refuse food when hungry), it should deal harshly with any tendency to do things that are wasteful or with adherence to a creed that espouses tenets that are "impossible." In the world of biological evolution, reality rules.

In his book *Freedom Evolves*, philosopher Daniel Dennett pointed out that from an evolutionary perspective, any characteristic of a living thing that appears to go beyond what is functionally necessary or useful cries out for explanation. "We don't marvel at a creature doggedly grubbing in the earth with its nose, for we figure it is seeking its food; if, however, it regularly interrupts its rooting with somersaults, we want to know why."[8] Looking at Muslims interrupting their lives to pray five times each day, at Jews refusing to use electricity or even ride in a car on their Sabbath, at Hindus circumnavigating the 52-km route around holy Mt. Kailash[vi] *making full-body prostrations on their knees the entire way*, or

---

vi. According to Hindu belief, Lord Shiva, the bane of sorrow and of evil, sits in a state of perpetual meditation at the summit of this mountain, along with his wife, Parvati. Climbing Mt. Kailash has long been forbidden so as not to disturb the holy couple.

Christians donating 10% or more of their income to their churches, evolutionists cannot help seeing the biological equivalent of truffle-pigs doing cartwheels.

Of course, religions almost always serve the interests of those who promote them, so there is nothing mysterious in the fact that shamans, ministers, priests, rabbis, imams, and rinpoches support religion, often to the detriment of the mainline followers. Evolutionary biologists are familiar with a similar phenomenon, in which natural selection generates arms races between potentially competing entities. Prey-catching adaptations on the part of wolves are typically not adaptive for elk. What's good for the lion is likely bad for the lamb.

But if there is little need to explain the adaptive value of religion from the perspective of its purveyors, its generals, and their associated high command, what about the much more numerous followers, the willing soldiers of the Lord? Or, another way of putting it: Insofar as there are genes that predispose their bodies to partake of religion, what is in it for those genes?

To be clear, there is no "God gene," despite the wildly exaggerated assertion by geneticist Dean Hamer.[9] Rather, there is a particular genetic variant, known as VMAT2, which—along with many others—helps code for the production of proteins that do much of the work in our brains: so-called neurotransmitters and neuromodulators. Different versions of VMAT2 exist in different people (the technical term is that it is polymorphic). And this, in turn, could contribute to why different people respond differently to different stimuli and situations. More specifically, Hamer found a weak but seemingly genuine correlation between the presence of the VMAT2 gene and a tendency to feel connected to the world and a willingness to accept things that cannot be objectively demonstrated. In a review of *The God Gene* in *Scientific American*, Carl Zimmer wrote that a more accurate title would have been "A Gene That Accounts for Less Than One Percent of the Variance Found in Scores on Psychological Questionnaires Designed to Measure a Factor Called Self-Transcendence, Which Can Signify Everything from Belonging to the Green Party to Believing in ESP, According to One Unpublished, Unreplicated Study."

There is, however, some evidence pointing to a general genetic underpinning when it comes to religion. A study characterized the religious inclinations of 31 pairs of fraternal twins who had been reared apart, comparing their pattern of similarity and difference with that found among 53 pairs of identical twins also reared apart. Fraternal twins share, on average, 50% of their genome, whereas identical twins are genetically identical, sharing 100% of their genes. Interestingly, when it came to religious tendencies, the correlation between the identical twins was roughly double that of the fraternals.[10] A similar result was found in an Australian study involving more than 4,000 twin pairs from Australia and England.[11] In a sense, therefore, we appear to be genetically hard-wired for religion. But what does this mean? Clearly, it isn't for a particular religion; there are more than 7,000 identified varieties.

Consider this: It has been well demonstrated that a particular human genetic variant, by modifying the way its carriers metabolize the neurochemicals dopamine and serotonin, generate a predisposition toward risk taking. This general inclination manifests itself in specific behaviors, such as a fondness for roller coasters, or for fast sports cars. This does not mean that there is a gene "for" roller coasters, or "against" sedate Volvo sedans. Rather, our genetic makeup often predisposes us in one direction or another, with the specifics determined by what's on offer. Not only are there no genes for Buddhism as opposed to Hinduism, or for Jewishness as opposed to Christianity, but also there are no genes for religion as opposed to atheism. But there can certainly be genes that make people more or less likely to believe things without empirical evidence, more or less likely to accept the authority of others, more or less likely to enjoy ritualized behaviors such as singing in a chorus, and so forth. Instead of thinking about genes "for" religion, it is more useful to consider genes that result in an openness or susceptibility or inclination for religion.

In addition, even if, as seems almost certain, there are no genes for counting or doing arithmetic, it is equally certain that there are genes whose effects include having the ability to do arithmetic. And there is no particular mystery why such a capacity hasn't been selected against: It can be very useful to keep track of the numbers of things, and very little liability. But what of religion?

A Brief Meditation on Ubiquity

Let's note, in addition, that even if there were a God gene, the evolutionary mystery would still be unsolved, since the deeper question would be: Why is there such a gene? Similarly, even if there were a God gene (and even if we understood its evolutionary history), this wouldn't say anything about whether or not there is a God. God could have implanted such a gene in the human genome for our edification and/or His greater glory. Alternatively, such a hypothetical gene could be as disconnected from reality as the fact that people have a predisposition—presumably, genetically influenced in some roundabout way—to take their sense perceptions as accurate when often they are not. (Thus, people are predisposed to think that the sun moves around the earth, that the earth itself is flat, and so forth.)

If it were demonstrated that there is a particular gene or combination of genes that generates religious behavior, or similarly, if it were found that there is a particular god-loving brain region, this wouldn't say anything about whether religion is correct, or whether god exists. Thus, one possible interpretation would be that people believe in God because they possess certain conglomerations of DNA or certain arrangements of neurons that, if real, might cause people to believe in a God or gods that are not necessarily real at all. A hard-wired biological underpinning for religious belief could thus somewhat undermine the divine legitimacy of that belief. Conversely, it might be claimed that a neuronal or genetic substrate for religious belief makes such belief more legitimate, implying that God implanted the appropriate genes or orchestrated the neuronal connections.

Responding to an article about the evolution of receptivity (for the positive spin) or susceptibility (the negative) to religion, a letter from the Rev. Michael P. Orsi argued as follows: "If religion is good for humans, as evolutionary biologists now seem to recognize, doesn't it seem reasonable that the Creator would design us with a congeniality to receive Him?"[12] One problem with this line of argument is that human beings have evolved with all sorts of perceptions that aren't necessarily true: for example, the perception that the world is flat, or that the sun moves around the earth.[vii]

Another is that we have numerous other predispositions that contribute to evolutionary success but certainly aren't admirable or worth retaining: for example, a tendency to homicidal violence, to rape on occasion, and so forth. Moreover, the notion that people may be inclined to believe in God because such belief has been reproductively useful would itself seem bad news for believers, who presumably would be more comfortable if people believed in God because He exists, not because our ancestors have somehow been bribed by natural selection to follow religion.

Sometimes the dictates of religion lead directly to increased biological fitness, suggesting that there are some aspects of religious practice that map directly onto evolutionary benefit. In orthodox Judaism, for example, intercourse is forbidden from the day menstruation begins until 7 days after it has ended. Then, after the woman cleanses herself in the mikva, a Jewish husband is expected to have sex with her when she returns. The result: intercourse when the woman is maximally fertile! At least as direct—and better known to most readers—is the Catholic Church's prohibition against not just abortion but even contraception. In fact, the most orthodox and fundamentalist religious traditions, including Christianity, Judaism, Islam, and Hinduism, are all vigorously pronatalist, frowning on any behavior likely to diminish reproduction. Typically included is intolerance of homosexuality, as well as resistance to divorce—except, notably, in cases of infertility or failure to "consummate" the marriage. On the other extreme, the Shakers, a peculiar sect that prohibited sex and thus the bearing of children, went extinct. Not surprisingly.

Religion is not an absolute human need, like breathing. There are no nonbreathers, noneaters, or nondrinkers, but lots of nontheists (i.e., atheists, including the present author). Nonetheless, according to Thomas Hobbes, himself a nonbeliever, "Religion can never be abolished out of human nature. An attempt to do so would just lead to new religions springing out of the old ones." Indeed, given its universality across human cultures as well as its

---

vii. So long as the perception in question does not reduce fitness, there is no reason for it to have been selected against.

stubborn persistence in the face of persecution, there seems little doubt that although the specifics of religious belief and practice are determined by the vagaries of personal situation and experience, our species was primed for religion, predisposed to engage in one kind or another, just as we are primed for language, sex, and sociality. But whereas it is relatively easy to imagine the adaptive value of language, sex, and sociality, religion is more puzzling.

In what might itself be testimony to the power of the religious impulse, even some great, deep-thinking evolutionary biologists seem to have checked their critical faculties at the door when it comes to examining religion. Thus, in his *Essays of a Biologist*, no less a scientific giant than Julian Huxley[viii] described religion as "the most fundamental need of man . . . to discover something, some power, some force or tendency, which was moulding the destinies of the world—something not himself, greater than himself, with which he yet felt that he could harmonize his nature."[13]

But the mere fact that something is widespread—even universal—doesn't necessarily mean that it is adaptive. Appendicitis is ubiquitous in our species. So is the common cold.

Appendicitis appears to be simply the unavoidable downside of a particular vestigial structure, and the common cold results from an arms race between human beings on the one side and the cold virus on the other. What about religion, which certainly seems to be something that human beings have evolved, for its own reasons? But what reasons? Religion has shown itself to be quite persistent—consider, for example, the stubborn survival of religion for decades in the Soviet Union despite vigorous efforts to wipe it out. In itself, of course, this doesn't say anything about whether it is good or bad, adaptive or maladaptive; our hearts' stubborn insistence upon beating, despite injuries and illnesses of various sorts, is "good" from the perspective of survival. But numerous pathogens and parasites are also stubborn about their continued existence—the fact that it is difficult to eliminate the tuberculosis bacteria or HIV doesn't mean that tuberculosis or AIDS is in any sense good for us.

---

viii. Brother of Aldous, the writer; half-brother of Nobelist Andrew; and grandson of Thomas, aka "Darwin's bulldog."

On the other hand, an equally strong case can be made against biologists being disdainful of religion, insofar as religion itself is almost certainly a product of biology. There is accordingly no more reason to derogate religion because it is in some sense biologically grounded than to disdain birdsong, wolf predation, or the long-distance migration of Arctic terns.

But the question persists: Given that religion has discernible downsides (as does birdsong, wolf predation, or the long-distance migration of Arctic terns), why has it evolved? How have its liabilities been compensated at the level of differential reproduction?

The Viral Meme Hypothesis

One possibility is that it hasn't happened, that *Homo sapiens* has been saddled with—or parasitized by—a tendency that is maladaptive. Not surprisingly, this idea comes from the fertile mind of a great evolutionary biologist who is also renowned (or infamous) as a vigorous opponent of religion: Richard Dawkins. Among Dawkins's many intriguing ideas, one of the most widely accepted has been that of "memes," which are essentially the cultural equivalent of genes. Whereas genes are entities of nucleic acid that reside in living bodies, memes are entities of memory and information that reside in society. Genes are inherited biologically, via reproduction; memes are acquired culturally, via teaching and imitation. Genes are Darwinian, projected across generations via reproduction and spreading by the process of organic evolution; memes are Lamarckian, acquired characteristics that are "inherited" culturally, passed along from ancestors to descendants, from parent to child, from adult to adult, rapidly and nongenetically via conversation, imitation, songs, schooling, books, radio, television, YouTube, email, Twitter, Facebook, and, yes, religious indoctrination.

Memes are increasingly acknowledged, to the extent that they have entered normal language. There is even a word— "memetics"—for the study of how memes originate and spread. Memes, the concept, have themselves become a meme! There is no doubt, as well, that religious memes spread like their sectarian relatives: The language and doctrine of religion, patterns of dress, song, prayer, and other traditions are promulgated among congregants, varying slightly (mutating) on occasion, but for the most part being copied with remarkable fidelity. And they also reproduce differentially, experiencing a kind of "selection," with certain ones outcompeting others, the winners prospering while the losers go extinct.

Michael Pollan's best-selling book *The Botany of Desire* provided many readers with a novel perspective on plant domestication, showing how cultivated plants—notably apples, tulips, marijuana, and potatoes—can be seen as agents in their own promulgation, not merely passive recipients of human attention but active manipulators of *Homo sapiens*. Actually, it's a perspective long known to evolutionary biologists in general, and devotees of memes in particular (also, as we'll see, parasitologists). Just as genes orchestrate the behavior of the bodies they create and within which they reside, memes are, in a sense, replicating agents that succeed in proportion as they induce their "bodies" (human societies) to help them—the memes—to proliferate. Tulips, for example, have done well appealing especially to the human penchant for beauty; apples, sweetness; marijuana, intoxication; and potatoes, control.

Turn, next, to "The Parable of the Sower" (Matthew 13), according to which "The Word of God is a seed and the sower of the seed is Christ," and good Christians are called upon to follow in Christ's footsteps. As Pollan pointed out, plants use seeds to spread themselves,[ix] and in the process, they employ us. We spread them, ostensibly for our own benefit, but at least as much to theirs. Who, then, is in charge, and can the same be said of religion? Perhaps human religions are a composite of "viral memes," perpetuated and spread for the sake of the religions themselves, manipulating human beings to their meme-ish benefit (as well as that of their priestly, rabbinic, imam-ish, and other human guardians) and to the disadvantage of those poor dupes—the congregants—who serve as unwitting hosts, carriers, or victims. Sowers of seeds may think they are in control, but the beneficiaries—and, in a sense, the ones calling the shots—are the seeds!

The technical phrase is "host manipulation." For example, the tapeworm *Echinococcus multilocularis* causes its mouse "host" to

---

ix. Of course, they also use pollen, for a delightful vowel-switch coincidence.

become obese and sluggish, making it easy pickings for predators, notably foxes, which—not coincidentally—constitute the next phase in the tapeworm's life cycle. Those the gods intend to bring low, according to the Greeks, they first make proud; those tapeworms intending to migrate from mouse to fox do so by making "their" mouse behave in a way that turns them into fox food. Highly adaptive for the worm, not so much for the mouse.

In another example of host manipulation adduced as a metaphor for the viral meme hypothesis, Daniel Dennett begins his book *Breaking the Spell: Religion as a Natural Phenomenon* by describing a creature much beloved of biologists, the lancet fluke or so-called brain worm, *Dicrocoelium dendriticum*. This creature hijacks the brain of an ant, inducing it to climb a blade of grass and hold on, whereupon the ant (and its accompanying worms) are eaten by sheep, cow, or horse, enabling the surviving worms to continue their life cycle. Dennett then asks whether anything comparable happens to human beings. His answer: "Yes indeed. We often find human beings setting aside their personal interests, their health, their chances to have children, and devoting their entire lives to furthering the interests of an *idea* [his emphasis] that has lodged in their brains."

Of course, for all the importance typically associated with various holy objects, it is the ideas of religion rather than their material trappings that are generally acknowledged to be what really matters, and doctrines and belief systems are not physical entities like a worm. But as with all memes, the key characteristic for our purposes—and theirs—isn't the structure of religious memes, but what they do. And what they do is promote themselves.

Christians make much about spreading the Gospel, disseminating seeds bearing the "good news" about Christ. Indeed, in many religions the Word itself trumps the lives of its practitioners. Among other things, it is this self-abnegation, often to the point of renunciation of various worldly pleasures, even celibacy and martyrdom, that demands the attention of evolutionary biologists. Bear in mind, for example, that Islam means "submission," and Muslims are proud of subordinating themselves to the dictates of Allah. But why? Has Allah deceived them, for His own benefit and their disadvantage, in the manner of a mouse-inhabiting tapeworm? Perhaps. Or is He using them for their own good?

Could be. Or is it the various ideas of Allah and His dictation to the prophet Muhammad that is the ultimate beneficiary? Again, maybe so. But if this is the case, why are so many people bamboozled into playing along?

The "viral meme hypothesis" is most convivial for atheists, since it puts religion in so unfavorable a light. At the same time, the validity of a hypothesis should never be judged by whether it supports one's prior convictions. Moreover, memes aren't necessarily pernicious; most of the time, in fact, they are likely to be either neutral hitchhikers or actually beneficial to their hosts (hence, their success). Useful devices, whether mnemonic or mechanical, prosper in proportion as they help their practitioners do so. Applied to religion, the presumption of memic malevolence is an easy misunderstanding to make, since the concept was introduced by Richard Dawkins, who is avowedly antireligious and who has argued that religion memes are comparable to viruses or other parasites, doing harm to their hosts. But, to repeat, it is also possible for memes to be neutral or even beneficial; indeed, the great majority of them probably are.

"Overshoot" Hypotheses

Memes aside, what are some other evolutionary hypotheses for religion, suggesting how it might benefit its practitioners? It is not sufficient simply to say that people worldwide turn to religion to meet certain needs, otherwise unmet: explaining great mysteries such as death or the meaning of life, or because it provides solace, a sense of belonging, meeting our "spiritual needs," and so forth. The problem is that these don't suffice as biology, which requires us to ask: Why do people need explanations for death, or for the meaning of life? Why do people need the solace that religion evidently provides, etc.? Why do people have spiritual needs? And by "why," we mean: What is the evolutionary payoff? We might ask, for example, why do people eat? Answer: because they get hungry. But why do they get hungry? Because hunger is a sensation generated by natural selection, a mechanism to get people to nourish themselves when such nourishment is necessary, which is to say, when it is adaptive to eat. If people have a universal hunger for God, why is that? Maybe God is a worldwide tapeworm, generating hunger for His own sake. Or maybe—warning: snark attack!—God yearns for the kind of worldwide worship that religion generates, so He has instilled a need for religion in human beings because He is fundamentally lacking in self-esteem. If God felt better about Himself, we'd all be atheists.

Getting serious, now, let's first examine possible payoffs to individuals. Once again, it isn't sufficient to conclude that religion provides answers to "deep questions" not otherwise answerable— unless we accept that these answers are more accurate and thus more fitness enhancing than those otherwise available. If that is your perspective, then you have your "scientific" answer and there's nothing more to say.

For the rest of you, let's start with something basic: a definition of religion. Daniel Dennett came up with a good one, not only useful but pleasantly simple: Religions are "social systems whose participants avow belief in a supernatural agent or agents whose approval is to be sought."[14] Each part of this deserves being "unpacked"—religions involve social systems rather than solitary activity, commitment to the supernatural as opposed to nature generally, and the seeking of approval, as opposed to, say, black magic or voodoo, for which the goal is to manipulate the super-natural for personal benefit.

A series of closely related hypotheses present themselves, all starting with traits that are otherwise adaptive, which then over-shoot their mark. Start with the importance of being attuned to the world outside ourselves. As useful as it is to know when it is getting dark, or where to find the nearest water hole, these are things that nonhuman animals can manage. A higher level of cognition—and, presumably, of benefit—involves knowing (or making a good guess) about what others are doing, and why, inter-preting underlying motives and attributing significance to things: A cracking sound might mean a predator stepping on a branch while sneaking up on you, or it might simply be a twig breaking in the wind. Better to assume the more consequential, even if there is a cost if it is, in fact, a false alarm.

Statisticians refer to two different kinds of error. Type I errors are false positives, thinking that something is true or significant when in fact it isn't. Type II errors are false negatives, thinking that something isn't genuine or meaningful when in fact it is. When it comes to interpreting underlying meaning or pattern in something, a type I error is inconvenient and even potentially costly, but not that big a deal—at least, not compared to a type II error. For example, if you hear a noise and figure it's a murderous villain when it's just a tree branch scraping against your window, the resulting type I error may cause you to lose some sleep, or to get out of bed unnecessarily. The alternative, a type II error, occurs if you hear a noise and decide it's merely a tree branch when in fact it's a lethal threat. For our ancestors on the African savannah who interpreted a rustling in the grass to be a snake when it was just a small rodent, such a type I error would have been troublesome but hardly lethal, whereas those who committed the opposite error—thinking it's a mouse when it's really a venomous snake—would have left fewer descendants. Hence, it's a good bet that we're predisposed to err on the side of false positives rather than false negatives.

A similar logical argument was made by the brilliant mathematician and devout Catholic Blaise Pascal, who maintained that God might (1) exist or (2) not, and that we might (a) believe or (b) not. Since the conjunction of situations 1 and b is liable to be very severe—that is, eternal damnation—best to play it safe, and bet on 1 and a. ("Pascal's wager" has never been very persuasive to me, since if nothing else, God would seem unlikely to be impressed by someone who based her "faith" on such reasoning; it is conceivable, however, that natural selection would have favored just this kind of risk-minimizing wager.)

Early human beings may thus have been especially prone to expand such an adaptive tendency to protect oneself, if need be by anticipating the worst and, in the process, being prone to over-interpret the world. Add to this, as well, the payoff of delving deeply into a version of Lenin's famous question: "Who, whom?": Who is doing what to whom? Who is planning what with—or against—whom? The result is a powerful inclination to see "agency" in the world, not only when it is really there but even when it isn't, especially when potentially directed at ourselves and thus important to us. "We find human faces in the moon, armies in the clouds," wrote David Hume in *The Natural History of Religion*, "and by a natural propensity, if not corrected by experience and reflection, ascribe malice and good will to every thing that hurts or pleases us"—sometimes not just to those things that hurt or please us, but to everything, period.

Renowned anthropologist Bronislaw Malinowsky argued similarly, suggesting that religion evolved as a consequence of humanity's restless intellect: "Like magic it [religion] comes from the curse of forethought and imagination, which fall on man once he rises above brute animal nature."[15]

The idea, in brief, is that human beings are especially prone to detect or imagine that these worldly agents are directed toward ourselves because sometimes they are, and when this is the case, better safe than sorry. The result is a human penchant for wielding an array of hyperactive agent detection devices (HADDs),[16] which aren't devices for the detection of hyperactive agents, but rather, detection devices that are themselves hyperactive, readily perceiving "agency" in the universe. Once again, the hypothesis is uncongenial to believers since it suggests that although agency detection devices were adaptive (and probably still are), when it comes to religion, we've been HADD.

Theory of Mind

As for attributing "agency" to entities outside ourselves, probably the trickiest—and, paradoxically, the most important as well—are those entities known as *others*. As we already briefly considered earlier, psychologists have been especially interested in what is known as Theory of Mind (ToM). This is the highly adaptive human capacity to "read someone else's mind," not implying extrasensory perception, but rather, the far more down-to-earth process of making assumptions that other beings have their own agendas, their own subjective sources of information as well as their own motivation, independent of our own. Put this all together and the result is a world that is populated not only by other things and creatures but also by things and creatures that are bursting with portents and meaning, all oriented toward ourselves.

Here is Dennett on how it works once people started populating the world with objects that move and whose actions could have consequences for themselves: "We experience the world as not just full of moving human bodies but of rememberers and forgetters, thinkers and hopers and villains and dupes and promise-breakers and threateners and allies and enemies." Not only that, but even inanimate objects can take on the aura or intentionality, or at least, of consequentiality for those weak-bodied (albeit strongly imagining) creatures who are so vulnerable to attack, and who therefore must rely on their ability to imagine events in order to flourish. Think of the clutching, grasping arms of a forest at night, or the building threat of accumulating storm clouds, or—on the positive side—the cheerful promise of a sunny day or the friendly, hopeful caress of a spring rain on parched fields. And then, consider that once the world is so populated with fitness-relevant agents, how tempting it must have been (and still be) to attempt to pacify, or otherwise influence them—that is, to seek their approval.

To this, add animism, the likely universal tendency to attribute motives even to things that are "animated" by altogether nonliving energies and impulses . . . and which, a few minutes ago, I just indulged when I muttered something about my computer not *wanting* to boot up. At other times, it spends time *thinking*, while *trying* to download a lengthy file, just as your car may *struggle* in low gear. After all, we all know—sort of—that plants *seek* the light, that rivers *try* to *reach* the sea, and, that when the sky is partly cloudy, the sun often *attempts* to break through.

Along the way, it is plausible that our ancient ancestors' Theory of Mind contributed not only to the personification of nature but also—quite naturally—to a belief in souls, spirits, and ghosts, which in one form or another is closely allied to most religious traditions. Once you attribute mind, an independent consciousness, to others, you have opened the door to the existence of something whose objective reality you accept but cannot see, touch, hear, or smell. In other words, you may well have taken a consequential step toward accepting something close to the Roman Catholic catechism, which describes the soul as "a living being without a body, having reason and free will."

In addition, as anthropologist Pascal Boyer has emphasized,[17] early human beings faced a particularly daunting problem when it came to death of a loved one, even beyond the practical issues of missing that person, losing his or her company, assistance, advice, and so forth: What to do with the corpse? The exigencies of microbiology make it impossible to keep a dead body around indefinitely, but once all that ToM has been generated—and not merely toward clouds and trees—how were our ancestors to turn off their assumptions and expectations about the dearly departed? After the body is buried, burned, or otherwise disposed of, what to do with the likely persistence of memory on the part of those left behind? One convenient ploy would be to argue that some part of the deceased person—moreover, a part that corresponds to the memory retained by the living—still persists, thus, perhaps, belief in the ongoing vitality of "souls" or "spirits" of the recently dead.

It probably didn't hurt that such belief also helped soothe anxiety among the living that some day, they too would join the dead. The prospect of literally being worshiped once dead might have been additionally reassuring, although at least some people, anticipating this outcome, have been rather cynical about it: *Vae puto deus fio* ("Dammit, I seem to be becoming a god"), the Roman emperor Vespasian is said to have complained on his deathbed. More important, however, than enabling the elderly to anticipate becoming a god, or at least, a venerated ancestor in the hereafter, might well have been the prospect of payoff in the here and now. If someone is getting close to becoming a powerful ghost or presiding spirit, it would seem wise to treat this person with deference and to cater to his or her needs and desires. And this, in turn, could motivate such people to urge the reality of ghosts and spirits.

It's only a small step from mollifying one's ancestors (living or dead) to propitiating or otherwise manipulating other underlying agents, not only ghosts and spirits but also other forces—human shaped or inchoate—that more closely approximate most people's conception of God. Of course, rivers and mountains, the sun and stars, not to mention rain and winter and summer don't have an obviously godlike appearance, so it is not altogether unreasonable to assume that they are manipulated by gods that, like the Wizard of Oz, pull the strings offstage. And of course, human faces are especially important to human beings, starting, we now know, in early infancy and continuing into adulthood as "pareidolia," the perception of patterns where none exists. The result is a wide-spread human tendency to see human faces and features in the most nonhuman of things: the Virgin Mary in a spilled ice cream cone, "Pope-Tarts," the face of Jesus in a tortilla—and we're on our collective way, not only to "primitive" religion, but to increasingly elaborate theology, with all the fixings.[18]

"If by 'God,'" wrote Carl Sagan, "one means the set of physical laws that govern the universe, then clearly there is such a God. But this God is emotionally unsatisfying . . . it does not make much sense to pray to the law of gravity."[19] Perhaps people pray, instead, to a god they see in a cloud.

Or elsewhere, maybe in the stars. It seems likely that our ancestors have been powerfully rewarded for recognizing patterns in the natural world: changes in the seasons, the flow of rivers, the migrations of animals. And indeed, it isn't surprising that we have a strong species-wide predisposition for "pattern recognition," for extracting genuine meaning from the world around us. Sometimes, those patterns may even be purely arbitrary and nonsignificant, such as those stars as seen from earth, the ones that are grouped— purely via human imagination—into constellations. It is most unlikely that there is a genuine Hercules up there, or Orion, or Leo, but there is undoubtedly a strong temptation to see "something" nonetheless—a temptation that is all the more italicized by the fact that for most of us, it takes real effort even to identify these presumed patterns!

But at least no harm is done in the process. In fact, some benefit can ensue, as for those African Americans prior to the end of the Civil War who made their way north, escaping slavery, by following the "handle" of the Big Dipper, which ended in the Pole Star, pointing north.

There is no question that the natural world has rewarded people who perceive it accurately, and it seems reasonable that in the process, the door has been opened to misperceptions, as well. But assuming that things don't flow in the other direction—that sacrificial offerings, prayers, ritual observances, and obeisances of various sorts don't really influence the physical world—why should people continue to put, literally, their faith in them? Wouldn't it be more adaptive to drop those belief systems that experience shows to be inaccurate or ineffective? It depends on the cost of persevering versus that of backing away. Moreover, the human tendency to stick with beliefs, even those manifestly unsupported by experience, is itself supported by a deep-seated inclination, namely, an almost desperate search, not only for patterns, but also for causal connections.

Cause and Effect

Not that religion necessarily induced believers to substitute erroneous, immaterial explanations for accurate, naturalistic ones. The great British anthropologist E. E. Evans-Pritchard, who spent decades studying the Zande of Africa, reported that these people weren't ignorant of day-to-day cause and effect. By the same token, most people in the modern world—even those who self-identify as devout—have no difficulty accepting the basic laws of physics as governing their daily lives.[x] Where the Azande used their religion, which graded imperceptibly into magic and witchcraft, was to explain the otherwise inexplicable specificity of events. For example, they knew full well that termites can cause a wooden house to collapse, but the Azande turned to witchcraft to explain why *this particular* house, with *these particular* people in it, happened to collapse at *that particular* time.[20]

Inhabitants of the modern Western world are similarly inclined to look for "deeper" explanations for specific events, looking for solace in particular in the aftermath of painful experiences. Why do bad things happen to good people? Why was my innocent daughter killed in a traffic accident? Why did the tornado come down where and when it did? It isn't simply a matter of narcissism and egocentrism—the notion that the cosmos is orchestrated with each of us specifically in mind (although it may well include that, too)—but also a genuine seeking for meaning in a world that for the most part proceeds without regard to our hopes, fears, or even our very existence.

In a now-classic research report, psychologist B. F. Skinner described "superstitious" behavior in laboratory pigeons.[21] These animals were being trained to respond to certain signals, such as a

---

x. Admittedly, this would seem to be contradicted by frequent recourse to prayer, which Ambrose Bierce, in his aptly named *Devil's Dictionary*, defined as requesting "that the laws of the universe be annulled on behalf of a single petitioner confessedly unworthy."

flashing light, by pecking a target whereupon they received a food pellet. Occasionally, Skinner's experimental subjects would develop a persistent tendency to do something seemingly irrelevant—at least from the viewpoint of the experimenter—such as fluttering a wing or twisting its head to the left. The birds had performed these actions on their own and then, simply by chance, were provided with food shortly thereafter, so they developed a fixed delusion, or what in human beings might be called a superstition, that the correlated experiences were causative. Such a presumption can certainly be adaptive; things correlated in nature are not uncommonly connected by cause and effect, so it can be a good strategy to assume some sort of "genuine" relationship. And people do it, too—think about the superstitions that sports fans, and even players, frequently develop: wearing a particular red cap while watching a game, doing a special kind of dance to induce rain, etc. One would think that over time, it is difficult to maintain the fiction that dances (or prayers) induce rain, but just consider the persistence of water witching in the supposedly advanced Western world (not to mention prayers). Add to this the ubiquity of efforts to apply various quack cures to human diseases, and the resulting mix is revealed to be especially potent, even for those inclined to draw a line between superstition and religion.

How many correlations are needed before two events are liable to be considered meaningfully connected? We don't know. But again, if the cost of believing in a connection—even if spurious—is low compared to that of being oblivious to those correlations that are genuinely causative and thus subject to being manipulated to human benefit or ignored only at substantial peril, then the required number may well be quite small. Add to this, moreover, the potency of placebo. That is, to a significant extent, prayers directed toward human health actually do work, compared with rain dances directed toward the inhuman skies. The immediate explanation is "placebo," the puzzling tendency of people to experience positive health benefits from procedures and substances in proportion as they believe that they will be beneficial.[xi]

---

xi. The story has it that Nils Bohr kept a horseshoe above his office desk in Copenhagen. When a visitor asked the great Nobel Prize–winning physicist whether he believed in such foolishness, Bohr responded that he absolutely did not—but he

Placebo works. On average, it has an efficacy rate of about 33%, with added benefits of very low cost, no side effects, and no risk of overdose. The word derives from the Latin "I please" and the reality has evidently been recognized long before the advent of modern medicine. Thus, in *The Charmides*, one of Plato's early Socratic dialogues, we read about a cure that consists of "a certain leaf, but in addition to the drug there is a certain charm, which if someone chants when he makes use of it, the medicine altogether restores him to health, but without the charm there is no profit from the leaf." But what's in the "charm," which is to say, why does placebo work? No one knows, but one possibility is that it serves as a signal of social caring and support, inducing the body to attempt healing itself.

But if the body has this capacity, why wouldn't individuals be selected to make such a healing effort even without placebos? (And this leads to yet another possibility, of a different sort: that the placebo effect is so mysterious in its own right that it deserves its own chapter in this book!) For now, however, the point is that the combination of HADD plus animism plus superstitious coincidence marking plus ToM plus placebo—in the case of early "medicine"—might have helped lay the foundations for religion.

Distinguishing "Adaptive" From "Good"

This brings us back to an underlying pattern, a kind of evolutionary misfiring in which one or more tendencies are adaptive and have therefore been positively selected for . . . but the system then goes awry and overshoots its original target, producing outcomes that if not actually maladaptive can be at least nonadaptive. Before we proceed, let's clear up a likely misconception. There may be a temptation for opponents of religion to embrace the prospect that religion is nonadaptive, thinking this means it is somehow "not good," and conversely for the devout, who might be disposed to resist this possibility, worrying that if religion is found to be nonadaptive, or worse yet, maladaptive, this would count as a strike against it.

---

had been assured that a horseshoe was likely to bring luck whether or not someone believed in it!

But there is no reason to think that if religion is nonadaptive, it lacks legitimacy or goodness, any more than if it turns out to be adaptive, it is therefore appropriate and laudable. There are numerous traits that were adaptive in our long evolutionary adolescence that are bad, ethically, for example, nepotism, violence, maybe even rape. And there are others that aren't adaptive but are by most assessments good: care for the sick, injured, elderly—especially if the recipients are unrelated to the aid giver, and even more so, if they are from a different group, and if the aid is provided anonymously. In short: The adaptiveness of nonadaptiveness of religion may help us understand how religion evolved, but it says nothing whatever about whether religion is good or about the existence or nonexistence of a deity.

Here are some additional hypotheses for the appearance and persistence of religion involving a process comparable to the phenomenon of overreach suggested by HADD. Take intelligence. There must have been a substantial fitness payoff to those of our ancestors who were especially clever: Smart proto-people were likely better at choosing friends, outwitting enemies, getting food, making tools, attracting mates, communicating effectively, caring for their offspring, and so forth. And although it is conceivable that there are separate modal "intelligences" for each of these dimensions—plus numerous others—it seems far more likely that at least to some extent, selection favored generalized IQ (with specificity as well). And part of being globally smart is to have an inquiring mind, inclined to ask questions and to interrogate the world with a searching need for explanations.

Darwin speculated that "primitive religion" evolved as a consequence. He wrote:

> The belief in unseen or spiritual agencies seems to be almost universal . . . nor is it difficult to comprehend how it arose. As soon as the important faculties of the imagination, wonder and curiosity, together with some power of reasoning, had become partially developed, man would naturally have craved to understand what was passing around him, and have vaguely speculated on his own existence.

There is a problem here, however. Why should our ancestors have "naturally" speculated on their own existence? More to the point, it is one thing to follow insights that are empirically valid and thus likely to be fitness enhancing, quite another to pursue purported insights that are incorrect (e.g., dances prevent or produce rain) or, at best, ambiguous. One explanation, consistent with evolutionary science, would be the overshoot hypothesis: Having generated a "naturally" inquiring mind, evolution has had to deal with an equally natural tendency to demand answers to its inquiries and, when verifiable answers haven't been available, to insist upon others to fill the intellectual void. If so, it shouldn't be surprising that religions typically provide responses to otherwise unanswerable questions, such as what happens to us after death, what is the purpose of life, or why do bad things happen to good people.

Here's an analogy. Engaging in sexual behavior is clearly adaptive. Moreover, since sperm are cheap and easily replaced, men in particular have been selected to be readily aroused by sexually relevant stimuli, which, during 99.99% of our evolutionary past, have been emitted exclusively by genuine, real-live women. But given their biological priming, men are also prone to being aroused by pornography, even though pixel images aren't "real" and cannot contribute to reproductive success. Maybe our species-wide yearning for answers (adaptive in itself, not unlike the especially male yearning for quick-and-easy sexual stimulation) renders human beings—women no less than men—similarly vulnerable to empty but superficially satisfying answer-giving stimuli in the form of religion.

The following is all the more startling and powerful, coming as it does from the "Meditations of Rene Descartes," one of the great philosophical and mathematical geniuses of all time, the founder of a branch of geometry and much else:

> But above all we must impress on our memory the overriding rule that whatever God has revealed to us must be accepted as more certain than anything else. And though the light of reason may, with the utmost clarity and evidence, appear to suggest something different, we must still put our entire faith in divine authority, rather than in our own judgment.

Theologians are understandably uncomfortable with the formulation known as "God of the gaps," by which God is invoked to explain gaps in scientific understanding, the problem for the devout being that as science advances, God becomes correspondingly smaller. Descartes' message can put "God of the gaps" in a different perspective, suggesting a need for many people—even some of the most brilliant and rational—to subordinate themselves to a higher authority. Maybe this relieves an otherwise intolerable pressure, one uniquely felt by a species endowed with the ability to explain many things, to explain *everything*.

Isaac Newton's theory of gravity—one of humanity's greatest scientific advances—was resisted by many at the time because, ironically, it seemed to smack of mysticism, operating as it does via "force at a distance." Newton agreed that the concept seemed absurd but added that he had been unable to figure out how it happened, and "I do not feign hypotheses."[xii] Yet that is much of what religion is. On second thought, it is less the *feigning* of hypotheses than the bypassing of them altogether: leaving the matter to God, and in the process, satisfying a widespread need for answers (of a sort).

A Consequence of Our Big Brains?

The distinction between science and religion is generally clear: The former ultimately relies upon logic and empirical falsification or validation, whereas the latter rests upon faith and authority. Nonetheless, much science is itself counterintuitive. We know with scientific certainty that the earth goes around the sun and not vice versa, that even a demonstrably "solid" object is mostly empty space, that species are mutable, and that in the miniature world of quantum events or the vast one of light-speed, "weird" things happen with space, time, mass, and energy. What is a large-brained creature, with a need to understand, to do with such facts? As anthropologist Clifford Geertz pointed out, people simply cannot look at the world "in dumb astonishment or blind apathy," so they struggle for explanations—objectively valid or not—resulting inevitably in beliefs.

---

xii. Interestingly, Newton was a devout if idiosyncratic Christian, writing far more about the Books of Daniel and Revelations than about all his work in mathematics and physics combined.

There remains another series of possibilities, all variants on the "adaptive overshoot" hypothesis, involving nonadaptive consequences of being so darned intelligent. For example, throughout the animal world, smarter species are those that rely more on learning and less on instinct, since instincts involve built-in, hardwired behavior patterns whereas intelligence involves the capacity to modify one's actions as a result of learning; indeed, the ability to learn is as good a definition of intelligence as we have. As a species heavily "into" learning, *Homo sapiens* is also predisposed to do much of that learning while young. We're born with big brains that, compared to most other animals, have relatively little that is built into them. And so, children are veritable learning machines, neural vacuum cleaners prewired to suck up what they can absorb of what they are taught, especially language and how the world works, particularly the complex rules of the social road. What about religion?

It is overwhelmingly true that people grow up following the religion into which they were born, which is to say, doing as they have been taught. Whatever the original adaptive value of religion, it may have persisted in large part because it is an accidental by-product of a program that is adaptive in most other respects: When young, believe what your elders tell you.[xiii] And when you grow up, do as they have done.

Parents may ruefully complain about the waywardness of their offspring, but the reality is that children are strongly predisposed to accept parental teaching, since such input is likely to be fitness enhancing ("This is good to eat," "Don't pet the saber-tooth," and so forth). This, in turn, makes children vulnerable to whatever else they are taught ("Respect the Sabbath," "Cover your hair") as well as—if we are to believe Freud, in *The Future of an Illusion*—downright needy when it comes to parentlike beings, leading especially to the patriarchal sky-god of the Abrahamic faiths.

Anthropologist Weston La Barre developed a similar argument in his book *Shadow of Childhood*, in which he proposed that prayer

---

xiii. Biologists distinguish between the evolutionary origin of a trait and the factors leading to its maintenance once it has evolved (and regardless of how it was initially derived). The "Early Learning Hypothesis" discussed here is an argument for religion's maintenance, not its origin.

is unique to our species, resulting from our prolonged, neotonous, developmental trajectory:

> No other animal when in distress or danger magically commands or prayerfully begs the environment to change its nature for the organism's specific benefit. Calling upon the 'supernatural' to change the natural is an exclusively human reaction. . . . [O]ne doubts that even herding animals like the many antelope species in Africa have gods they call upon when they fall behind the fleeing herd and are about to be killed by lions, wild dogs, cheetahs or hyenas. Antelope infancy and parenthood do not present such formative extravagancies. And in the circumstances the belief itself would be highly maladaptive.

In his *Autobiography*, Darwin straddled the fence between thinking religion was learned—acquired via experience—and inherited: "Nor must we overlook the probability," he wrote,

> of the constant inculcation in a belief in God on the minds of children producing so strong and perhaps an inherited effect on their brains not yet fully developed, that it would be as difficult for them to throw off their belief in God as for a monkey to throw off its instinctive fear and hatred of a snake.

It isn't clear to a modern biologist how the inculcation of religion could produce "an inherited effect," but let that pass. (In much of Darwin's writing—which, after all, preceded any knowledge of genetics—there are assumptions of Lamarckism, the "inheritance of acquired characteristics," since shown to be fallacious.) The key point for our purposes is Darwin's conviction that religion is something to which human beings are strongly predisposed, and that part of that predisposition is a susceptibility to learning that begins in childhood, and which is itself adaptive— even though its expression with regard to religion might be non-adaptive or even maladaptive. Given the huge payoff that comes with learning, and the fact that nearly all the time, parents have much genuine survival value to pass along to their children, it is likely that the latter would be quite open—one might even say susceptible and vulnerable—to parental teachings with respect to religion, too. In fact, it is difficult to imagine a simple genetic algorithm that would screen out religious indoctrination but permit other parental teaching to be absorbed.

Deference to experts provides a similar situation. Most people aren't jacks-of-all-trades. At least, they are better at some things than at others. We trust the auto mechanic to be good at fixing cars, the dentist to be good at fixing teeth, and so on. Even in the early history of *Homo sapiens*, some of our ancestors must have been better at hunting, others at making tools, and yet others at being in touch with occult powers (or at least, who claimed to be). Just as a susceptibility to parental teaching may have greased the skids for susceptibility to religious indoctrination, a generally adaptive respect of expertise may have been extended to those who claimed spiritual expertise as well.

Here is yet another adaptive overshoot hypothesis: Maybe religion serves a Grand Inquisitor function. A famous chapter in Dostoyevsky's novel *The Brothers Karamazov* takes us back to the Spanish Inquisition, during which the Grand Inquisitor explains that "Nothing is more seductive for man than his freedom of conscience, but nothing is a greater cause of suffering." He goes on to explain that organized religion—in the form of the Roman Catholic Church—has lifted that burden by mentally enslaving their subjects and telling them what to believe and what to abjure.[xiv] For our purposes, the hypothesis would be that as a result of our species-wide intelligence, we find ourselves stuck with a species-wide problem: a tendency to think too much, to get so wrapped up in the endless array of possible actions that we are essentially paralyzed, unable to function effectively and altogether miserable.

Enter, then, religious authority, ritual and holy writ, which—like Dostoyevsky's Grand Inquisitor—tell the believer what to do, how to do it, and when, thereby relieving him or her of the terrible burden of too damned much freedom and excessive thought. We might call this the antidithering hypothesis.

There is, in fact, a growing body of research in social psychology that speaks to the problem of "choice overload," which shows that too many choices is a troublesome thing.[22] In a now-famous experiment, psychologist Sheena Iyengar (currently a professor of business at Columbia University) set up a tasting booth outside a busy supermarket in California. On offer: either 6 flavors of jam or

---

xiv. Dostoyevsky was a devout Russian Orthodox believer, for whom the villain wasn't religion, and certainly not Christianity, but Roman Catholicism.

24 flavors, with the options alternating every few hours. The results? More people stopped at the table when 24 flavors were displayed . . . but fewer people bought any. The difference turned out to be quite dramatic: Whereas only 3% of those at the 24-flavor booth purchased any product, at the 6-flavor booth, the number shot up to 30%.

Consequentially, perhaps, for our purposes, Sheena Iyengar has also shown that fundamentalists are generally more optimistic than those associated with more liberal religious traditions. "Members of more fundamentalist faiths experienced greater hope, were more optimistic when faced with adversity and were less likely to be depressed than their counterparts,"[23] she writes. "Indeed, the people most susceptible to pessimism and depression were the Unitarians, especially those who were atheists." As with her jam-tasting study, Dr. Iyengar interprets this difference as due to differences in the amount of choice available: fundamentalist faiths (which, in her sample, included Jews, Muslims, and Hindus as well as Protestants and Catholics) allow less latitude among their members. Thus, they are closer to the Grand Inquisitor's ideal.

Additional By-Products

Yet another variant on the adaptive overshoot model is another variant on HADD, discussed earlier, focusing on the human tendency to see—and sometimes imagine—the world as populated by other beings, in this case not so much an inclination to perceive agency as to engage in a kind of basic taxonomy. Thus, people don't need to be biologists to have recognized that there are many different kinds of living things, of which human beings are just one. Considering that many religions find themselves at odds with evolutionary biology, it is ironic that there is a connection between the universal identification of many kinds of living things and the fact that we are one among many—but not at the top of the heap. Most people likely know, deep in their hearts, that they aren't omniscient or omnipotent. So, given that that there are many different kinds of creatures, and that people are deeply aware of this diversity, isn't it possible that some people, at least, "naturally" imagine that there must be yet another kind, one that in fact possesses those divine qualities that we know that we lack?

Some readers may balk at the notion that to be religious means to perceive God as a "creature," pointing out that sophisticated theologies generally perceive the divine as beyond material substance or specific form, and not even acting in traditional space or time—something like Paul Tillich's concept of the divine as the Ground of all Being, or Spinoza's account of God as immanent in all of nature. The reality, however, is that most people who practice religions, all over the world, do in fact personify God as some sort of creature or organism, typically an anthropomorphic one who (not that) "hears" prayers; "sees" whether we do the right thing or not; can be angered or pacified, implored or cajoled; and in any case "acts" in real time. That is, for the overwhelming majority of people, the great bulk of the time, God is another species! Typically, God is thought to be smarter than us, bigger than us, stronger than us, but not a purely abstract phenomenon, a divine essence independent of time and space; in fact, God typically resembles our own organicity—hence, perhaps, the powerful tendency to multiply the gods, an inclination against which the major monotheistic religions constantly struggle.

But why should human beings need to posit the existence of yet another creature in their universe? (Aren't there already enough?) Try this: We start life, at least according to many developmental psychologists and psychoanalysts, with the illusion of omnipotence, or if nothing else, the sense that the world revolves around us and our needs. With increasing maturity, however, comes the growing realization that we are not the center of the universe and, moreover, that we are neither omnipotent nor omniscient. It is an important lesson, and one that every healthy adult learns. But our early experience, especially with parents, induced us to think that someone must be in charge; since we learn that this does not include either our parents or ourselves, this leaves a rather large hole in our image of the world and how it works. Enter God.

In the European tradition, there is a long history of recognizing the *Scala Naturae*, or natural ladder of existence, including various worms and bugs, snakes and birds, and mammals and then people, and then—why not?—God. If so, then God evolved out of an initially adaptive tendency to classify and clarify the diversity of life forms, combined with a developmental awareness of our own limitations as well as the shortcomings of our parents. (Relevant here, as well, is Freud's celebrated account, in *The Future of an Illusion*, of religion as an "infantile neurosis," in which people imagine God as a substitute for the parent who falls short.)

Closely allied to these adaptive overshoot hypotheses is another: religion itself as a by-product. It isn't strictly necessary that all biological traits have been directly selected for. Sometimes, they arise as a side effect of something else that has been favored by natural selection, such that we are mistaken in considering the trait in question to be an adaptation at all. Consider, for example, the redness of blood. It is possible that blood has evolved its particular color because natural selection favored individuals who, when hemorrhaging, are camouflaged against the blood-red sky of a setting sun. But probably not. More likely: It just happens that oxyhemoglobin is bright red, not because the color per se is adaptive, but simply as a nonadaptive consequence of the biochemistry of efficient oxygen transport.

In the case of religion, another variant on the by-product connection seems more plausible. Sometimes, a highly adaptive trait is so closely allied to the development of a particular by-product that the two cannot effectively be separated. The benefit conveyed by the adaptive characteristic may simply outweigh the slight drawback of the other, so that evolution has "created" both, even though it only actually favored one. Nipples, for example, convey no discernible fitness payoff when borne by a man, but are clearly functional as baby-feeding nozzles when at the tip of a woman's breast. The embryonic process that creates nipples in girls is too intimately tied to its highly adaptive anatomical outcome to have been segregated by evolution into dramatically different male and female versions, even though the result is nonfunctional one-half the time. And so, men have nipples as a nonadaptive consequence of its payoff among women. Maybe the "deep-question answering" component of religion is like a male nipple, a nonadaptive tag-along consequence of something else—intelligence and curiosity—that has been favored by natural selection.

Natural selection has also endowed us with a need for social connection. Babies can't survive unless connected to one or more adult caregivers, adults require other adults, and so forth.

For anthropologist Barbara King, human beings "evolved god" because of their need for "belongingness." She writes that

> Hominids turned to the sacred realm because they evolved to relate in deeply emotional ways with their social partners, because the resulting mutuality engendered its own creativity and generated increasingly nuanced expressions of belongingness over time, and because the human brain evolved to allow an extension of this belongingness beyond the here and now.[24]

Developmental psychologists and evolutionary biologists would doubtless agree about the merits and allure of belonging, insofar as this leads to caring and being cared for, but what is the adaptive significance of cozying up to the ineffable? If, as King suggests, the bedrock payoff of religion comes from "the belief that one may be seen, heard, protected, harmed, loved, frightened, or soothed by interaction with God, gods, or spirits," then what in the real world has anchored human biology to this bedrock? A feeling of belongingness sounds lovely, as does the contentment that comes from having a full belly, but to be adaptive, one ought to have a genuinely full belly. No matter how exalted, feelings divorced from reality can be misleading delusions . . . unless the satisfying belongingness conveyed by religion is a by-product, hitchhiking on the highly adaptive feelings evoked by being part of a sustaining social network. In this case, the proximate gratifications provided by caregivers, lovers, family members, and friends can also power a connection to coreligionists as well and—by extension—perhaps connection to a perceived God, too.

Proximate Payoffs

Similar reasoning leads to another set of hypotheses involving adaptive overshoot and/or by-products, involving other immediate (proximate) effects of religious observance. Let's note, first, that although scholars tend to focus on the intellectual or doctrinal aspects of religion, most people who actually practice a faith seem to be more aware of their subjective experience, how they feel when praying, singing, making what they see as personal contact with the divine. Darwin himself had trained for the Anglican ministry and, as a young novitiate biologist aboard the *H. M. S. Beagle* briefly anchored off Australia, he had witnessed the ecstatic side of religion as practiced by a group of aboriginals and was shocked, shocked by the "nearly naked figures, viewed by the light of blazing fires, all moving in hideous harmony . . .."

It isn't surprising that a typical representative of buttoned-down Victorian religious practice should have found such rites disturbing. But almost certainly, rituals of the sort witnessed by Mr. Darwin are far closer to the many traditional, animistic, pantheistic, and diversely experiential kinds of religious practice that characterize "primitive" religions, and that, in one form or another, still engage practitioners today. Singing, dancing, and swaying; engaging in prayers whether ritualistic or extemporized; taking in the sights, sounds, and smells of religious observance, often in special places with unusual colors, patterns, or architecture; and repeating phrases whose exact meaning may be completely unknown but that are nonetheless deeply satisfying, nearly always in concert with others: These are typically the flesh-and-blood stuff of religion, far more than the fine points of theological doctrine. What may look like "hideous harmony" to an intellectualized, emotionally buttoned-down 19th-century European observer can be downright ecstatic for a participant.

Reacting to what he saw as the excesses of the Enlightenment, William Blake wrote his great poem, "Mock on, mock on, Voltaire, Rousseau," which continues with the lines: "Mock on, mock on: 'tis all in vain!/You throw the sand against the wind,/And the wind blows it back again," and ends: "The Atoms of Democritus/And Newton's Particles of Light/Are sands upon the Red Sea shore,/Where Israel's tents do shine so bright."

For Blake, and likely for the great majority of religious practitioners, the rationality of science and the arcane details of theological doctrine are merely sand compared to the bright, shining allure of Israel's tents. The emotional heat of Jerusalem is more seductive than the cold rationality of Athens.

Although religions often entail demanding, painful, and even sometimes life-threatening initiation rituals (more on this later), for the most part, believers report that their religious practice makes them feel good: cleansed, purified, relaxed, at peace, made whole, renewed, refreshed, connected, and so forth. Maybe the adaptive value of religion lies here, in the ecstasy or simply the "inner peace" so often promised—and frequently provided. Bear in mind, however, that it doesn't work simply to say that religion exists and persists because it provides spiritual fulfillment, ecstatic joy, inner peace, etc.—because this posits a need (for spiritual fulfillment, and so forth) that in itself has no evident evolutionary payoff. It is like saying that religion exists because people have a need for it, which doesn't help us at all.

On the other hand, the panoply of personally satisfying religious payoffs begins to make sense in the light of adaptive overshoot and by-products. As noted by psychiatrist Michael McGuire and anthropologist Lionel Tiger, religious ritual can result in heightened levels of certain pleasurable brain chemicals, such as oxytocin and vasopressin, which in turn generates a kind of physiological "brain soothing." This is consistent with the views of path-breaking American philosopher and psychologist William James, who argued that the key to religion lies in its personal impact: In his masterpiece, *The Varieties of Religious Experience*, James defined religion as "the feelings, acts, and experiences of individual men in their solitude, so far as they apprehend themselves to stand in relation to whatever they may consider the divine." What really matters, for James, is religious "experience" and how good it feels.

Freud may accordingly have missed the boat when he averred that religion "comprises a system of wishful illusions together with a disavowal of reality, such as we find nowhere else but . . . in a state of blissful hallucinatory confusion."[25] Or rather, perhaps he didn't take his observation seriously enough: If an experience is sufficiently blissful, whether illusory or not, then rather than disavowing reality, it becomes its own reality, one that is subjectively and powerfully compelling.

As for *why* this happens, why religion so often feels so good, once again there is uncertainty. Thus, it is one thing to identify brain regions that "light up" during communal singing, repetitive chanting, ecstatic devotions, or even quiet, meditative prayer, and ditto for identifying the neurochemicals likely to be released—and, moreover, it isn't surprising that people find themselves inclined to engage in activities that activate those brain regions and release those chemicals, so long as they are perceived, subjectively, as pleasurable. But it is quite another thing to figure out why those brain regions and neurochemicals, along with their pleasurable sensations, are activated as a result of these devotions.

Back once again to the example of hunger: It occurs as a mechanism that induces people to do something (eat) that is ultimately in their evolutionary interest (nourish their bodies). So, two other possibilities present themselves. For one, maybe religion represents not so much an overshoot or by-product as a hijacking of neuroanatomic and neurochemical mechanisms that exist for other, more clearly adaptive reasons, in the same manner that chemical addictions, for example, may arise when certain substances (marijuana, cocaine, and so forth) evoke brain pathways that have evolved for other reasons. Call it the addiction hypothesis.

Or for another, maybe—like hunger—the subjective gratifications of religious practice exist because religions provide a proximate route toward genuinely fitness-enhancing activities. Accordingly, we now turn to some more adaptive possibilities.

Notes

1. Wilson, E. O. (1999). *Consilience*. New York: Knopf.
2. Armstrong, K. (1993). *A history of God*. New York: Knopf.
3. Mencken, H. L. (1949, 1982). *A Mencken chrestomathy: His own selection of his choicest writing*. New York: Vintage
4. Pinker, S. (2009). *How the mind works*. New York: Viking.
5. Russell, B. (1928). *Sceptical essays*. London: Allen & Unwin.
6. Benthall, J. (2010). *Returning to religion: Why a secular age is haunted by faith*. Taurus.
7. Wilson, E. O. (1978). *On human nature*. Cambridge, MA: Harvard University Press.
8. Dennett, D. C. (2003). *Freedom evolves*. New York: Viking.
9. Hamer, D. (2004). *The God gene: How faith is hardwired into our genes*. New York: Doubleday.
10. Waller, N. G., Kojetin, B., Bouchard, T., Lykken, D., & Tellegen, A. (1990). Genetic and environmental influences on religious attitudes and values: A study of twins reared apart and together. *Psychological Science, 1*(2), 138–142.
11. Martin, N. G., Eaves, L. J., Heath, A. C., Jardine, R., Feingold, L. M., & Eysenck, H. J. (1986). Transmission of social attitudes. *Proceedings of the National Academy of Science of the United States of America, 83*, 4364–4368.
12. Letter to the editor. (2009, November 22). *The New York Times*.
13. Huxley, J. (1929). *Essays of a biologist*. New York: Alfred A. Knopf.
14. Dennett, D. (2006). *Breaking the spell*. New York: Penguin.

15. Malinowski, B. (1931). The role of magic and religion. In W. A. Lessa & E. Z. Vogt (Eds.), *Reader in comparative religion*. Evanston, IL: Row Peterson.
16. Barrett, J. (2000). Exploring the natural foundations of religion. *Trends in Cognitive Science, 4,* 29–34.
17. Boyer, P. (2001). *Religion explained: The evolutionary origins of religious thought.* New York: Basic Books.
18. Guithrie, S. (1995). *Faces in the clouds.*
19. Sagan, C. *The varieties of religious experience.*
20. Evans-Pritchard, E. E. (1976). *Witchcraft, oracles and magic among the Zande.* Oxford: Clarendon Press.
21. Skinner, B. F. (1947). "Superstition" in the pigeon. *Journal of Experimental Psychology, 38,* 168–172.
22. Schwartz, B. (2004). *The paradox of choice: Why more is less.* New York: Ecco.
23. Iyengar, S. (2010). *The art of choosing.* New York: Twelve.
24. King, B. *Evolving God.*
25. Freud, S. (1927, 1989). *The future of an illusion.* New York: Norton.

CHAPTER EIGHT

Religion II: Social Bonding and Morality

S CIENCE IS QUITE NEW. Until recent times, it probably didn't pay to spend a lot of time and effort trying to figure out the natural world, since its secrets just weren't very accessible. To be sure, our ancestors were well advised to know where game is likely to be found and how to avoid enemies, make a spear, prepare a meal, court a mate, and so forth, but the overwhelming reality is that the deeper aspects of reality itself were simply not penetrable to early *Homo sapiens*. Insofar as this is true, religion—during its formative eons—may have been adaptive as essentially a labor-saving device, a way of keeping our ancestors from wasting their time, beating their heads against the stone walls of their own ignorance and impotence.

Taking Things "On Faith"

The labor-saving hypothesis resembles the antidithering and grand inquisitor hypotheses discussed earlier, in that all three take as their starting point the downside of an otherwise adaptive human trait: intelligence. They differ, however, in that the labor-saving hypothesis imagines that early religion contributed more positively (adaptively) to human success rather than simply developing as a response to one of our species-wide liabilities—namely, sometimes being too smart for our own good.

The Book of Job provides an especially powerful indictment of human ignorance. Toward the end of the story, God appears as a voice out of a whirlwind and forces Job to confront how little he (and all people, especially 3,000 or so years ago) actually know of the world: "Have you comprehended the expanse of the earth? Declare, if you know all this" (Job 38:16–18). "What is the way to the place where the light is distributed, or where the east wind is scattered upon the earth"? (Job 38:24). "Do you know the ordinances of the heavens? Can you establish their rule on the earth?" (Job 38:33). The voice of God goes on to describe various mysterious aspects of natural history, ranging from "leviathans" and "behemoths" to birds and the number of grains of sand on a beach. Most important, Job raises the ancient problem of theodicy—how to reconcile the existence of pain and suffering in the world with God's presumed goodness and omnipotence. To this, God's answer is simple: Don't ask!

Better to stop all the vain theorizing, the wondering and worrying, the half-assed attempts to figure things out and simply believe and do as you've been told! Stick with the tried and true? Not exactly. In fact, the "answers" from religious authorities—at least when it comes to explaining objective phenomena of the natural world, from the structure of the solar system to the matter of human origins—have more often been *untrue*. But at least they have a long history of having been tried, with no great harm having resulted. The labor-saving hypothesis could as well be called the "stop worrying about things you won't understand and in any event can't do anything about hypothesis."

It isn't all that unrealistic or as far-fetched as might be imagined by the scientifically inclined nor as critical of religion as believers might fear. After all, even devoted pro-science atheists (such as this book's author) take all sorts of things "on faith," without actually having personally tested their validity. I believe in the existence of atoms, in the germ theory of disease, that the moon causes the tides, and that $E = mc^2$, and not because I've investigated any of these things first-hand. Rather, I take the words of those

I trust, plus the chain of logical sequence that involves them. It saves me a lot of time and trouble to adopt an almost religious perspective in these and many other cases.[i] Isn't it reasonable, at least, to think that our ancestors may have found religion similarly useful as a labor- and time-saving device?

Add to this the possibility that religion can provide reassurance, a kind of ideological Prozac (i.e., antidepressant) for those disappointed with the circumstances of their current lives, combined with the doctrinal equivalent of Xanax (an antianxiety medication) for those worried about their eventual death. The English poet Rupert Brooke is best known for writing "If I should die, think only this of me/That there's some corner of a foreign field that is forever England." But for all his sentimentality, Brooke took a gimlet-eyed view of religion's promise of a reassuring afterlife. Here is his cynical take on "Heaven," as imagined by fish:

. . . This life cannot be All, they swear,
For how unpleasant, if it were!
One may not doubt that, somehow, Good
Shall come of Water and of Mud;
And, sure, the reverent eye must see
A Purpose in Liquidity.
We darkly know, by Faith we cry,
The future is not Wholly Dry.
Mud unto mud! -- Death eddies near --
Not here the appointed End, not here!
But somewhere, beyond Space and Time.
Is wetter water, slimier slime!
And there (they trust) there swimmeth One
Who swam ere rivers were begun,
Immense, of fishy form and mind,
Squamous, omnipotent, and kind;
And under that Almighty Fin,
The littlest fish may enter in.
Oh! never fly conceals a hook,
Fish say, in the Eternal Brook,
But more than mundane weeds are there,

---

i. Note the "almost," since there is a crucial difference between scientific "belief" and its religious counterpart: The former is susceptible to empirical testing and confirmation.

And mud, celestially fair;
Fat caterpillars drift around,
And Paradisal grubs are found;
Unfading moths, immortal flies,
And the worm that never dies.
And in that Heaven of all their wish,
There shall be no more land, say fish.

For Marx, religion was the opiate of the masses. For Brooke, it offered reassurance . . . at least for credulous fishes. The Brookeian hypothesis can even be rendered compatible with evolutionary biology, if piscines (or people) who were calmed and reassured by the promise of heavenly bliss in an Eternal Brook might as a result be calmer, more confident, and therefore likely to experience higher fitness *this* side of heaven.

Rational Choice

For another hypothesis involving a positive selective payoff, consider the argument for religion as a rational choice. When social scientists refer to something as resulting from "rational choice," they mean that it owes its existence to the fact that it somehow maximizes the payoff that comes from doing it. Thus, there is a rational choice argument for what people purchase, how much schooling they obtain, where they decide to live, even who they court or marry. Economists are especially fond of such arguments, and their discipline is largely founded on the presumption that human beings are rational "utility maximizers," with utility meaning essentially anything that people find to be in their interest: happiness, health, wealth, and so forth (most often, wealth).

The rational choice hypothesis for religion has been especially championed by sociologists Rodney Stark and Roger Finke.[1] Not surprisingly, this approach is far more approving and supportive of religion than are most of the hypotheses we have encountered thus far. "It now is impossible," write Stark and Finke, "to do credible work in the social scientific study of religion based on the assumption that religiousness is a sign of stupidity, neurosis, poverty, ignorance, or false consciousness, or represents a flight from modernity." It is one thing, after all, to debate whether religious believers are correct in that God (or gods) actually exist, after all, not to mention whether their particular religion is the correct way to worship Him, Her, or Them. It is another to ask whether such worship is, in its own way, rational. People—often perfectly intelligent and rational ones—put their faith in any number of false gods, from Marxism to laissez-faire capitalism, Freud to Derrida. Just think, for example, of how hard-headed, data-minded investors have often bestowed money on stocks that turned out to be worth next to nothing. Rationality can go awry.

But at the same time, seemingly irrational actions can be motivated by an underlying logic that is in fact subject to a precise calculus, in which benefits end up exceeding costs, thus yielding a net positive payoff. Take romance, which, in popular imagination at least, is totally driven by emotion, hormones, more than a touch of insanity resulting from the magical impact of Cupid's arrow, or some equivalent. "Who can explain it, who can tell you why?" we are asked in the song *Some Enchanted Evening*. And the question is immediately "answered" in a way that fits closely the style of God speaking to Job out of the whirlwind: "Fools give you reasons, wise men never try!"

But in fact, when romance is stripped of its, well, romance, and examined with a cool, Darwinian eye, when it is designated "mate selection" and analyzed in terms of how it accords with the evolutionary prescription whereby the decisions of most living things accord with the expectations of fitness maximization, we find that romance (even its human manifestations) is typically a rational choice after all. People tend to choose mates that maximize their fitness. People may tend to choose religion for the same reasons—although in neither case are they likely to be consciously aware of the factors behind their choice.

Thus, depending on circumstances, religious commitment can increase personal wealth—not merely that of the preachers, but of parishioners, too—if being part of a belief network enhances access to a trade and business network, improves one's reputation for reliability, and so forth. More generally, it can increase one's "social capital." If a religiously based society has established the firm expectation of religious practice (regardless of the initial cause for this expectation), it can quickly become a self-generating system, especially if the norm is to exclude or actively attack nonparticipants.

Groucho Marx famously quipped that he wouldn't want to be a member of any group that would accept him. Most people wouldn't want to be excluded from a group that would shun, injure, or kill them if they remained outside. Under such circumstances, necessity could quickly be presented—and perceived—as a virtue.

Add to this certain health-related payoffs (whether or not placebo generated), as well as some or all of the hypotheses already discussed, and religious commitment can emerge as a highly rational choice, despite the fact that it might perch atop a mountain of irrational rubble. Thus, even though we don't currently understand why natural selection might have promoted religion via its placebo payoff, for example, once such a payoff exists, it can make sense for individuals to partake.

Lest I misrepresent the rational actor thesis, however, it should be clear that it does not necessarily endorse a view that religion arose and endures purely because of its practical, this-world payoffs. Stark and Finke, for example, are quite clear about the special appeal of the supernatural in general, and of God in particular. As they see it, a religion without God would be

> like expecting people to continue to buy soccer tickets and gather in the stands to watch players who, for lack of a ball, just stand around. If there are no supernatural beings, then there are no miracles, there is no salvation, prayer is pointless, the Commandments are but ancient wisdom, and death is the end. In which case the rational person would have nothing to do with church. Or, more accurately, a rational person would have nothing to do with a church like that.

Robert Wright's book, somewhat misleadingly titled *The Evolution of God*, similarly emphasizes the practical, self-serving, and thus rational components of religion, although with a different twist.[2] Wright's basic point is that people have the ability to recognize win–win opportunities (trade, mutual tolerance, etc.) and that this recognition, in turn, gives rise to religion, which expands the "moral circle" and enables everyone to benefit as a result. This approach says very little about why religion evolved in the first place, or—more crucially—why religion rather than some other mechanism has been called upon to perform this function. Moreover, there is nothing in Wright's speculation that requires or explains the distinctive feature of religion: its evocation of the supernatural. But it might well shed light on the secular successes of religion, here in the very natural world.

Group Coordination and War

The hypotheses we have examined thus far, whatever their merit, have been limited in one crucial aspect: All have been concerned with the evolution of religion as a phenomenon of individuals, whereas religious practice is overwhelmingly social. Even our proffered definition, from Daniel Dennett, spoke of religion as a "social system," thereby distinguishing it from, say, superstition or "magic," preoccupations that are fundamentally solitary.

At the other explanatory pole from William James and his concern with religion as something subjectively experienced, there is Emil Durkheim, founder of sociology, who wrote his masterpiece, *The Elementary Forms of Religious Life*, at about the same time as James's magnum opus. For Durkheim, "religion is first and foremost a system of ideas by means of which individuals imagine the society of which they are members and the obscure yet intimate relations they have with it." Just as picnic goers note that there is no such thing as a solitary ant, there is no such thing as a religion-of-one; for Durkheim, and most scholars, religion "must be an eminently collective thing," whose crucial dimension is social more than individual. Here is another, better known definition from Durkheim: "A religion is a unified system of beliefs and practices relative to sacred things, that is to say, things set apart and forbidden—beliefs and practices that unite into one single moral community called a Church all those who adhere to them."

It is worth noting that when small nonreligious social groups were compared with those that had been organized around explicitly religious themes, the religious ones were on average four times more likely to remain in existence the following year than were their secular counterparts.[3] Thus, there appears to be something about organizing a group around shared religious belief and practice that makes it more likely to endure. But what?

One possibility is that almost by definition, and in contrast to groups organized around secular themes (politics, age, shared hobby, etc.), religion provides more social glue, generating enhanced cohesion—which includes greater staying power for the group as a whole—simply because of its more densely structured rules and social patterning, which typically include songs, chants, ceremonial events, prohibitions and requirements, and so forth. If so, then this contributes to the prospect that religion may indeed prosper as a kind of viral meme, operating by virtue of its positive impact on groups themselves, rather than within the minds of individual practitioners and believers.

The origin of the word *religion* is uncertain, but seems most likely to involve the Latin word *religare*, meaning "to bind together." Perhaps it is this unifying, binding aspect of religion that explains not only its emotional appeal but also its adaptive function. Groups do better when their actions are coordinated, when individuals subordinate their immediate personal interests to the benefit of the greater community. It seems plausible, therefore, that religion developed and prospered because it bound people together, creating groups that were more coherent and thus more successful than were groups lacking religion, and which, as a result, were more "atomic," individualistic, and selfish.

Prominent among the possible group-oriented benefits of religion would have been enhanced coordination, notably when it came to the high risk, high payoff associated with coordinated violence—which is to say, warfare. After all, human beings are a very social species, whose major threats have derived—ironically—from other social units of the same species. *Homo sapiens* is unusual in living in social groups whose major enemies are other social groups. Usually, animals that live in large social units do so to obtain protection from predators, not from others of their own species, although there are exceptions, such as colonies of social insects (notably ants) and some nonhuman primates including chimpanzees and, on occasion, baboons and gorillas. Insofar as early hominids and even prehominids experienced violent and sometimes lethal competition with other groups, it seems likely that the better organized, more coherent groups were victorious. And when it comes to mechanisms that generate such cohesion, religion ranks high.

Anthropological accounts of primitive warfare among contending tribes are replete with examples of how tribal religions help generate and shore up enthusiasm and mutual commitment. Religious rituals, with communal dancing, singing, chanting, body decorations, and various forms of blessings on the part of shamans, priests, and other consecrated elders are intimately associated with preparing warriors for battle. In many cases, religious faith also serves to discourage defection, with threats of social ostracism in this world and often eternal damnation in the next helping to ensure compliance. The promise of afterlife rewards—of which the supposed 72 dark-eyed virgins awaiting Islamic suicide "warriors" is a notorious but not unusual example—can help motivate otherwise improbable actions that are fitness reducing for the practitioner but potentially beneficial for the warring society of which he or she is a member. Beyond this, assurances of immediate battlefield success, even in the face of seemingly long odds, can—if believed by the believer—translate into an enhanced prospect of success . . . or at least, reduced likelihood of catastrophic defeat, if it makes the believer more likely to fight.

It may have worked wonders for the ancient Israelites. "When thou goest out to battle against thine enemies," we read in Deuteronomy 20:1, "and seest horses, and chariots, and a people more [numerous] than thou, be not afraid of them, for the Lord thy God is with thee, which brought thee up out of the land of Egypt." Such promises might not be altogether adaptive, when we consider other examples, such as the assurance—surprisingly common, especially among colonial people fighting against western armies possessing guns—that their religion will render them invulnerable to bullets. But in much primitive war, when there was an enormous price to be paid by the side that turned and ran, religiously based reassurance could have been hugely helpful. Not unlike placebo: Those who believed in the cure (promise of victory) were more likely to experience it.

Other creatures engage in highly destructive warlike activities, notably ants, which, like human beings, occupy a pinnacle of social evolution. Unlike people, however, their coordination is achieved (at the level of proximate causation) by pheromones and, at the level of ultimate causation, by unusually close genetic relatedness among the colony members.[ii] People, lacking either of these

---

ii. It's a long story, but briefly, ants are "haplodiploid," as a result of which workers are exceptionally close, genetically, to each other. This appears to contribute significantly to their self-sacrificial behaviors.

factors, have used religion. On the other hand, there are many highly social birds and mammals that have attained remarkable levels of cooperation but without anything even approximating religion. It is one thing, however, to cooperate in building a nest or migrating to a new feeding territory, quite another to risk your life in lethal, organized encounters; maybe human beings, lacking the instinctive social repertoire of weaverbirds, elephants, dolphins, or chimpanzees, needed something else to generate cooperation in the face of such dangerous activities as war.

It is clear, for example, that the early Aztec empire owed its extraordinary success not only to the ferocity of its warriors but also to the coordinated and thus highly effective aggression by which the Aztec armies attacked their neighbors. And it is also clear that the major driving force behind this spectacularly effective organized violence was provided by the Aztec religion itself, which insisted that in the absence of tens of thousands of sacrificial victims, angry gods would destroy the earth.

Writing of the extraordinary military success of the Aztec (Mexican) armies prior to Cortes, a pair of anthropologists note that

> The Mexicas' sacrificial cosmology gave them the competitive edge needed for such victories: fanaticism. The unending hunger of the gods for mass sacrifices also generated the tireless dynamism of Mexica armies, a persistence which allowed them to wear down some of the most obstinate of their opponents.[4]

I hope it will not seem unduly disrespectful to suggest that when the Aztec empire slaughtered the vanquished to nourish their sun god with the blood of these victims, the deity in question probably was not really made healthier or happier, and thus, the Aztecs themselves were probably not *directly* aided by their bloodthirsty and immensely demanding worship practices.[iii] Thus, it seems unlikely that in the absence of these sacrifices, the sun god would have become enfeebled, forgetful, or churlishly disinclined to rise in the morning and warm the Aztecs' world. More likely, these and other egregious excesses were adaptive for the practitioners in

---

iii. It has been suggested, however, that the human protein thereby made available may have constituted a genuine nutritional payoff.

another way—notably, by providing a motivating force around which their triumphal military exploits were able to cohere.

Long before such highly structured empires as the Aztecs, success in war and its earlier antecedents of organized violence and intertribal raiding would have given the upper hand to early human groups that were more cohesive than their competitors—and nothing promotes such cohesion more powerfully than shared religion. Part of this cohesion presumably involved encouraging tolerance and restraint toward other group members (more on this shortly). But in-group cohesion likely posed a problem for groups, tribes, and ultimately states that sought to engage in war: Having taught that killing others within one's group is bad, how to justify the killing of others, outside the group? Religion could have pitched in here, too. Thus, objective observers agree that one of the ethical downsides of religious practice involves the frequent exhortations to kill followers of other religions (or deviationists from the accepted orthodoxy).

There are cases, at least in recent times, of religion standing athwart political power. One thinks of Martin Luther King Jr. and the civil rights and antiwar movements in the United States, the Catholic Church in opposition to Soviet-backed authoritarianism in Eastern Europe, Buddhist peace programs around the world, and so forth. It is also true, however, that religions have contributed to means of social and political control by supporting governmental power. It is unclear which was the predominant orientation of religion in its long evolutionary infancy, but the likelihood is that religious and political leadership has long been mutually supportive, and that religious and secular power have long been hand in hand, if not one and the same. Divine commands have long been a convenient way to get people to follow orders, even though more recently, governments have discovered how to obtain loyalty without necessarily relying on such pressure.

It can certainly be argued, therefore, that religion doesn't only promote within-group cohesion, but it also generates schisms, competition, and war. This raises the question of whether religion is an aid in waging successful war or a cause of war. In many cases, however, it can at least be argued that religion isn't the fundamental, underlying basis for organized violence, which involves competition among polities or ethnic groups, squabbles between leadership elites, misunderstandings and personal animus, ambition, fear, etc., so much as it provides an organizing principle and rallying point once wars have been generated for these and other reasons. It is debatable, for example, whether the hostility between Jew and Muslim in the Middle East is literally caused by their religious differences or whether these differences serve as proxies for differences arising when groups contend for the same real estate.[iv] Ditto for most of the other iconic cases of "religious wars," such as between Hindu and Muslim in India/Pakistan, Catholic and Protestant in Northern Ireland, and so forth. There seems little doubt, in any event, that once war breaks out, groups that are more coherent and whose population is more disposed to altruistic, self-sacrificial devotion, if called for, would be more likely to prevail—and here, religion may provide the winning margin, now and in the past.[v]

Additional Social Benefits

Religion's pro-social, pro-group orientation could well have provided other benefits in addition to heightened success in warfare. And anthropological evidence suggests that such benefits might have begun paying dividends quite early in human prehistory. Thus, current hunter-gatherers such as Australian aboriginals, Kalahari bushmen, indigenous peoples of the Amazon, and so forth—who are farthest removed from elaborate technology and thus seem closest to what our earlier ancestors may have resembled—are overwhelmingly egalitarian in their social structure, typically with strong inhibitions against excessive individuality, taking more than one's share, etc. Nicholas Wade[5] makes the intriguing suggestion that religion developed early in human prehistory in association with the switch from a presumed hierarchical social organization like that of modern baboons, macaque

---

iv. There is, after all, a large population of Christian Arabs.

v. There are counterexamples, however. In the 1980s, for example, millions of Iraqis chose their nationalist, Iraqi identity over their Shiite religious connection, making war against Shiite Iran in the name of the Iraqi state.

monkeys, and chimpanzees to the egalitarianism that presumably characterized early human societies.

During such a transition (if, indeed, it occurred), a problem would have arisen: How to organize and orchestrate the behavior of the various group members—especially how to curb tendencies to be a freeloader, a show-boater, or any other kind of independent spirit whose individuality and independence threatened the cohesion and thus the success of the group? Given that religion is an effective way of subordinating the individual to the group, it could well have provided one of the answers.

Writing of the Nuer people of Sudan, famed anthropologist A. E. Evans-Pritchard noted that "if a man wishes to be in the right with God he must be in the right with men, that is, he must subordinate his interests as an individual to the moral order of society."[6] Religions often include an explicit threat that the nonbelieving nonparticipator will be punished, which, not surprisingly, makes deviance less likely, and which leads in turn to yet more group cohesion and coordination.

The punitive aspects of religion, in addition to keeping participants in line, provides an additional payoff: To some extent, it frees others from the odious task of being an enforcer or punisher. Moreover, the punishment can be magnified (at least in concept) to include eternal torment. As for the fact that there may well be nothing to back up such a threat, consider the mirror image of placebo, and the fact that the mere expectation of harm can—at least on occasion—actually cause harm to frightened believers who anticipate the worst. (Think, for example, of the well-documented impact of "black magic" and "voodoo," whereby serious belief that one is about to be harmed generates physiological responses such that genuine harm actually takes place.)

In addition, just as hoped-for outcomes sometimes occur, simply by chance alone—as with rain that may serendipitously follow a rain dance, thereby giving undeserved credence to the dance—negative outcomes are readily interpreted as divine retribution for religious back-sliding. Consider Rev. Jerry Falwell's claims about 9/11:

> The ACLU has got to take a lot of blame for this. And I know I'll hear from them for this, but throwing God . . . successfully with the help

of the federal court system . . . throwing God out of the public square, out of the schools, the abortionists have got to bear some burden for this because God will not be mocked and when we destroy 40 million little innocent babies, we make God mad. . . . I really believe that the pagans and the abortionists and the feminists and the gays and the lesbians who are actively trying to make that an alternative lifestyle, the ACLU, People for the American Way, all of them who try to secularize America . . . I point the finger in their face and say you helped this happen.

And this observation, from a senior Iranian imam, who claimed that the "un-Islamic" behavior of certain "loose" women is responsible for earthquakes: "Many women who do not dress modestly lead young men astray, corrupt their chastity and spread adultery in society, which increases earthquakes," claimed the cleric Hojatoleslam Kazem Sedighi. (Iran, it should be noted, is one of the world's most earthquake-prone countries.) "What can we do to avoid being buried under the rubble?" Mr. Sedighi went on to ask during a Friday prayer sermon. His answer: "There is no other solution but to take refuge in religion."[7]

A Route to Morality

This leads us to yet another possible group-related payoff of religion, the ostensible connection between religious belief and social morality. Concerning the idea that religion serves as a way of discouraging deviancy, Nicholas Wade points out that this helps explain an otherwise puzzling feature of religion, the fact that it is almost universally assumed that gods care about what people do. "Why," asks Wade,

should human sexual affairs or dietary preferences matter in the least to immortal beings living in a spirit world? The assumption makes little sense unless the gods are viewed as embodying a society's moral authority and its interest in having all members observe certain rules of social behavior.

It has often been argued, as Ivan Karamazov did in *The Brothers Karamazov*, that "without God, all things are permissible." Although agnostics and atheists vigorously maintain otherwise, many believers claim that religion is a prerequisite for moral behavior. And although sometimes the proposition is more narrowly stated—"only *my* religion will guarantee moral behavior"—not uncommonly, the claim is made that fundamentally, all religions are the same, and therefore belief in some religion, any religion, is key, such that which one hardly matters.

This perspective is itself illuminating, suggesting that maybe there really is a sense in which all religions are the same, in that they help steer people from self-interest toward group interest. Thus, late in his life, Jurgen Habermas, for most of his career a staunch supporter of Enlightenment values, has begun arguing in favor of moderating reason with religion, because of the latter's capacity for generating "morally guided collective action."[8] Let's note, first, that religious people can certainly be hypocritical and immoral, and that religious commitment is no guarantee of morality (plenty of horrors have been perpetrated in the name of religion). Nonetheless, it is also worth acknowledging that much of social life depends on people having confidence in the motives and reliability of their colleagues. Legal restraints and criminal sanctions go only so far; most of our interactions—and nearly all of our economic exchanges—assume at least a minimal degree of shared values. Significantly, people are far more likely to feel comfortable when interacting with someone else who shares their religion, with the implication that as a result the other's motivations are more comprehensible and thus more trustworthy. Insofar as this is so, then religion serves as a societal lubricant no less than a glue.[vi]

There are comebacks to this social morality hypothesis for the evolution of religion. Although shared moral codes may be necessary for societies to survive without destroying themselves, it isn't clear that these codes must derive from religion. Thus, many animal species engage in elaborate social systems (bees, ants, wasps, chimpanzees, bonobos, baboons, gorillas, zebras, blackbirds, even many reptiles and fish) without wielding anything resembling religion. In such cases, biology provides the equivalent of moral codes

---

vi. It is sometimes said that the two necessities for a happy life are duct tape and WD-40: the former for keeping things together that would otherwise move when they shouldn't, and the latter for helping things move when they need to and otherwise wouldn't.

that regulate such activities as altruism, selfishness, communication, courtship, competition, parental care, and so forth. Are people notably bereft of biology in this respect, such that were it not for religion, human social life would be impossible, intolerable, or, at least, less efficient and acceptable? Japan, for example, lacks rigid religious beliefs but has lots of social cohesion.

At the same time, it is not that easy to discount the various group-level payoffs that may be associated with religion, if only because religion is such a group-oriented phenomenon, whose practitioners often experience a fervent sense of togetherness. And for a social species such as *Homo sapiens*, togetherness is itself a powerfully satisfying experience, just as social isolation can be terrifying. When given the choice, few resist the promise—as stated in the song from Rodgers and Hammerstein's *Carousel*—that "You'll Never Walk Alone."

Maybe the personal payoff of religious devotion (the satisfied sense of spiritual and existential fulfillment that so impressed William James) serves as a proximal mechanism getting people to participate, in return for which they gain the various social and evolutionary benefits. Just as hunger gets us to eat, which ultimately nourishes the body, perhaps evolution has outfitted human beings with a spiritual hunger, which induces them to follow one religion or another, as a result of which they experience less personal loneliness, fewer doubts, and greater efficiency in their daily lives.

God as Alpha Male

It is also possible that religious belief—and particularly, faith in one or a small number of very powerful deities—derives from a this-worldly primate tendency to worshipfully obey a dominant leader. Jay Glass has made the interesting argument that "In the original state of nature, for both animals and humans, loyalty to a Supreme Being (aka dominant male, king, warlord, etc.) offered protection from enemies and provided the necessities to sustain life. Those that did not put their faith and trust in a god-like figure did not survive to produce the next generation."[9] The jewel in Glass's argument is his reworking of the 23rd Psalm, as it might describe members of a chimpanzee troop speaking of the dominant male:

PSALM XXIII	THE CHIMP'S PRAYER
The Lord is my shepherd;	The dominant male is my leader;
I shall not want.	I shall not want.
He makes me to lie down in green pastures	He makes me to lie down in green pastures
He leads me beside still waters.	He leads me beside still waters.
He restores my soul.	He quells my anxiety.
He leads me in the paths of righteousness for his name's sake.	He shows me how to survive for his name's sake.
Yea, though I walk through the valley of the shadow of death,	Yea, though the jungle is full of threats,
I will fear no evil, for You are with me.	I will fear no evil, For you are with me.
Your rod and Your staff they comfort me.	Your strength and Your vigor they comfort me.
You prepare a table before me in the presence of my enemies.	You protect me from other animals.
You anoint my head with oil.	You bless me.
My cup runs over.	My cup runs over.
Surely goodness and mercy shall follow me all the days of my life; and I will dwell in the house of the Lord	I feel safe in your territory as long as I am in your troop; I submit and accept your dominance
Forever.	Forever.

This rendering overstates the degree of affiliation between "average" chimp and dominant male(s), but it nonetheless deserves more attention than it has received.[vii] Nonetheless, monotheism isn't universal, nor is worship of male god(s)—both of which are implied by Glass's thesis. Thus, his book, *The Power of Faith*,

---

vii. Its author is outside the traditional scientific/academic establishment, which probably explains much.

overstates the role of the dominant male as leader of the pack, not only in animal societies, but in human religion as well. It also focuses too intently on chimpanzees, omitting, for example, bonobos, which may if anything be more closely related to *Homo sapiens*, but among whom dominant males are something of an oxymoron.

In addition, it seems likely that insofar as a primate troop member "worships" his or her leader, at least the existence of that leader is undeniable, along with (in most cases) the negative consequences of deviation. On the other hand, to my knowledge, God seems on balance less likely to strike down disbelievers than a dominant animal is to punish would-be rebels. Disbelief in God thus seems less costly (at least in the short term) than is failure to honor and obey one's flesh-and-blood leader. Yet, as we shall soon consider, it is also possible that religion has established and maintained itself precisely by exacting temporal punishment against apostates, which not only harkens back to Richard Dawkins's hypothesis of religious belief as parasitic meme but also provides a potential mechanism whereby religion could conceivably be selected for at the level of groups.

There seems little doubt, in any event, that numerous payoffs can be derived by followers of religion no less than those following a dominant, secular leader, who participate in a group whose shared followership results in greater coherence and thus enhanced biological and social success.

Last-Gasp, Extra Effort, and Don't Panic

One such payoff was glimpsed by historian Walter Burkert, who argued that religion helps induce people to make a last-gasp effort when otherwise they might stop trying. "Although religious obsession could be called a form of paranoia," wrote Burkert,

> it does offer a chance of survival in extreme and hopeless situations, when others, possibly the nonreligious individuals, would break down and give up. Mankind, in its long past, will have gone through many a desperate situation, with an ensuing breakthrough of *homines religiosi*.[10]

On the surface, this seems plausible, but it begs a crucial question: If religion has proven adaptive because it evokes greater confidence, increased effort, or enhanced probability of a last-gasp attempt that occasionally yields success and thus enhanced fitness, why aren't people primed to make such efforts in any event, without religion no less than with it? The issue raised is similar to the mystery of the placebo effect, encountered earlier. Thus, if believing in something (the efficacy of a medicinal cure, the prospect of divine intervention on the battlefield or in response to a final, last-gasp effort) contributes to success, then why the necessity of belief? Wouldn't selection favor bodies curing themselves via those immunologic mechanisms that are evidently already available, or people making other efforts on their own behalf—even without much prospect of success—regardless of whether they were motivated to do so by religious faith?

There is also a converse of making extra efforts because of religious conviction: remaining calm in the face of disaster. Here is Zora Neale Hurston's description of the Okeechobee Hurricane and its resulting flood of 1928:

> Ten feet higher and far as they could see the muttering wall advanced before the braced-up waters like a road crusher on a cosmic scale. The monstropolous beast had left its bed. Two hundred miles an hour wind had loosed is chains. . . . [T]he wind came with triple fury and put out the light for the last time. They sat in company with others in other shanties. . . . [T]hey seemed to be staring at the dark, but their eyes were watching God.

Most likely, the extra effort and don't panic hypotheses don't hold water with regard to individuals, since selection should indeed favor making that extra effort and/or avoiding panic any time the ultimate benefit—to the individual—exceeds its cost. However, let's imagine that making the "ultimate sacrifice" is indeed counterevolutionary . . . for the individual. It could nonetheless be beneficial for the group. So, selection could possibly operate to favor religious conviction, if it worked at the group level, in which case Burkert's extra effort hypothesis might provide some biological momentum. Similarly, if it is beneficial to avoid panic, then people should have been selected to do so, without any necessary prod from religion. But maybe "watching God" under times of severe stress helped provide the kind of preservative pause that was adaptive after all.

Connected to Consciousness?

There's more. The evolution of religion could be linked in a curious way to the evolution of consciousness. As our ancestors evolved consciousness (see Chapter 9), they may well have become increasingly aware—consciously, for the first time in the history of life on this planet—that they had personal interests that didn't necessarily coincide with the social norms and traditions of their social unit. Groups function better, with less friction and more cohesiveness, when their members don't lie, steal, or murder (also, of course, when they don't covet their neighbor's wife, and so forth). But individuals are often inclined to do precisely these things, and more. In the absence of consciousness, such inclinations are likely to be acted upon, whereas once individuals become aware of their own selfish propensities and sensitive to the drawbacks they pose to the "greater good," the stage could be set for explicit statements of social prohibitions and expectations, and for people's willingness—however reluctantly—to go along.

Early human beings' emergent awareness of their own selfishness, although beneficial to the individuals in question, would have been detrimental to the group, insofar as it would have induced them to be less reliable "team players." It is at least possible, therefore, that groups responded by seeking to establish supraindividual norms—enforced via what we now call religion—which were then imposed on otherwise rebellious individuals: "Do these things, even if you'd rather not, because God commands it," while at the same time, the group benefits.

The above considerations add cogency to Voltaire's celebrated observation that if God didn't exist, we'd have to invent him—in order to reap some of the payoffs that religion provides. Can we carry this a step further and conclude that if God didn't exist, natural selection would have had to evolve Him . . . if not for the good of the participating individual, then for the benefit of the greater group?

There is a common denominator uniting the various hypotheses we have just considered, namely, that religious commitment involves forswearing certain personal gains while benefiting other individuals. Insofar as this basic pattern has contributed to the evolution of religious belief and practice, then the puzzle of religion's origin corresponds with another puzzle: the evolution of altruism. Darwin struggled with this matter, asking how selection could favor traits that helped others while harming those who manifested those behaviors. He concluded that

> A tribe including many members who, from possessing in a high degree the spirit of patriotism, fidelity, obedience, courage and sympathy, were always ready to aid one another, and to sacrifice themselves for the common good, would be victorious over most other tribes; and this would be natural selection.

Even Darwin was occasionally wrong, and this appears to be one such case. The process he described above would not be "natural selection," but its close cousin, group selection. Natural selection is defined as "differential reproduction," leading to the crucial question, "Differential reproduction of what?" Biologists understand that the fundamental units of natural selection are individuals and—more precisely yet—their constituent genes. Differential reproduction *of groups*, on the other hand, is a different matter, and one that is highly contentious among evolutionists.

Group Selection 101

This is an important matter, deserving a brief detour, both because it highlights an interesting scientific debate in general and because it goes to the heart of the hypotheses we have just been discussing for the evolution of religion. It is tempting to think that natural selection works to promote the success of groups, especially when these groups compete with each other. If individuals could somehow be persuaded to give up their interest in maximizing their personal reproductive success and instead agree to subordinate some of their selfishness to the overall greater good, then the groups of which they are members would do better as a result, whereupon the constituent individuals would do better, too.

Shouldn't they give up a bit to get even more in return? And shouldn't such a tendency be favored not simply by ethical appeal to the human conscience, but also by the hard-wiring of natural selection?

In most cases, the answer is no.

This is because even though self-sacrifice might help groups do better in competition with other groups, it would necessarily mean that *within* their groups, altruists would be worse off than selfish individuals who refused to go along. Economists call it the "free-rider problem," experts in game theory talk about "defectors" or "cheaters," while for biologists, it's a matter of self-interested individuals enjoying a higher fitness than their more selfless, group-oriented colleagues. Even if groups containing altruists—whose altruism might incline them to share food, sacrifice themselves in defense of others, and so on—are better off than are groups lacking altruists, the problem is that those altruistic food sharers and other-defenders would be trumped by free-riders, defectors, and cheaters who selfishly looked out for number one.

Mathematical models have demonstrated that whereas altruism could, in theory, evolve via group selection, the constraints are very demanding. Among other things, the difference in reproductive success between altruists and selfish cheaters would have to be quite low, whereas the disparity between groups containing altruists and those lacking them would have to be very high—and in actuality, the opposite is typically true. It makes a big difference whether you are a self-sacrificing, group-oriented altruist or a selfish, look-out-for-number-one SOB. Moreover, although the differences between successful and less successful individuals is likely to be very great, disparities in the reproductive rates of groups are likely to be much more sluggish. Not surprisingly, no clear examples of group selection among nonhuman animals have been identified.

On the other hand, things just might be different when it comes to *Homo sapiens*.[11] Compared to other creatures, our own species is extraordinary in the degree to which we stick our noses into each other's business: snooping; gossiping; wondering who is doing what and when; who is toeing the line and who is shirking; who said what to whom; who attended church, synagogue, mosque, or the ritual fire dance and who stayed home; who sacrificed a goat and who held back; who engaged in the expected observances and who deviated from the rules.

Of course, every species is unique. That's how we are able to identify each as a distinct species! Human beings aren't unique when it comes to enforcing social cooperation via punishment of noncooperators. Thus, dominant meerkat females attack and may even kill subordinates who attempt to breed[12]; among the brilliantly colored superb fairy wrens of Australia, males punish "helpers" who flag in their helping[13]; honeybee workers destroy eggs laid by other workers (by doing so, they police their siblings who would produce offspring to which they are less closely related than they are to the queen's direct offspring)[14]; cleaner fish that nip the fins or gills of those they are supposed to be cleaning are punished by their clients[15]; and something equivalent even occurs among plants: Soy beans cut off the flow of nutrients to root nodule bacteria that fail to supply the host plant with the nitrogen-based protein normally associated with such microorganisms.[16]

Nonetheless, human beings are still unusual in the degree to which they are able to enforce their sociocultural traditions. Far more than other animals, among which cooperation typically occurs at a limited one-to-one scale, people have long been obliged to partake in distinctly group-oriented and group-sustaining behaviors as a result of which selection might have been able to operate at the level of such groups, free of the self-directed undermining that would occur if individuals were permitted to opt out.

If so, then the various group-oriented benefits suggested for religion just might have been selected for after all. Certainly, religion is among the more prominent behaviors that are enforced at the group level. Those who deviate from its rules, obligations, and precepts—the heretics, apostates, and plain old-fashioned shirkers—have long been punished, often severely. According to Verse 9:74 of the Qu'aran, Allah will allot to apostates grievous penalty both "in this life and in the Hereafter," and indeed, defecting from Islam (apostasy) is a capital crime in many Muslim countries.

Nor is Islam unusual in coming down hard on any who deviate from religion's expectations—which, of course, is precisely what we would expect if religion (whatever its benefits to the group) is enforced via social sanctions powerful enough to generate group-level selection on its behalf. Ostracism, for instance, is enforced by nearly every religion, as punishment for leaving the fold. Renouncing the Mormon faith results in complete isolation from friends and family, a devastating experience even now in the 21st century, and something that must have been yet more severe for early human beings who were, if anything, more isolated and dependent on their immediate social network.

There is direct biblical support for ridiculing and isolating non-believers . . . and for much more. Psalm 14, for example, begins, "The fool hath said in his heart, 'There is no God.' They are corrupt, they do abominable works, there is none that doeth good." In Numbers 15:32–36, we are given an account of someone discovered picking up sticks on the Sabbath, whereupon Moses, after consulting with God, commanded that the guilty party should be stoned to death.

Skipping church on Sunday was a crime in Shakespearean England, punishable by a fine of 20 pounds sterling (approximately 1 year's salary), while frequent offenders risked being hanged, drawn and quartered. And a country that prides itself in promoting freedom of religion was notably reluctant to institute freedom *from* it. Thus, in the late 18th century, many states and local jurisdictions in the United States passed blasphemy laws that carried severe punishments for religious dissenters. First offenders could have a hole bored in their tongue, while repeat offenders risked execution. And even today, anyone aspiring to high political office is well advised to keep his or her atheism under wraps.

In short, a strong case can be made that religions conform to many—perhaps all—of the requirements for group selection. David Sloan Wilson is a biologist who has long championed the general theory of group selection, and although his perspective (some might say his fervent ideology) has not been embraced by most evolutionists, there is growing, grudging acknowledgment that group selection might have been significant in human evolution in general, and in the evolution and maintenance of religion in particular. To summarize the argument: Group selection might have been important in human evolution, in part because of the strong sociocultural pressure for sticking to social norms—which in turn would have worked against the tendency to be a selfish nonaltruist (read: nonfollower of the group's religion).

In addition, there could well have been substantial competition among early proto-human groups, manifested via primitive warfare. Under such conditions, more organized and cohesive groups could well have been more successful, while at the same time, individuals within such groups who were resistant to cohesive norms—such as religion—would have had a difficult time prospering or even, perhaps, surviving.

The objective truth or falsity of religious claims may thus be less important than the impact they have—whether they induce their followers to do things that are, on balance, in their interest. "Clearly," writes Wilson,

> I need to accurately perceive the location of a rabbit to hit it with my throwing stick. However, there are many, many other situations in which it can be adaptive to distort reality. . . . Even massively fictitious beliefs can be adaptive, as long as they motivate behaviors that are adaptive in the real world."[17]

Such as cooperating.

For Wilson, "Religions exist primarily for people to achieve together what they cannot achieve alone." He suggests, accordingly, that there has been group selection for religions, with various forms coming into existence, competing with each other, some replicating themselves more successfully than others and some going extinct, not unlike what happens among individuals and genes.[18] Science writer Nicholas Wade is similarly persuaded, pointing out that religion "can unite people who may share neither common kinship, nor ethnicity nor even language." If religion evolved in the context of group selection, the drama must have played out over tens of thousands of years (or more), among groups of pretechnological, early human beings living in small social units, within which individuals likely knew each other very well, and who would certainly have shared kinship, ethnicity, and language.

Wade's argument suggests not only that religion initially evolved in the context of group selection but also that it continues to offer survival benefits even in a world of huge nation-states: "When nations feel their existence is at stake, they often define their cause by religion, whether in Europe's long wars with Islam, or Elizabethan England's defiance of Catholic Spain, or the Puritans' emigration to New England, or the foundation of Israel." Overlooked here is that these and so many other conflicts, in which religion supposedly provides a protective function, would not arise if the various religions in question weren't being practiced. Thus, much of the Israeli–Arab conflict is generated by the fact that overwhelmingly, Israelis are Jewish and Arabs are Muslim. Can we say that religion unified and thus protected the Puritans against persecution in Europe—given that if they weren't self-identified as Puritans, they wouldn't have been persecuted in the first place?

Maybe we can, since once the labels Puritan, Anglican, Jew, or Muslim have been affixed, they might indeed help rally the troops and induce them to remain committed to the larger social unit. Although "mega-group selection" (as with nation-states) doesn't answer the fundamental question of how religion could have been adaptive in the first place, there seems little doubt that it could contribute to the success of groups already designated as consisting of one religious affiliation or another. Moreover, as we have seen, group selection in its more intimate and biologically relevant context could well have been instrumental in the initial evolution of religion.

Group selection remains controversial among evolutionary biologists. It has been invoked, in the past, when attempting to account for seemingly altruistic behaviors, actions that impose a cost on individual participants, while possibly conveying a compensating benefit to the larger group. When it comes to the evolution of religion, group selection also appears an attractive explanation, and for the same reason. (In the extreme case, after all, people literally sacrifice themselves for their religion.) This, in turn, leads to yet another debate, one that is even more fraught than that over group selection itself, and which goes beyond technical disputes among biologists: the extent to which religion equals morality. After all, altruism is often considered a cornerstone of morality, and many people consider that religion is a prerequisite for moral behavior more generally.

This book is not the right venue to examine this dispute. Suffice it to note there is no evidence that religious people are any more moral or law abiding than are agnostics or atheists. On the other hand, it is probably significant that every major religion takes some responsibility for teaching morality. Of these pedagogic efforts, the Ten Commandments are best known to Westerners, but certainly not unique. Note, however, that in most tribal societies, moral precepts do not come from religion; more often, they derive independently from interpersonal patterns and social expectations. But even in such cases, religion may yet be ethically consequential when it comes to the important function of achieving peace among strangers from within the same society, a need that arises when populations become so large that people encounter same-society members who were not previously known. Under such circumstances in the nonbiological "evolution" of societies, religions probably contributed adaptively by proclaiming that killing a fellow tribe member, for example, is offensive to the gods or to God.

But isn't this unnecessary, since we have laws that mandate what we should and shouldn't do?

The Long Arm of Religion

Bear in mind, first, that secular legal institutions are likely to be very recent developments in the human evolutionary experience. And second, the "long arm of the law" isn't necessarily all that long, whereas religious requirements and prohibitions, insofar as they are incorporated into the subjective belief systems of each participant, are much harder to sidestep. "Unlike secular authority," writes biologist Kenneth Kardong,

> supernatural authority is always watchful, a daily and nightly spiritual judge of private personal conduct. Indoctrinated early with myths, legends, and worship of supernatural beings, the individual comes to regard the supernatural not as fanciful concoctions of imagination but as organic, vital, actual forces in everyday life. From the watchful eye of spiritual forces there is no hiding, no escape. Private actions and intimate thoughts lie open to spiritual inspection. Commit a sin, and a local god soon knows it. A temptation arises and the conscience begins to squirm. With a god watching over the sinner's shoulder, fortitude is more likely found to resist.
>
> Civil authority may be foiled but demands by supernatural beings are not easily ignored. For the sinner with an active conscience, natural misfortunes are easily found to apparently punish the misdeed. Everywhere lies evidence of divine displeasure. Compelling reasons

for the sinner to return to pious behavior abound—crop failure, death of an infant, disease, plague, injury, lightning, floods, drought, fire, storms, or thunder. All these misfortunes can be spiritually sobering. A culture embeds the authority of these spiritual inquisitors in an individual through regular and frequent worship, sacrifice, and prayers. Religious practices impress upon an individual the power of intangible spirits to inspect private behavior and enforce acceptable codes of conduct. The result is an internalized judicial system. It is called a conscience.[19]

There are other respects in which the purported connection between morality and religion is relevant to the question of religion's adaptive significance. Here the key word is "purported." Thus, although it is unlikely that religion actually makes people act more ethically, its crucial contribution might well be that it gives rise to an *expectation* of such behavior.

Among the orthodox Jews who predominate in the diamond market in Manhattan, for example, exchanges involving large amounts of money are often based on a simple handshake. And even though departures from intrareligious solidarity certainly occur—for example, Ponzi scheme investment crook Bernard Madoff was described as an observant Jew, and most of his victims were also Jewish—there is little doubt that members of a religious community are especially likely to trust others from within that same community. Indeed, many commentators on the Madoff scandal noted particular outrage caused by the fact that Mr. Madoff had taken advantage of "his own people," thereby deviating from the expectation of intrareligious ethical solidarity.

The following proposition has not been tested empirically, but seems likely: Interpersonal trust within a given religion will be greater in proportion as the religion imposes onerous costs upon its members. Groucho Marx once famously quipped that he wouldn't want to join any club that would accept him as a member, presumably because its standards would necessarily be too low! An influential article by economist Lawrence Iannacocone, titled "Why Strict Churches Are Strong," argued similarly that the more onerous the rules, the more committed the membership.[20] Iannacocone found that when it is easy for members to opt out, levels of benefits are lower, to which we add that the confidence of each participant in the degree to which her coreligionists are committed is also likely to be higher. If you don't know whom to trust, it is generally a good bet to rely on those who have gone through demanding initiations and paid substantial dues, like yourself.

It probably isn't a coincidence that many religions require not only that their devotees give money, or a commitment of time, but that they undergo painful rites, often involving genital mutilation—known less pejoratively as circumcision. An important consideration in evolutionary biology revolves around the question of "honest signaling." The idea is that it is easy, perhaps too easy, for an individual to communicate something about himself: how healthy he is, or what a good father he would be, or what a reliable partner in other respects. Since talk is cheap, in many species natural selection has favored messages that cannot readily be faked, such as a deep croak among toads (small individuals are limited to higher frequencies), fancy feathers among peacocks (weak individuals cannot muster the energy to grow such outlandish accoutrements), and so forth. Maybe even Groucho Marx would trust membership in a religion that demanded much of its congregants.

In many human interactions—perhaps most of them—participants are vulnerable to being deceived by others. Interactions often involve what evolutionary biologists call "reciprocal altruism," in which someone helps someone else, at some cost to the helper (the initial altruist). But such behavior can be richly rewarded—and thus not actually be altruistic at all—if the initial recipient pays back her debt when the tables are turned, and the altruist is needy and the recipient is in a position to repay the debt. Such systems are vulnerable to exploitation, however, if the beneficial reneges on her obligation and refrains from repaying the initial donor. Although it is often possible to protect oneself from social predators, effective defenses are time and energy consuming; it is more efficient, albeit far from foolproof, to rely on shared membership in the same social club, ideally one that has already established certain ethical rules of the road. And it is at least possible that religious affiliation sometimes fills this role, generating trust that coreligionists are less likely to renege on their reciprocal obligations. This would help make sense of the widespread assumption that religion is somehow a prerequisite for moral behavior.

In public opinion polls, for example, Americans have consistently said that they would prefer to vote for a president who is of their own religious faith, but overwhelmingly, that they would rather vote for someone of a different faith than for an atheist. President Dwight Eisenhower (not especially devout himself) reportedly opined that the US government only makes sense insofar as it is founded on "a deeply felt religious faith," adding "and I don't care what it is." Even in such a supposedly secular venue as a US court of law, witnesses routinely swear to tell the truth on a Bible, adding "so help me God."

The assumption that religiosity is intimately connected to moral reliability isn't new, nor is it limited to the United States, which is—for better or worse—the most devout country in the Western world. Thus, when John Locke, one of the preeminent philosophers of tolerance, religious and political, penned his celebrated *Essay Concerning Toleration* (1689), he explicitly excluded atheists from his list of those who merited tolerance: "Those are not at all to be tolerated who deny the being of a God. Promises, covenants, and oaths, which are the bonds of human society, can have no hold upon an atheist."

According to historian Edward Gibbon, writing about a century after Locke, "The various modes of worship, which prevailed in the Roman world were all considered by the people as equally true; by the philosopher, as equally false; and by the magistrate, as equally useful."

Most observers of religion agree that when it comes to morality and ethical behavior, the balance sheet of most religions is difficult to interpret, although it is plausible that the "usefulness" of religion extends to natural selection (operating presumably on groups), no less than to Roman magistrates (presumably operating via its effect on rendering social relations more predictable and citizens more law abiding). Religions certainly claim to be a source of positive moral values, and they are typically perceived as such by their proponents. On the other hand, religious persuasion can be a source of intolerance and violence, and no small amount of hypocrisy. It is one thing, however, to ask whether, on balance, religions are morally beneficial, yet something different to inquire whether they are *biologically* beneficial by virtue of their moral teaching and the social confidence and coherence—whether objectively justified or not—that they generate.

In summary, the jury is still out on whether religion evolved via group selection, which, in turn, might have favored those groups that were more violently cohesive during war and morally cohesive during peace. It seems highly likely, however, that natural selection, whether acting at the level of individuals or of groups, has been responsible for the existence as well as the perseverance of religion.

If so, it may also have been responsible for one of the more peculiar and fascinating aspects of our mental lives: the fact that we are such divided creatures, capable of both extraordinary rationality and critical thought on the one hand and blind, unquestioning faith on the other—and the fact that when it comes to religion, the latter typically predominates. No less a skeptical rationalist than David Hume famously noted that "reason is and ought only to be the slave of the passions." The "is" part seems clear, and not surprising. After all, *Homo sapiens* and probably its antecedents as well have been practicing various forms of religion for tens of thousands of years, whereas scientific inquiry, for example, is only a few centuries old. It is just barely 150 years since Darwin's *Origin of Species*. Our understanding of the microbial basis of disease is even newer. Relativity is only about a century old, and we've only started using computers.

The passions—religious and otherwise—are much older, and their roots are deep indeed.

Sweet, Like Sugar?

The likelihood is that on balance, religion was adaptive for human beings, at least in the past. But is it still? Clearly, in some cases it has been grotesquely maladaptive: parents in Jonestown, Guyana, poisoning their children and themselves, followers of "Heaven's Gate" castrating and then killing themselves—all the better to be whisked away onto the passing comet, Hale-Bopp, and so forth. As to other, more mainstream religions, the jury is still out, and the question goes beyond the purview of the current book.

A useful metaphor might be found—strangely enough—in the human fondness for sugar. Why is sugar sweet? For the evolutionary biologist on the lookout for ultimate explanations, the answer does not involve glucose, sucrose, fructose, and so forth, all of which are chemicals that give rise—proximally—to the sensation of sweetness when consumed by a human being. After all, an anteater would probably protest that sugars aren't sweet at all; rather, ants are.

Sweetness, when it comes to evolutionary considerations, is thus in the mouth of the taster. Anteaters have been honed by natural selection to be positively influenced by the taste of ants, just as giant pandas adore bamboo shoots and koalas are partial to eucalyptus. Almost certainly, members of the species *Homo sapiens* find sugars sweet because we are primates, who evolved as fruit eaters, and fruit, in turn, is maximally nutritious when ripe, and ripeness correlates with being sugar laden (so as to attract birds and mammals—including primates—which spread their seeds after eating them).

Today, people can indulge their species-wide sweet tooth, a preference that was clearly adaptive among our ancestors, but by consuming "empty calories" in the form of cakes, cookies, candies, and soft drinks. The result is an adaptive inclination gone awry, especially since we no longer need ripe fruit as a major source of calories, on top of the fact that our ingenuity has endowed ourselves with the ability to cater to a "need" without conveying any of the original payoff. In fact, it does us harm.

Is there something similar in our predisposition to religion? Thus, although we cannot as yet conclude which biological factors made religion adaptive in our species' infancy, it is at least possible that it—or some behaviors currently subsumed under the term *religion*—was once adaptive. But just as a fondness for sweets used to be adaptive but is now troublesome and sometimes downright dangerous, the same may apply to religion. Of course, our penchant for sweetness can be used for our benefit—as in the *Mary Poppins* song, "a spoonful of sugar makes the medicine go down"— there can be substantial beneficial aspects of religion, too.

Also, just as there are substitutes for sugar—saccharine, aspartame, etc.—aren't there also substitutes for religion? These chemical substitutes are sought because of the payoff to satisfying the craving but without the undesired calories; is there an equivalent for religion? Interestingly, devotees have argued for various "sugar substitutes" such as LSD, marijuana, or psilocybin, although no one has thus far come up with "God in a pill" as satisfying as that which—somehow or other—natural selection managed to invent.

Notes

1. Stark, R., & Finke, R. (2000). *Acts of faith: explaining the human side of religion.* Berkeley, CA: University of California Press.
2. Wright, R. (2009). *The evolution of God.* New York: Little Brown.
3. Sosis, R., & Alcorta, C. (2003). Signaling, solidarity, and the sacred: The evolution of religious behavior. *Evolutionary Anthropology, 12,* 264–274
4. Conrad, G. W., & Demarest, A. A. (1984). *Religion and empire.* Cambridge, UK: Cambridge University Press.
5. Wade, N. (2009). *The faith instinct.* New York: Penguin.
6. Evans-Pritchard, E. E. (1971). *Nuer religion.* London, UK: Oxford University Press.
7. *The New York Times* April 20, 2010.
8. Habermas, J. (2010). *An awareness of what is missing: Faith and reason in a post-secular age.* New York: Wiley.
9. Glass, J. D. (2007). *The power of faith: Mother nature's gift.* Corona del Mar, CA: Donington Press.
10. Burkert, W. (1996). *Creation of the sacred: Tracks of biology in early religions.* Cambridge, MA: Harvard University Press.
11. Wilson, D. S., & Wilson, E. O. (2007). Rethinking the theoretical foundation of sociobiology. *Quarterly Review of Biology, 82,* 327–348.
12. Young, A. J., Carlson, A. A., Monfort, S. L., Russell, A. F., Bennett, N. C., & Clutton-Brock, T. C. (2006). Stress and the suppression of subordinate reproduction in cooperatively breeding meerkats. *Proceedings of the Natural Academy of Sciences of the United States of America, 103,* 12005–12010.
13. Mulder, R. A., & Langmore, N. E. (1993). Dominant males punish helpers for temporary defection in superb fairy wrens. *Animal Behaviour, 45,* 830–833.
14. Ratnieks, F. L., & Visscher, P. K. (1989). Worker policing in the honeybee. *Nature, 342,* 796–797.
15. Bshary, R., & Grutter, A. S. (2005). Punishment and partner switching cause cooperative behaviour in a cleaning mutualism. *Biology Letters, 1,* 396–399.
16. Kiers, E. T., Rousseau, R. A., West, S. A., & Denison, R. F. (2003). Host sanctions and the legume-rhizobium mutualism. *Nature, 425,* 78–81.
17. Wilson, D. S. (2002). *Darwin's cathedral.* Chicago: University of Chicago Press.
18. Wilson, D. S. (2002). *Darwin's cathedral.* Chicago: University of Chicago Press.
19. Kardong, K. V. (2010). *Beyond God.* Amherst, NY: Prometheus Books.
20. Iannacocone, L. (1994). Why strict churches are strong. *American Journal of Sociology, 99*(5), 1180–1211.

CHAPTER NINE

On the Matter of Mind

W HEN IT COMES TO constituting a hallmark of the human species, the opposable thumb just isn't very impressive. Ditto for our largely hairless torsos, even our bipedalism. What stands out, far more, is our big brains and our capacity for sophisticated thought. Yet we know very little about thought itself, neither how we go about it as individuals, nor what caused us as a species to have evolved into such highly cognitive creatures. Accordingly, here is paradox along with mystery: As clever as we are, we aren't smart enough to figure out why we became so clever! Consistent with our approach throughout *Homo Mysterious*, in this chapter we'll focus on the evolutionary side of the mystery: Why did natural selection make us—at least by our own standards—the smartest species on earth?

This question has received considerable attention, from some very clever people, and yet, the answers remain elusive.

A Proximate Glance

Even more elusive, it seems, is the mystery of proximate causation. Thus far we have pretty much ignored these "how" questions, and although this chapter will continue in this vein, it is worth noting that when it comes to scientific mysteries, there may be none more daunting than *how*—in proximate terms—we achieve intelligence, consciousness, and the range of subjective perceptions and sensations that constitute every person's innermost life. There seems an almost unbridgeable gap between physiological, anatomic, electrochemical events such as packets of neurochemicals and waves of ion-based depolarization passing along nerve cell membranes—which biologists are beginning to unravel and understand in astonishing detail—and those innermost sensations that all of us experience.

Connecting the "stuff" of the physical world with that of our subjective consciousness has long been the third rail of biology. Touch it and maybe you won't die, but you are unlikely to get tenure! It helps, of course, if you are a Nobel laureate, such as Francis Crick or Gerald Edelman, but until recently it appeared that even their attempts to pin down the electrical-chemical-anatomical (or whatever) substrate of mental phenomena would go the way of Einstein's doomed search for a unified theory of everything. This may yet be the case, but the situation has nonetheless changed dramatically of late, such that inquiry into the neurobiology of mental experience has become one of the hottest, best funded, and most media attracting of research enterprises, along with genomics, stem cells, and a few other newly favored subdisciplines.

For literally centuries, it was perfectly acceptable for philosophers to ponder consciousness, because after all, no one really expected them to come up with anything real. Descartes' renowned *cogito ergo sum* ("I think, therefore I am"), for example, was modified thusly by Ambrose Bierce: *cogito cogito, ergo cogito sum* ("I think I think, therefore I think I am"), to which Bierce added that this was about as close to truth as philosophy is likely to get! Bierce, once again, noted that the chief activity of mind "consists in the endeavor to ascertain its own nature, the futility of the attempt being due to the fact that it has nothing but itself to know itself with."

But now we have microelectrodes recording from individual neurons, computer modeling of neural nets, functional MRIs, and an array of even newer 21st-century techniques, all hot on the trail of how mental processes emerge from "mere" matter.[i] Cartesian dualism is on the run, as well it should be.

Admittedly, there are some exceptions, proving that imbecility runs deep, especially in the curious world of the consciousness credulous. Take the remarkable popularity of the charlatan cinema "What the Bleep Do We Know?" with its faux scientific assertion that consciousness is an active force by which we can impact the world, not to mention showcasing such ludicrous—and persistently unreplicated—claims as this: Water supposedly forms different kinds of crystals as a result of being exposed to "fields of consciousness" embodied in written messages such as "You're a fool" (no crystals or ugly ones) as compared to "I love you" (beautiful, heart-warming symmetrical delights). With such friends, the serious study of mental events hardly needs enemies.

This chapter, however, shall seek neither to bury nor to praise neurobiology, but to point instead to another side of bona fide inquiry that has received all too little attention, even as neurobiology has advanced. I refer to the question of why our higher mental processes exist at all. Accordingly, let's grant a "how" to thought, intelligence, consciousness and those various perceptual events known as "qualia" (our experience of "red," "cold" or "love," for example) and agree that somehow or other, energy and matter come together and produce them, via electrochemical and anatomical events, some of which we understand and others yet unknown. And let's get back to the "why."

Big Brains

It is quite possible, after all, to imagine a world inhabited by highly competent zombies, who go about their days responding appropriately to stimuli—basking, perhaps, in the warm sun, obtaining suitable nutrients at opportune times, even repairing themselves

---

i. In a sense, Bierce is still correct, in that even with the aid of such powerful prosthetic devices, we are still limited—and presumably always will be—by the fact that in the end, we have nothing but our own minds and brains to know ourselves with.

and producing offspring—but lacking intelligence or any inner mental life whatsoever.

There is an old and not terribly funny joke—of the type known generically as a "shaggy-dog story"—that involved a "potfer." After several minutes of lengthy and irrelevant narration, the joke's victim is led to ask, "What's a potfer?" whereupon the joke teller triumphantly announces the punch line: "Cooking." So, what's a brainer? Most people would answer "Thinking." Or maybe "feeling." Or "controlling one's body." Most evolutionary biologists, however, are likely to disagree with all of these, pointing out that the adaptive significance of brains is both more basic and more multidimensional and complex: promoting the fitness of bodies within which they reside or, more precisely, the fitness of those genes that are responsible for producing the brains in question.

Brains may or may not be good at making sense of the world, or thinking great thoughts, or providing vivid subjective experiences to its possessors, or adroitly controlling their bodies. It is even possible, one can imagine, to be too brainy for one's own good, which brings up another story, this one told by the landscape architect Ian McHarg: It was the aftermath of World War III and our planet had been reduced to radioactive cinders. In the deepest recesses of the ocean, the few exiguous survivors—a motley group of primitive, amoeboid creatures—have just decided they are going to try once again, but before they separated, ready to initiate, once more, that old evolutionary process, they take a solemn vow: "This time, no brains!"

Brains, in short, can be a problem. For evolutionary biologists, they definitely are. The question is, "Why did our brains become so large, so quickly?" which often boils down to "How do/did they contribute to fitness?" The answers have not been easy to obtain. Or rather, they have been too forthcoming. Just as Mark Twain once pointed out that it was easy to stop smoking—he had done it hundreds of times!—it is easy to identify the adaptive significance of the extraordinarily large human brain: It has been done dozens of times.

As we'll see, there are hypotheses suggesting that human braininess is a result of selection for tool use, tool making, cooperative hunting, defense against predators, defense against other proto-humans, and so forth, not to mention the suggestion by Alfred

Russell Wallace that the elaborate functional complexity of our cerebrum, and especially its remarkable cognitive and artistic capacities, must be due to something supernatural (intelligent design for intelligence itself). There is also Stephen Jay Gould's patently absurd suggestion that our mental capacities must be a random, nonadaptive happenstance, specifically a result of "surplus" brain tissue.

Why is this absurd? For the same reason that evolutionary biologists agree that high intelligence and large brains need to be explained at all, in contrast to the assumption of most people that intelligence is always a good thing and therefore needn't be "explained." It is possible for natural processes to accumulate large quantities of stuff, like gravel at the base of a glacier, or fresh water flowing down a river, but not if the process is governed by natural selection, in which benefits must exceed costs. And a brain is very, very costly. Its 100 billion nerve cells are highly nonrandom, hooked together via perhaps 100 trillion carefully orchestrated connections. Such a device is devilishly difficult to encode, requiring more than its fair share of precious DNA. Moreover, even after it is constructed, the human brain is extraordinarily expensive to maintain.[1] It uses up an inordinate amount of metabolic energy: Although it occupies only about 2% of the body's weight, it accounts for roughly 20% of our total metabolism, compared to 10% or so for most mammals, including chimpanzees. If brain tissue has ever been surplus, it would long ago have been selected against, or turned into fat, not mental athleticism. (And although some people can be accused of being "fat-headed," this isn't the usual implication.)

For an animal like ourselves, a product of natural selection like all other living things, to have evolved a brain like this, we must have needed it very, very badly. But for what?

There is little doubt that brain size is importantly linked to intelligence as well as to other higher mental faculties. In 1935, J. A. Hamilton conducted laboratory-based breeding experiments, selecting for maze-bright and maze-dull rats. By the 12th generation of such artificial selection, the maze-bright and maze-dull strains had brain weights that differed by 2.5 standard deviations. This experiment is a sort of accelerated test of evolutionary change, showing a dramatic association between brain size and cognitive ability.[2]

On the other hand, although brain size generally correlates with intelligence, the pattern is not invariant. Albert Einstein, for example, had an unusually small brain, measured by volume . . . but not by output. And Neanderthals had larger brains than Cro-Magnon *Homo sapiens*, who eventually replaced them, perhaps via direct head-to-head (brain-to-brain?) competition. But Neanderthal brains were also constructed somewhat differently, with relatively fewer neurons in the frontal and prefrontal lobes, where higher intellectual pursuits evidently reside.

Primates are smaller bodied than many other mammalian groups, but even little ones such as squirrel monkeys are typically smarter than their big grazing cousins such as antelopes or giraffes. As a result, biologists interested in comparing the intellectual anatomy of different species have been inclined to employ, among various measures, one that reflects relative brain size and is known as the "encephalization quotient," defined as the ratio between actual brain mass and predicted brain mass for an animal of a given size. The encephalization quotient for reptiles is roughly 0.05; for birds, 0.75; for chimps, around 2.3; for gorillas, 1.6; and for people, 7.5. Hominid encephalization began increasing roughly about 1 million years ago, peaking roughly 35,000 to 20,000 years before the present. The modern human brain evolved not only in size, however, but also in complexity, such that it is fully three times the size of the chimpanzee brain, but has only a 25% advantage in the number of neurons. On the other hand, human brains have much higher numbers of synapses and interconnecting branches, such that it is often said that our brains are the most complex things in the universe (although in all fairness, we probably should consider who—or what—is telling us this "fact").

The picture is genuinely complex, almost as much as thought itself, but it is nonetheless clear that (1) within certain limits, there is a correlation between brain mass and overall intelligence and (2) both these traits increased quite dramatically in the course of human evolution. It is also clear that for this to have happened, smarter individuals must have somehow experienced a fitness advantage over those who were less intellectually endowed. Altogether unclear, however, is the basis for this advantage, although there are many contenders.

Tools and Language

We can start with some of the obvious ones. For a long time, it was believed that the use of tools was a unique human specialty, to the extent that the Latin term *Homo faber* ("man the maker" or "builder") had seriously been proposed. Moreover, it is easy to imagine that our ancestors' unusual skills in this regard could well have set up a kind of self-catalyzing positive feedback, in which those early proto-humans who were better able to employ tools—and who gained a distinct survival and reproductive advantage as a result—were likely smarter than their less handy fellows. The result was a neat conceptual scheme that explained the rapid evolution of human brains and intelligence.

Then Jane Goodall discovered that chimpanzees use sticks to "fish" for termites, which they avidly consume. Her mentor, Louis Leakey, was ecstatic at the news, responding that "Now we must redefine 'tool,' redefine 'man' or accept chimpanzees as humans." Those struggling to retain the status of human uniqueness without engaging any of Leakey's redefinitions quickly adopted a fallback position: Human beings were unique in *making* tools, not just using them. But then Goodall pointed out that prior to their tool-assisted fishing expeditions, chimps run their fingers along suitable sticks, removing leaves and twigs, thereby fashioning a bare implement all the better to insert into termite mounds. So much for the uniqueness of tool making. (Perhaps one benefit of recurring efforts to define human uniqueness is that they spur field primatologists to keep disproving the latest definitions!)

Even if neither tool use nor tool making is unique to *Homo sapiens*, there is no question that human beings are extraordinary among animals in the extent to which they create and employ tools, leading to the prospect that adroitness with tools constituted an important selective agent for increased intelligence and brain size. After all, we are physically modest creatures, lacking impressive canine teeth or claws, unable to fly or burrow rapidly underground, not especially fleet of foot, vulnerable to being killed and eaten by a range of predators, and not terribly well equipped to capture or kill other animals. It seems likely that intelligence helped make up for our numerous physical deficits: Those among our ancient primate ancestors who were smart enough to fashion and use tools—defined broadly to include weapons, digging implements, carrying devices for small vegetables or invertebrates, animal hides as primitive clothing, and so forth—would likely have experienced a distinct reproductive advantage. The result would be selection for intelligence and thus big brains.

There is, however, a problem. Fossil evidence now shows quite conclusively that our ancestors began using tools *before* they evolved especially large brains, although this finding isn't necessarily fatal to the hypothesized connection between tools and intelligence: Even if we started using tools as average-brained apes, once the "discovery" was made, the payoff associated with their manufacture and adroit use could still have generated a positive feedback loop that rapidly selected for high IQ.

A bigger problem, however, is that there are many other arenas wherein intelligence and evolutionary fitness seem likely to have been joined, making it difficult (perhaps impossible) to identify an evolutionary prime mover. Take language, which—like tool making—is often trumpeted as a defining human characteristic. As with tool making, there are animal examples that approach the human situation: for example, the famous "dance of the bees," by which these insects convey remarkably accurate information about food sources; the use of predator-specific alarm calls by certain primates (different vocalizations for aerial predator, ground predator, and snakes); and the presence of distinct vocal dialects passed along via learning from adult birds to nestlings. Nonetheless, and again as with tool making, there seems little doubt that the difference between human language and that of nonhuman animals is so great that it may well be qualitatively discontinuous.[3] Symbolic thought——a key component of thought generally—depends crucially upon language, such that the two may not even be separable.

In any event, whether a difference of kind or merely of degree, the extraordinary elaboration of human language—with its complex syntax and use of symbolic verbal structures—could very well have conferred a huge reproductive advantage upon those early hominids able to make good use of it. Language may even be our most important "tool." With language, we can plan ahead, explain the past, convey information, strategize with others, etc. It is easy to envisage scenarios by which those who had greater linguistic mastery also enjoyed greater evolutionary fitness. They would have been able to share information and to learn more efficiently, as well as to teach, to plan and strategize, and to coordinate their actions with a level of specificity and precision that simply is unavailable to creatures essentially limited to playing charades. As with the invention, deployment, and modification of tools, once language skills began to emerge, their existence could well have generated a positive feedback loop: In the newly established linguistic environment, there would presumably have been yet more payoff to those able to employ language effectively.

Even so, the precise evolutionary course whereby language skills evolved, and we along with them, remains obscure:

> To understand why humans are so intelligent, we need to understand how our ancestors remodeled the ape symbolic repertoire and enhanced it by inventing syntax. Wild chimpanzees use about three dozen different vocalizations to convey about three dozen different meanings. They may repeat a sound to intensify its meaning, but they don't string together three sounds to add a new word to their vocabulary.
>
> We humans also use about three dozen vocalizations, called phonemes. Yet only their combinations have content: we string together meaningless sounds to make meaningful words. No one has yet explained how our ancestors got over the hump of replacing "one sound/one meaning" with a sequential combinatorial system of meaningless phonemes, but it's probably one of the most important advances that happened during ape-to-human evolution.[4]

Traditionally, when trying to identify the evolutionary basis of human intelligence, researchers have focused on such payoffs as enhanced success in obtaining food, avoiding or defeating predators, surviving despite a challenging environment, and so forth. But there is also a darker possibility.

Competition and Climate

Perhaps the most threatening and important environmental challenge faced by our ancestors was . . . other people. We are now and presumably have always been group-living creatures, and it is entirely possible that intergroup competition (primitive warfare, possibly including cannibalism) exerted powerful selective pressures during the evolution of prehuman hominids. It is discouraging to contemplate the prospect that our crowning quality—our large brains and highly effective minds—may have evolved in the service of killing others of our own species or, at the least, keeping them from killing us.[5] But it is distressingly easy to posit ways in which this could have happened.

Other studies also point to a significant role for competition, although not necessarily revolving around primitive warfare as such. Thus, after examining 175 hominid craniums from 1.9 million to 10,000 years ago, one research team concluded that social competition—as inferred from population density—was key to the threefold increase in hominid brain size since *Homo habilis*.[6]

Other routes to human braininess have also been proposed. An interesting one connects human brain evolution to fluctuations in the earth's climate, and has been particularly championed by biologist/author William H. Calvin. In his book *A Brain for all Seasons*,[7] Calvin argues that we evolved intelligence as a way of coping with a rapidly changing physical environment. Earth's climate began fluctuating significantly about 10 million years ago, one consequence of which appears to have been the Ice Ages, starting around 2.5 million years ago. Another result is that as the earth became drier and cooler, the tropical forests that had previously covered much of northern and eastern Africa began to retreat, transitioning first into savannah and grassland, and in some parts, to desert. Animals that had been adapted to arboreal life had to adapt; included among these were our ancestors, who evolved bipedalism, perhaps as a way of standing up among the grasses and thus freeing their hands for gathering food and for using weapons and other tools.

It is conceivable, as well, that a little-appreciated aspect of savannah life contributed in its own independent way to the evolution of human intelligence: Seeing potential prey as well as predators from a distance could have selected for an ability to anticipate events and plan ahead. Such visually based opportunities were not likely experienced by forest-dwelling creatures, whose encounters are more immediate and thus unplanned. At the same time, adopting a ground-dwelling lifestyle would probably have made our ancestors more vulnerable to predation by big cats, hyenas, and so forth, which in itself would have put an evolutionary premium on those early hominids best able to cope with these threats. And if nothing else, intelligence would seem to fit the bill as a multipurpose "coping mechanism."

Calvin argues that intelligence can be defined as effective adaptation to the environment, and that the early hominid environment required a whole lot of prompt adaptation:

> Although Africa was cooling and drying as upright posture was becoming established 4 million years ago, brain size didn't change much. The fourfold expansion of the hominid brain did not start until the ice ages began, 2.5 million years ago. Ice cores from Greenland show frequent abrupt cooling episodes superimposed on the more stately rhythms of ice advance and retreat. Whole forests disappeared within several decades because of drastic drops in temperature and rainfall. The warm rains returned with equal suddenness several centuries later. The evolution of anatomical adaptations in the hominids could not have kept pace with these abrupt climate changes, which would have occurred within the lifetime of single individuals. But these environmental fluctuations could have promoted the incremental accumulation of new mental abilities that conferred greater behavioral flexibility.

There is a growing consensus among atmospheric scientists that the earth experienced a series of dramatic, even catastrophic heating and cooling within the last few million years. The mechanism is complex, involving interruptions of the thermohaline circulation of the North Atlantic as a result of increased freshening of its water, which in turn can be a consequence of brief but intense periods of global warming. The pattern, then, would entail heating (presumably nonanthropogenic) followed by dramatic and possibly even catastrophic *cooling*. The argument goes that such "whiplash" climate cycles drove selection for large brains insofar as they conferred the ability to adapt to rapidly changing environments. If, for example, rapid cooling produced lots of grassland, this would have resulted in a relative abundance of large grazing animals, which, in turn, would have selected for the now-familiar "man the hunter" lifestyle.

In a very real sense, human culture—defined broadly, to include everything that we transmit nongenetically—is our most important biological adaptation, and pretty much whatever contributed to our ancestors' ability to generate, employ, and transmit culture would have been selected for, with intelligence being a necessary substrate. Culture is not necessarily opposed to biology; rather, it is humanity's primary biological adaptation. The same may be true of intelligence. Moreover, it is a good bet that intelligence and culture are intimately related: Intelligence is a prerequisite for us to pick up whatever culture we are born into or migrate into. Hence, it may be highly significant that human beings are both the cultural creatures par excellence and the world's most intelligent.

We may also be the only animals to have been substantially affected by group selection, a process that could well have been directly involved in the evolution of human intelligence. Thus, the payoffs associated particularly with enhanced communication and the teaching and learning of new skills could have enabled proto-humans to outcompete other groups lacking such skills and the benefits they provide. Closely allied to this is the reality of Lamarckian, nongenetic transfer of information, another payoff to intelligence, and one that could have rebounded not only to the benefit of individuals and genes but also to groups.

When it comes to asking "Why did human beings evolve to be so intelligent?" we are left, therefore, with an abundance of suspects. This isn't necessarily a bad thing, since unlike investigators in a criminal case, those of us trying to solve the mystery of human intelligence are under no pressure to pin the rap on a single perpetrator. Maybe there were many.

Here are some other suspects.

Sex and the Brain

When looking for the adaptive value of intelligence, researchers traditionally think in terms of its contribution to survival (hence hypotheses based on tools, language, environmental adaptation, warlike competition among groups, etc.). It is also possible, however, that much of our vaunted intellect evolved as a result of sexual selection. Earlier, we considered the suggestion—especially associated with evolutionary psychologist Geoffrey Miller—that the human capacity for and appreciation of the arts is attributable to mate choice, specifically the interaction between showing off and choosing the best possible mates.

Miller's hypothesis was not developed with an eye toward explaining the arts, but rather as a way of solving the mystery of human intelligence more generally. The idea is that since brains are expensive, any traits—such as artistic or linguistic skills—that require big brains and hence intelligence would have been selected for as a fitness indicator. The result would therefore have been more intelligent descendents sporting bigger brains, not so much because of any practical, survival-related benefit of intelligence as such, but because their ancestors had impressed members of the opposite sex with their overall genetic quality, perhaps including disease and parasite resistance. In the process, badges of physical fitness would have morphed into traits conferring evolutionary fitness as well, through the mediation of sexual choice. It is possible, as well, that studies measuring heritability of intelligence are at least in part measuring heritability of disease resistance instead.[8]

If theorists such as Miller are correct, then intelligence was favored not so much because of its intrinsic merits, but because it offers a relatively unfakeable and thus honest signal of biological sturdiness[9]—a bit of a takedown for those of us who value intelligence as an end in itself.

In this regard, it is worth noting that taxonomic groupings that contain large numbers of especially smart animals such as cephalopods, elephants, and apes typically aren't notably abundant or ecologically successful in other respects. Maybe intelligence isn't all that it is cracked up to be. As we have already seen—and as the sexual selection hypothesis requires—brains are very costly. Since larger brains are found only in creatures with larger bodies, perhaps those larger brained (hence, more intelligent) animals such as ourselves are successful because of our body size plus our opposable thumbs rather than our brainpower. After all, dinosaurs were successful for tens of millions of years—far longer than *Homo sapiens* have yet prospered—and their brains were notoriously unimpressive.

Maybe the evaluative deck is stacked in favor of those people who already value intelligence, perhaps more than it deserves. Thus, *Homo sapiens* who concern themselves with the adaptive value of big brains and heady intellection are especially likely to be those in universities, research institutes, or other avowedly intellectual communities, including the "intelligent reading public" so beloved of book publishers such as Oxford University Press, and who are therefore likely to be strongly represented among those reading this book. But what if intelligence isn't the immense asset that most of us in these communities like to think?

Here, accordingly, is some food for thought: At present, high intelligence correlates with *decreased* reproductive success.[10] This may or may not have implications for human beings of the future, but nonetheless, it probably doesn't detract from the generalization that among people in the past, intelligence and evolutionary fitness were evidently closely and positively linked for a million or more years, during which hominids were evolving such large brains, and becoming us.

If the sexual selection theorists are correct, one wonders as well about the situation of ancestral women. Although both sexes can be expected to have exercised preference for smart sexual partners (in fact, this was likely true even if survival selection rather than sexual selection was the driving force), women would have been uniquely stuck with a major *negative* consequence of such a choice. Women, not men, get pregnant and give birth. And because of our species' penchant for bipedalism,[ii] the human birth canal has been substantially and dangerously narrowed over evolutionary time, such that selection for increased head size has literally bumped up against the anatomically mandated narrowing of women's pelvic girdle. Most quadrupeds drape their internal organs from their backbones, like salamis hanging in a butcher shop. But with bipedalism, the human pelvis has necessarily rotated, partly to provide basinlike support for our abdominal organs but in the process, restricting the birth canal. As a tragic result, one of the most common sources of perinatal morbidity and mortality is "cephalopelvic disproportion," when the baby's head is too large for the mother's pelvic opening.

Earlier, we encountered a Goldilocks hypothesis, whereby men were hypothesized to choose women whose breasts and thus

---

ii. A phenomenon that poses its own evolutionary mystery, while also likely contributing to the role of tools: By becoming bipedal, a species frees its forelimbs for possible use of tools. At the same time, there are other possible evolutionary drivers for bipedalism, including enhanced line of sight, ability to appear larger and thus intimidate predators as well as other humans, even presenting a diminished target for the tropical sun's potentially dangerous rays.

reproductive prospects were "just right." When it comes to female choice of intelligent men as sexual partners, Goldilocks just might have been at it again, generating babies whose heads are large—probably as large as possible. But not too large. Just right.

Other ideas also concern themselves with a possibly disproportionate role of women—specifically, mothers—in selecting for human intelligence, aside from choosing their reproductive partners. For example, if maternal intelligence contributes substantially to reducing childhood and infant mortality, this could itself select for greater intelligence—for people generally and for intelligence in women most especially.[11] This smart-mother hypothesis requires that childhood mortality rates are otherwise high, which they certainly were during most of our evolutionary history. It also assumes an inverse correlation between maternal IQ and childhood mortality, which also appears valid,[12] although this line of thought is inconsistent with the fact that there is currently an inverse relationship between maternal IQ and reproductive success in modern technological societies.[13] One can nonetheless argue that such a correlation was likely obtained during the 99.99% of our evolutionary past when most of our humanness evolved.[iii]

When discussing a different evolutionary mystery—menopause—in Chapter 3, we looked into the possibility that the prolongation of human childhood may have been intimately connected to the termination of women's reproduction and the consequent ability and inclination of grandmothers in particular to help care for their grandchildren. It may be equally valid to reverse this association and consider that human intelligence may owe much to our prolonged childhood, which is lengthier than that of any other primate.[14] If so, then our intelligence also owes much to mothers as well as grandmothers, whose attentiveness would have helped select for our extended juvenile period, a time during which we almost literally fill our brains with the stuff of experience and thus of intelligence (fathers, too, or at least so I'd like to think).

---

iii. This leads to the paradoxical possibility that when it comes to deciding upon the adaptive basis of our intelligence, intelligence itself may be an impediment, insofar as it induces us to come up with too damned many hypotheses, as well as counterarguments for each, followed by counter-counterarguments, ad infinitum.

Assortative mating—in which "like prefers like"—could amplify this tendency: Males who are smarter could presumably have been more effective resource and protection providers as well as teachers of their children. If they mated with females who were especially good at keeping their offspring safe, as well as obtaining and preparing optimum nutrition and also providing them enhanced learning opportunities, the resulting positive feedback could have contributed substantially to the evolution of intelligent offspring. This effect may well have become even more pronounced as early human ancestors migrated "out of Africa," since inclinations leading to survival and success in the Pleistocene environment where much human evolution occurred would presumably have been strongly selected for and could well have become "instinctively" fixed. It is when our ancestors encountered a new environment (Ice Age Europe and Asia, the discovery of agriculture, urbanization, and so forth) that maternal as well as paternal IQ would have become especially relevant.

Social Intelligence

When we referred previously to "social competition" as a possible driver of increased human brain size and intelligence, the implication—as with hypotheses invoking primitive warfare—was that the key interactions were those taking place between competing groups. There is another array of emerging hypotheses that also point toward social competition, but of another sort: within-group and mostly nonviolent. The term of art is social intelligence,[15] and in its sneakier form, "Machiavellian intelligence."[16]

The key point here is that social living is a two-edged sword. On the one hand, it provides many opportunities not available to those whose lives are more solitary: taking advantage of strength in numbers when it comes to catching prey (think about wolves pulling down a moose), keeping predators at bay (including perhaps other groups of the same species), sharing information and expertise, and so forth. But on the other hand, social life has its downsides: the need to share food or other important resources, increased risk of disease transmission, and so forth. It also sets up numerous hurdles as well as opportunities for success, since social living establishes its own complicated array of challenges.

Zoologist Richard D. Alexander put it succinctly (albeit with perhaps more certainty than such a complex subject warrants):

> The real challenge in the human environment throughout history that affected the evolution of the intellect was not climate, weather, food shortages, or parasites—not even predators. Rather, it was the necessity of dealing continually with our fellow humans in social circumstances that became ever more complex and unpredictable as the human line evolved.[17]

Natural selection operates for the most part on the reproductive success of individuals and their constituent genes rather than for the good of the group as a whole. As a result, there is a constant tug-of-war among individuals (and their genes), each struggling to maximize its payoff, and not necessarily someone else's. This issue is ameliorated, but definitely not eliminated, by the fact that maximum success is often achieved by cooperating rather than competing—because insofar as cooperation is motivated by the payoff available to each participating individual, every individual is nonetheless motivated by considerations of personal advantage. In other words, even while cooperating, individuals will have been selected to maximize their benefit in doing so. If this sounds Machiavellian, then welcome to the Machiavellian hypothesis for the evolution of intelligence, which basically says that intelligence has arisen because of the payoff to individuals who are able to evaluate social situations and come up with their personally optimal responses. And this process in turn is recursive, since it conveys a benefit to those who are able to detect the self-serving maneuvers of others and use them to enhance one's own situation—or at least, to keep one's payoff from being diminished as a result.

The result is survival and success of the socially adept and thus mutually beneficent, as well as of the cunning and manipulative and thus diabolically self-serving. For example, social intelligence promotes differential reproduction of those who are able to establish useful coalitions to defend their interest and compensate, perhaps, for a lack of size or strength by making strategically helpful alliances with others who are equally intelligent.

Nonhuman primates engage in an almost dizzying variety of complicated social calculations, including short-term bonds for mating as well as long-term associations (essentially, friendships) based on the status, need, and potential contributions of all participants. A dazzling series of field experiments conducted among free-living baboons, for example, showed that individuals are able to assess social dominance as well as the genetic relationships of others in their troop and to keep these traits in mind, juggling the pros and cons of various actions accordingly.[18]

For social intelligence to be directly selected for, it is also necessary that social success correlate positively with reproductive success, something that seems intuitively likely, and that has been demonstrated convincingly in a research report whose title well describes its key finding: "Social Bonds of Female Baboons Enhance Infant Survival."[19] In short, individuals who succeed in effectively navigating the complexities of social life are those who succeed in getting copies of their genes projected into the future. Although our antecedents were not baboons, it seems more than likely that a similar process occurred in ancestral human beings.

Social success—and thus reproductive success—likely correlates double-fold with the ability to employ high levels of rational thought. Of these payoffs, the obvious one relates to direct benefits of simply being smart: ability to anticipate future events, deal with present ones, adjust one's behavior to that of one's colleagues and competitors, and so forth.

But a possible secondary benefit might also be involved: the payoff in terms of social prestige and dominance of simply being able to defeat one's enemies (and friends) when it comes to argumentation. Thus, the possibility exists that rationality and the ability to express one's most cogent thoughts in the social arena have evolved not because such a capability permits the speaker and listener to approach greater insight into the actual nature of the world, but rather, to help catapult those especially good at rational arguing into positions of success and power.[20] Maybe what's really being favored is the ability to impress others, or even to bamboozle them. Machiavellian indeed.

Much attention has also focused on the ability to detect cheaters. For biologists, cheating means pretty much what it means for everyone else: failure to abide by the rules, in a way that gives oneself a higher payoff than fairly entitled. Much social life involves exchanges, if not of actual items, then of attention, assistance, time and energy, and obtaining benefits as well as assuming costs and running risks. And sadly, in the process, there is a strong temptation to take more than one gives. It may be in the interest of a wolf, for example, to get a nice big chunk of moose meat, but at the same time, to hold back just a little when it comes to actually killing the moose, letting others take on the more risky duties. Achieving an optimal payoff almost certainly requires a degree of pro-social intelligence (to function adequately within the constraints and opportunities of a pack), along with Machiavellian intelligence, to deceive one's pack mates when possible, as well as to detect the wiles of would-be deceivers and avoid being suckered by them.

When Shakespeare wrote in *As You Like It* that "the dullness of the fool is the whetstone of the wits," this may be one of the very few cases in which his particular wit fell short—at least as devotees of the Machiavellian intelligence hypothesis see it: It is more likely that the sneaky, manipulative, high-grade intelligence of our smartest, most Machiavellian colleagues has been the whetstone of our own.

An especially important social exchange involves what is known as "reciprocal altruism," essentially "you scratch my back, I'll scratch yours." It provides an important route whereby natural selection can favor apparent altruism, even between individuals who are not genetic relatives. I say "apparent altruism" because a true reciprocal exchange actually isn't altruistic at all, since everyone ends up ahead: The initial beneficiary is helped, and then, when the situation calls for it, he or she repays the favor, so that the original back-scratcher gets its needs met, too.

The problem—and for many species and situations it is an insurmountable one—is that such exchange systems are vulnerable to cheaters, individuals who accept aid but then do not reciprocate. In fact, despite the fact that reciprocal altruism seems theoretically feasible, only rarely has it been clearly demonstrated in animals— presumably because of the ubiquitous temptation to cheat. Human beings are a notable exception: We are reciprocators par excellence, and it is at least possible—indeed, likely—that natural selection has favored a high level of intelligence in *Homo sapiens* as a way of countering the Machiavellian tendency to cheat, by endowing us with the ability to identify individuals and to hold them socially accountable. Just as selection could have favored a particular kind of Machiavellian intelligence that facilitates conniving and cheating, it could also have favored the additional intelligence needed to assess the trustworthiness of others and to hold them to a fair standard.

There are other aspects of social intelligence that might have been selected for among our ancestors, essentially as a complex, multifaceted response to the diverse challenges of social living, of which Machiavellian considerations are but one component. Anthropologist and evolutionary psychologist Robin Dunbar has made the argument that as group size increases, natural selection for greater intelligence—particularly, social intelligence—is likely to have intensified. In addition to the cleverness needed to compete and cooperate successfully in large social groups within which interactions are intense, increases in group size exert substantial pressure simply to keep the details and nuances of many different relationships in mind at the same time.

The issue is less fraught when social groups are essentially homogeneous, as we assume is the case with, for example, a school of herring. But when groups are highly structured and heterogeneous, with individuals recognizable as individuals, carrying with them the weight of their particular qualities as potential coalition members, competitors, mates, genetic relatives, etc., the payoff to ability to retain and juggle these relationships—that is, to be socially intelligent—increases.

Group size is essentially a proxy for social complexity; as group size increases, the number of possible interactions increases geometrically. So if intelligence evolved because of the payoff it provides in solving social problems, there should be a positive correlation between group size and brain size. There is. Dunbar has shown that neocortex size varies directly with group size in many mammals.[21] Small-brained monkeys tend to have simple social structures, baboons experience more complex social groupings and have larger brains, and chimps more so yet. And human beings? The most, and the largest. Dunbar also suggested that physical grooming, as found among nearly all nonhuman primates, eventually gave rise to language among human beings, since both activities serve to modulate interactions among individuals. As Dunbar sees it, when early human social groupings became too large for ancestral humans to keep track of each other via direct physical contact, evolution favored the ability to maintain "contact" verbally, via language, and with it, dramatically increased intelligence and brain size.

An interesting hypothesis, this, but once again, not quite a "slam dunk." For one thing, social insects, for example, have complex social relationships but very simple brains and a "language" that is chemical rather than verbal. In addition, who is to say that the correlation didn't proceed in the other direction, with higher intelligence having evolved for some other reason or reasons, itself making social relationships more complex? This could be because as individuals became smarter, their interactions would likely have become more sophisticated and elaborate, conferring yet more benefit upon those who were smart enough to navigate these complexities effectively. If so, then instead of social complexity being a cause of intelligence, it might have arisen largely as a result.

Just as most biologists agree that the generation of diversity is quite likely the major adaptive significance of sex, maybe the adaptive value of intelligence is that it allows us to cope with diversity and complexity in general, whether environmental or social. If so, it is also paradoxically the case that intelligence itself may generate diversity—at least, diversity within social settings—which in turn creates an interpersonal environment that favors yet more intelligence.

The boundaries may well be porous and indistinct between selection for intelligence as a result of social pressures and selection for intelligence as a means of prospering in a given ecological niche. If our ancestors grew smart as a consequence of selection for ability to master difficult habitats, there is no reason to doubt that evolution could eventually have transferred mastery over the environment to mastery over other individuals in the same group and, via primitive warfare and intergroup competition, between different groups as well. In a similar process, it is widely agreed that certain dinosaurs initially evolved feathers as an aid to thermoregulation, after which selection acted on these devices to achieve a new payoff: flight, and a new group of animals, called birds. Maybe our own soaring intellects and flights of imagination were similarly achieved, having evolved initially in response to one kind of payoff (involving ecological challenges) and then later transferred into another (involving social challenges).

Domain Specificity

There is a common thread connecting the above "social intelligence" hypotheses, namely, the supposition that aside from potentially direct survival benefits vis-à-vis obtaining food, avoiding predators, and competing mano-á-mano with other proto-human groups, we evolved our intellects at least in part in the context of living complex and demanding social lives. And this approach, in turn, fits with an important emerging concept: that our brains have not evolved as all-purpose, generic, logical problem solvers. Rather, human mental functioning is increasingly seen by evolutionary psychologists as divided into a toolkit of diverse and distinct mental modalities, each adapted to solve a particular kind of survival-and-reproduction challenge.

Even among psychologists whose orientation is distinctly nonevolutionary,[iv] there has long been serious debate about whether anything like generalized intelligence exists at all. Beyond the discussion of such things as "emotional intelligence" and the distinction between performance IQ and components of intelligence associated with verbal or mathematical capabilities, the perspective of evolutionary psychologists in particular is that human intelligence is essentially divided into various "domain-specific" modes. John Tooby and Leda Cosmides have been especially vigorous in promoting this approach, with a series of studies demonstrating that people are endowed with intelligence designed to detect cheaters in situations of social exchange, as opposed to conditions of pure logic.[22]

We have already noted that the human mind did not develop as a calculator designed to solve logical problems. Rather, it evolved for a very limited purpose, one that is ultimately no different from

---

iv. And I must concede, regretfully, that such psychologists still exist. My hope is that eventually the term "evolutionary psychology" will disappear, with the recognition that all psychology has to be evolutionary. Not yet, however.

that of the heart, lungs, or kidneys; that is, the job of the brain is simply to enhance the reproductive success of the body within which it resides (and in the process, to promote the success of the genes that produced the body, brain and all).

This is the biological purpose of every mind, human as well as animal, and moreover, it is its *only* purpose. The purpose of the heart is to pump blood, the lungs exchange oxygen and carbon dioxide, and the kidneys work to eliminate toxic chemicals. The brain's purpose is to direct our internal organs and our external behavior in a way that maximizes our evolutionary success. That's it. Given this, it is remarkable that the human mind is good at solving any problems whatsoever, beyond "Who should I mate with?" "What is that guy up to?" "How can I help my kid?" and "Where are the antelopes hanging out at this time of year?" There is nothing in the biological specifications for brain building that calls for a device capable of high-powered logical reasoning, or solving abstract problems, or even providing an accurate picture of the "outside" world, beyond what is needed to enable its possessors to thrive and reproduce.

Here is a particularly revealing example, known as the Wason Test. Most people's performance on this simple test reveals a pronounced inability to solve a simple logical problem, combined with remarkable cleverness when the same situation is reframed as a variant in one's socio-Machiavellian intelligence.

Imagine that you are confronted with four cards. Each has a letter of the alphabet on one side and a number on the other. You are also told this rule: If there is a vowel on one side, there must be an even number on the other. Your job is to determine which (if any) of the cards must be turned over to determine whether the rule is being followed. However, you must only turn over those cards that *require* being turned. Let's say that the four cards are as follows:

S   4   A   7

Which ones should you turn over? (Remember, you want to assess this rule: If there is a vowel on one side, there must be an even number on the other.)

Most people realize that they don't have to inspect the other side of card "S." However, a large proportion respond that the "4" should be inspected. They are wrong: The rule says that if one side is a vowel, the other must be an even number, but nothing about whether an even number must be accompanied by a vowel. (The side opposite a "4" could be a vowel or a consonant; either way, the rule is not violated.) Most people also agree that the "A" must be turned over, since if the other side is not an even number, the rule would be violated. But many people do not realize that the "7" must also be inspected: if its flipside is a vowel, then the rule is violated. So, the correct answer to the above Wason Test is that "S" and "4" should not be turned over, but "A" and "7" should be. Don't feel badly if you had trouble with this; fewer than 20% of respondents get it right.

Next, consider this puzzle. You are a bartender at a nightclub where the legal drinking age is 21. Your job is to make sure that this rule is followed: People younger than 21 must not be drinking alcohol. Toward that end, you can ask individuals their age, or check what they are drinking, but you are required not to be any more intrusive than is absolutely necessary. You are confronted with four different situations, as shown below. In which case (if any) should you ask a patron his or her age or find out what beverage is being consumed?

#1	#2	#3	#4
Drinking Juice	Over 21	Drinking Beer	Under 21

Nearly everyone finds this problem easy. You needn't check the age of person #1, the juice drinker. Similarly, there is no reason to examine the beverage of person #2, who is older than 21. But obviously, you had better check the age of person #3, who is drinking beer, just as you need to check the beverage of person #4, who is underage. The point is that this problem set—which is nearly always answered correctly—is logically identical to the earlier set, the one that causes considerable head scratching, not to mention incorrect answers.

Why are the second problems so easy, and the first so difficult? Cosmides and Tooby, who have extensively researched different variants on these two problems, conclude that the key isn't logic itself—after all, they are logically identical—but how they are positioned in a world of sociobiological reality. Thus, whereas the first is a matter of pure logic, disconnected from the real world, the second plays into issues of truth telling and the detection of social cheaters. The human mind, Cosmides and Tooby point out, is not adapted to solve rarified problems of logic, but is quite refined and powerful when it comes to dealing with matters of cheating and deception.[23]

The card example just described is a special case of the more general phenomenon, known as a "conditional rule." Such rules are simple statements, familiar to logicians: "If P then Q." The rule is violated if, in a given situation, P is true and at the same time, Q is false. There are lots of ways of stating such conditional rules, all of which are more or less familiar: for example, "If some-one lives in Miami, he or she experiences warm weather"; "If someone loves chocolates, then he or she will buy some on the way home"; "If someone is skiing, then it is winter." It turns out that only about 25% of subjects do a good job of detecting violations of such rules. On the other hand, if the rule is something like this— "If you attend a movie, you must buy a ticket"—then people are much better at detecting violations: About 75% get it right!

Once again, people tend to perform poorly at the Wason task, except when it is presented in terms of possible rule violation—not violations of rules of logic, but of rules governing social exchange. The take-home message here seems to be that when it comes to the evolution of our "higher mental faculties," an important driv-ing force has involved protecting a potential cooperator from being exploited by someone who takes without giving (thus violat-ing the expectations of reciprocity) or who simply doesn't play by the rules of social exchange.

Those rules are important, and not simply when it comes to good manners. Indeed, good manners themselves are important precisely because they indicate that someone can be trusted. Second only to interactions among family members (kin selection), it appears that being a reliable reciprocator is the cornerstone of social life. As Yogi Berra reputedly summed it up (sort of): "Always go to other people's funerals, or else they won't come to yours."

Food for Thought?

As yet, no one can say exactly how important the "social brain" and Machiavellian intelligence have been, and how they stack up against the various other drivers of human intelligence. Ironically, a problem with these hypotheses is that they are, if anything, too plausible. If human intelligence skyrocketed because our ancestors lived in social groups surrounded by other, comparable individuals, each with his or her agenda, and which in turn drove the evolution of elaborate mental capacities so as to maneuver effectively in such fraught interpersonal traffic, why didn't the same thing happen to other species? Wild horses and wildebeest live in large social groups: Why haven't they evolved minds as sapient as ours along with fancy brains to undergird them? And what about ants?

Here's a possible answer: Maybe the driving forces behind human intelligence were multifactorial, a perfect storm of several different adaptive pressures and opportunities, no one of which would have been sufficient in itself but which, combined, produced those intellects we so proudly identify as quintessentially ours. Maybe being essentially weak bodied turned out to be a paradoxical asset, inducing our more intelligent forebears to be favored over the duller ones. Maybe the elaboration of language, combined with discovery of tools, added to rapidly changing environments, along with vigorous competition (potentially warlike as well as more subtle, within-group), plus sexually selected preferences . . . all added up to a unique and intelligence-favoring configuration of circumstances that simply didn't arise for other species.[v]

If so, then we should also consider yet another possible driver— or at least, facilitator—of human intelligence: cooking. *Cooking?*

It's less weird than you think. Cooking is intimately connected to fire, the "conquest" of which has long been intuited as crucial, although until recently, its actual biological payoff was obscure. Primatologist Richard Wrangham (a student of Jane Goodall) has proposed that it isn't fire as such, but cooking that made us human, big brains and all.[24]

Wrangham points out that the greatest change in brain size leading to *Homo sapiens* occurred in the transition from *Homo habilis* to *Homo erectus*. And perhaps not coincidentally, ancestral jaws,

---

v. After all, if they had, then presumably we would be intelligent kangaroos or codfish or penguins, basking in our cleverness all the while tasking that cleverness to try to figure out how it arose!

teeth, and intestines became smaller at the same time that our brains got bigger.

Cooked food increases food safety by killing pathogens; it expands and enhances taste and retards spoilage. It enables us to eat foods that would otherwise be simply too tough. But none of these advantages is as important as a little-appreciated aspect: Cooking increases the amount of energy our bodies obtain from food. "The extra energy," Wrangham argues,

> gave the first cooks biological advantages. They survived and reproduced better than before. Their genes spread. Their bodies responded by biologically adapting to cooked food, shaped by natural selection to take maximum advantage of the new diet. There were changes in anatomy, physiology, ecology, life history, psychology and society.

As Wrangham sees it, by cooking meat or plants or both, digestion was facilitated, allowing our guts to grow smaller and more efficient. It would also have modified our time and energy budgets. Thus, he calculates that if our ancestors were limited to raw food—much of it only barely digestible and whose calories and nutrients are otherwise largely unavailable—they would have been obligated to spend many hours each day just chewing. There are animals, of course, who do just that: cattle, howler monkeys, and tree sloths, for example. Clearly, not all animals require the high-quality, nutrient-dense foods that cooking made available to our forebears. Termites do quite well digesting cellulose. But they aren't very intelligent, or rather, their cleverness is limited to their evolved biochemical techniques of breaking down wood.

Digestion itself requires far more energy than most people imagine. By getting much of that energy from fire and using it instead of our own bodily resources to unlock much of the nutritional value in food, ancestral cooks freed up additional energy to grow big brains, which, as we have noted, consume enormous amounts of energy. One can spin the story farther, as Wrangham does: Fire's warmth would have facilitated our shedding body hair, which in turn enabled us to run farther without overheating. Instead of eating on the run or at the immediate scene of a kill or patch of yummy tubers, we would have gathered around a cooking fire, thereby perhaps emphasizing the need for benevolent socialization—maybe even table manners. Insofar as the cooking fire also provided protection, it might have enabled our ancestors to sleep on the ground instead of in the trees, while further terrestrial adaptations—such as bipedalism—could have facilitated additional tool use and the ability to carry food, wood, tools, babies, and so on. The cooking hypothesis has the added benefit of reversing the standard assumption—namely, that human beings created technology—by suggesting that technology created human beings. We cook, therefore we are . . . smart.

Of course, all this is sheer speculation, but if you have read thus far, you know that speculation hasn't kept us from hypothesizing in other respects.

Pressing on, further speculation suggests that not all the impacts of primitive cooking would have been salubrious. In particular, Wrangham proposes that if cooking became a female specialty, it might have contributed to the social subordination of women, insofar as they were expected to stay home and prepare dinner while the men went off in search of cookables. Of course, it could also be argued that under this "Homo cooker" scenario, women—as guardians of the crucial kitchen—would have become more central and thus more important, rather than less. A bigger problem with this hypothesis, however, is that there is no evidence, as yet, that early *Homo erectus* actually used fire.

Wrangham's cooking hypothesis does not exhaust the possible linkage between human intelligence and nutrition. A highly regarded quartet of anthropologists from the University of New Mexico has suggested a model that makes explicit use of some of the distinctive landmarks in human life history.[25] Making a long and convoluted story short, their argument is that the human life pattern, compared to other mammals in general and primates in particular, is distinctive in experiencing a very long life span, extended time of juvenile dependence, assistance in childrearing provided by older postreproductive individuals (many of them relatives), and male assistance in childrearing. Our species is also distinctive, of course, in being very intelligent, which leads the four anthropologists to suggest that these phenomena are connected.

As they see it, the crucial factor uniting the four key life history traits to high intelligence is a dietary shift toward "high-quality, nutrient-dense, and difficult-to-acquire food resources." The logic, in the scientists' own words, is as follows:

> First, high levels of knowledge, skill, coordination, and strength are required to exploit the suite of high-quality, difficult-to-acquire resources humans consume. The attainment of those abilities requires time and a significant commitment to development. This extended learning phase, during which productivity is low, is compensated for by higher productivity during the adult period and an intergenerational flow of food from old to young. Because productivity increases with age, the investment of time in acquiring skill and knowledge leads to selection for lowered mortality rates and greater longevity. The returns on investments in development occur at older ages. This, in turn, favors a longer juvenile period if there are important gains in produc-tive ability with body size and growth ceases at sexual maturity.
>
> Second, we believe that the feeding niche that involves specializ-ing on large, valuable food packages promotes food sharing, provi-sioning of juveniles, and increased grouping, all of which act to lower mortality during the juvenile and early adult periods. Food sharing and provisioning assist recovery in times of illness and reduce risk by limiting juvenile time allocation to foraging. Grouping also lowers predation risks. These buffers against mortality also favor a longer juvenile period and higher investment in other mechanisms to increase the life span.
>
> Thus, we propose that the long human life span co-evolved with lengthening of the juvenile period, increased brain capacities for information processing and storage, and intergenerational resource flows, all as a result of an important dietary shift. Humans are special-ists in that they consume only the highest-quality plant and animal resources in their local ecology and rely on creative, skill-intensive techniques to exploit them. Yet the capacity to develop new tech-niques for extractive foraging and hunting allows them to exploit a wide variety of different foods and to colonize all of earth's terrestrial and coastal ecosystems.

As complex and resourceful as it is, the human mind—whatever the selection forces that caused it to evolve—also possesses a stub-born fondness for simple, unitary explanations. And this, in turn, generates resistance to multifactorial models such as this one! But the fact that our minds often prefer simple interpretations (e.g., that the earth is flat, that the sun moves through the sky, etc.) doesn't make them true. When it comes to its adaptive value, moreover, the human brain evolved to promote its own reproductive success, and not with any mandate of understanding itself. Best to be patient, therefore. As with the other hypotheses we have considered thus far, the final word on cooking as well as the role of nutrition and life history parameters has not been spoken. Or written. And perhaps not even imagined.

Purloined Intelligence?

Finally, we need to confront the most obvious possible adaptive value of intelligence, one that might be called the Purloined Letter hypothesis, after the short story by Edgar Allan Poe, in which the police tore apart someone's apartment, seeking in vain a letter that was "hidden in plain sight"—right there on the suspect's desk, and thus so obvious that it was overlooked. The idea is simply that greater intelligence was selected for because it led to higher survival (and thus reproduction). Much cynical amusement is generated, at least in modern times, by the so-called "Darwin Awards," in which people get themselves killed as a result of behaving stupidly. And indeed, it is at least a reasonable hypothesis that there is—or at least, was—a correlation at the other end of the population distribution as well: Smarter people may indeed have survived and reproduced more successfully than stupid ones, independent of their social or Machiavellian intelligence.[26]

But wouldn't such pressures apply to all living things? And if so, why don't we observe highly intelligent earthworms, oysters, or even radishes? For one thing, intelligence is expensive as we have already noted; it requires a complex and metabolically costly brain. And for another, it is at least possible that human beings are uniquely intelligent because we have placed ourselves on a path where high intelligence has become uniquely valuable, even necessary.

The evolution of technology, for example, while providing early *Homo sapiens* with distinct evolutionary advantages, may well have also subjected our ancestors to distinct risks: Cutting themselves with their ingenious tools, endangering themselves by their newfound ability to confront and (usually but not always) overcome other large animals, constructing structures that provide shelter but also the risk of collapsing on their builders, and so forth. As Spider Man aficionados often point out, with great power comes great responsibility . . . and also an increased risk that some people—likely, the least intelligent—will screw up.

If so, then human beings might have created for themselves a kind of one-way ratchet, with the increasing complexity of their own innovations being not only a consequence of their intelligence but also amplifying the importance of such intelligence as a survival mechanism. The rapid spread of early human ancestors from our African birthplace throughout the world could also have enhanced the import of intelligence as a straightforward Darwinian benefit, especially as our great-, great-grandparents encountered a wide range of new and challenging environments, from desert and forest to mountain and oceanside. All the while, the Darwinian, reproductive impact of smart survivors versus stupid losers would have been enhanced by the fact that early mortality on the part of the latter would also have left their orphaned offspring with lower survival and reproductive prospects, a kind of evolutionary double jeopardy.

Consciousness

We have been concerned thus far with intelligence rather than with consciousness. The two are doubtless related, however, in that both rely upon complex neural architecture, such that it is easy to assume that they are inextricably connected. But it ain't necessarily so. Computers, for example, are highly intelligent. They can defeat the best human grandmasters and perform very difficult calculations, but they don't (yet?) show any signs of possessing an independent and potentially even rebellious self-awareness like HAL in Stanley Kubrick's movie *2001: A Space Odyssey*. At the same time, it is an open question whether a creature—or a machine—can be conscious without being intelligent, although this seems probable, if only because most people would acknowledge that someone who is moderately or even severely retarded (and thus not very intelligent) can nonetheless be conscious.

Consciousness may well be a *sine qua non*, necessary but not sufficient for humanness, all of which leads inevitably to the question: Why has consciousness evolved?

First, let's try to define it, or at least, to gesture in that direction. If nothing else we can refer once again to Supreme Court Justice Potter Stewart's oft-repeated observation concerning pornography: We may not be able to define consciousness, but we know it when we experience it. Indeed, one of the persistent conundrums awaiting anyone who grapples with consciousness is that whereas we perceive ourselves to be conscious, we can never be certain that anyone else is.

Here, nonetheless, is what seems like a reasonable definition of consciousness: a particular example of awareness (whatever that is!), characterized by recursiveness in which individuals are not only aware but also aware that they are aware. By this conception, many animals are aware but not strictly conscious. My Boxer dog, for example, is exquisitely aware of and responsive to just about everything around him—more so, in many cases, than I. I *know*, however, that I am conscious because I am aware of my own internal mental state, sometimes even paradoxically aware of that about which I am *un*aware.

On the other hand, I have little real doubt that my dog *is* conscious, although I can't prove it (ditto for my cats and horses). A more satisfying stance, therefore—empathically as well as ethically—is to give in to common sense and stipulate that different animal species possess differing degrees of consciousness. This may be more intellectually satisfying as well, since postulating a continuum of consciousness is consistent with this fundamental evolutionary insight: cross-species, organic continuity.

In any event, the "why" question is as follows: Why should we (or any conscious species) be able to think about our thinking, instead of just plain old thinking, full stop? Why need we know that we know, instead of just knowing? Isn't it enough to feel, without also feeling good—or bad—about the fact that we are feeling? After all, there are downsides to consciousness. For Dostoyevsky's Grand Inquisitor, consciousness and its requisite choices compose a vast source of human pain (one that he obviated by telling people how to think and what to believe). For Ernest Becker,

> The idea [of consciousness] is ludicrous, if it is not monstrous. It means to know that one is food for worms. This is the terror: to have emerged from nothing, to have a name, consciousness of self,

deep inner feelings, and excruciating inner yearning for life and self-expression—and with all this yet to die.

And for Carl Sagan, who argued that consciousness is closely tied to the benefit of imagining events that have not yet occurred, "The price we pay for anticipation of the future is anxiety about it."

There are also some practical problems. As a result of excessive "self-consciousness," we are liable to trip over ourselves, whether literally when attempting to perform some physical act best done via the "flow" of unreflective automaticity or cognitively because of the infamous, chattering "monkey mind" so anathematized by Eastern traditions and that may require intense meditation or other disciplines to squelch. Even on a strictly biological basis, consciousness seems hard to justify, if only because it, like intelligence, evidently requires a large number of neurons, the elaboration and maintenance of which is energetically expensive. What is the compensating payoff?

One possibility—a biological null hypothesis—is that maybe consciousness hasn't been selected for at all; maybe it is a nonadaptive by-product of having brains that exceed a certain size threshold, regardless of why those brains have been selected. A single molecule of water, for example, isn't wet. Neither are two, or, presumably, a few thousand, or even a million. But put enough of them together in the same place and we get wetness—not because wetness is adaptively favored over, say, dryness or bumpiness, but simply as an unavoidable physical consequence of piling up enough H^2O molecules. Could consciousness be like that? Accumulate enough neurons—perhaps because they permit its possessor to integrate numerous sensory inputs and generate complex, variable behavior—wire them up, and presto, they're conscious?

Personal confession: At this point, I would dearly love to support this hypothesis, if only to demonstrate my willingness to entertain the possibility that some important human traits might in fact be nonadaptive. (After all, I have already been less than welcoming to the best-known candidate for a nonadaptive by-product, the curious case of female orgasm.) But the argument simply isn't persuasive, mostly because given the undeniably large costs of building and maintaining complex brains, it is almost unimaginable—to any fully conscious brain thinking about itself—that such an elaborate organ would evolve and persist unless it offered distinct reproductive benefits. It is so easy to become unconscious that one could readily imagine that any characteristic that is so specific, detailed, and vulnerable as well as expensive must be the result of positive selection—or else we would likely have big brains and thus elaborate sensory input, motor control, and so forth, but without consciousness.

Alternatively, it seems far more likely that consciousness really *is* adaptive. If so, then at minimum, at some time in the past, those who were conscious had to have been more fit than those who weren't. More precisely, genes that contribute to consciousness must somehow have been more successful than alternative alleles in getting themselves projected into the future. One possible avenue toward this end would be if consciousness endowed its possessors with the capacity to play "what if" games, to engage in trial and error in one's head. The Germans speak of so-called *gedanken* (thought) experiments, which involve running through various scenarios in one's imagination without actually having to undergo the risk of doing so in real life. As philosopher Karl Popper put it, this "permits our hypotheses to die in our stead." It is difficult to see how anyone could perform such calculations without sufficient conscious awareness of self to allow imaginative projection into the future.

Alternatively, consciousness could also benefit us by operating in the opposite domain, that of immediate sensations instead of imagination. It could, in short, enable its possessor to overrule the tyranny of pleasure and pain. Not that pleasure and pain are inherently disadvantageous. Indeed, both are imbued with considerable adaptive significance: The former is a proximate mechanism encouraging us to engage in activities that are fitness enhancing, and the latter, to refrain from those that are fitness reducing. But what about things that are fitness enhancing in the long run, but unavoidably painful in the short? Or vice versa?

Overeating, for example, might feel good but be nonetheless detrimental. In this case, perhaps a conscious individual can say to himself, "I want to gnaw a bit more on this gazelle leg, but I'd better not." Or vice versa, something that feels acutely bad might be ultimately beneficial, requiring a conscious override of the usual rule of thumb that induces us to avoid pain: "I don't want the highly unpleasant sensation of having my infected tooth pulled out, but if I do it, I'll be better off." Once an individual starts mulling things over, essentially talking to herself about herself, she may be en route to consciousness, and with powerful adaptive momentum.

Part of this adaptive momentum might emerge directly from what is otherwise a likely downside of consciousness, as reflected in the earlier quotation from Ernest Becker. Thus, let's grant that an important aspect of consciousness is explicit awareness of one's own mortality. Numerous thinkers have already suggested, moreover, that one result of such awareness is a widespread, concerted effort to "live forever," typically through various attempts at symbolic immortality: commissioning or constructing literal images of oneself, monuments, or other indications of continued presence in an otherwise transitory world, or in other ways striving to achieve something by which one's name, reputation, influence, etc., will live . . . if not forever, at least longer than one's own perishable flesh.

The next possible step (which I had conceived by myself but recently discovered had earlier been proposed by evolutionary biologist Lonnie W. Aarssen) is an easy step to imagine—at least for evolutionists: Maybe awareness of mortality isn't merely a tangential consequence of consciousness but its primary adaptive value, if it has the effect of inducing people to seek yet another way of rebelling against mortality: by reproducing.[27] If so, then consciousness as we normally recognize it (of self, others, of one's perception of a rainbow, and so forth) may be a complex side effect of the real biological significance of consciousness: of our mortality and the prospect of having children—and grandchildren, etc.— in response. If so, then people endowed with such conscious awareness would presumably give rise to more children, grandchildren, etc., thereby selecting for the underlying cause.

Even more intriguing, perhaps, than consciousness as a facilitator of impulse control or override, or as a means of enhancing our ancestors' fitness by inducing them to transcend their own impending death, is the possibility that it evolved in the context of our social lives, which, as we have seen, privileges a kind of Machiavellian intelligence whereby success in competition and cooperation is a function of intellectual capacity. Consciousness and intelligence are closely allied, such that consciousness may itself be a key part of Machiavellian intelligence. If intelligence has been serviceable in part as a way of helping our ancestors successfully navigate the twists and turns of complex social life, the same could have been true of consciousness. Thus, if intelligence provided the raw horse-power needed to perform difficult social calculations, conscious-ness could have yielded the information necessary to direct all that energy by enabling early human beings to imagine another's situation almost as well as our own.

The more accurate our perception of where others are "coming from," the better able we are to act benevolently in their interest or—more likely—to serve our own.

Consciousness is not only an unfolding story that we tell our-selves, moment by moment, about what we are doing, feeling, and thinking. It also includes our efforts to interpret what other indi-viduals are doing, feeling, and thinking, as well as how those others are likely to perceive oneself. Call it the Burns benefit, from the last stanza of the Scottish poet's celebrated meditation *To a Louse*: "O wad some Pow'r the giftie gie us/To see oursels as others see us!/It wad frae monie a blunder free us/An' foolish notion . . . ."

If, as sometimes suggested, character is what we do when no one is looking, maybe consciousness is precisely a Robert Burnsian evo-lutionary gift, our anticipation of how we seem to others who *are* looking. And maybe it evolved, accordingly, because it helped free us from many a blunder and foolish notion by enabling our con-sciously endowed ancestors to realize (in proportion as they were conscious) that, for example, seeming too selfish, or insufficiently altruistic, or too cowardly, too uninformed, too ambitious, too sex-ually voracious, and so forth would ill serve their ends. The more conscious our ancestors were, according to this argument, the more able they were to modify—to their own benefit—others' impres-sions of them, and thereby to enhance their own evolutionary suc-cess. If so, then genes "for" consciousness would have enjoyed an advantage over alternative genes "for" social obtuseness.

Twice earlier, first when speculating about the possible adaptive significance of art—specifically, storytelling—and again when considering the evolution of religion, we briefly examined Theory of Mind (ToM), which is something of a "hot topic" among cogni-tive psychologists. Essentially, ToM is a sophisticated cognitive mechanism whereby its possessors infer the mental attributes of others. After all, the minds of others are especially interesting to people, just as flowers are interesting to hummingbirds and rivers are interesting to otters: Our survival and reproduction depend upon them.

Achieving a ToM—that is, a valid notion about the minds of other people—is to succeed in a kind of mind reading, not literally, of course, but rather to have gained the benefit of insights into what is going on inside another's head, so as better to predict his or her behavior. It might be possible to make accurate inferences of this sort without consciousness, but it seems likely that the greater the consciousness by individual A, the more successful she will be in constructing a valid model of the inner workings and thus the eventual behavior of individual B. It is one thing to conclude, without reflection, "That fellow is angry and hence, dangerous" because of his recent behavior. It is likely to be more fruitful, however, to say—to oneself—something like, "He seems angry, just as I was when something similar happened to me. Since I responded in such-and-such a way at that time, I bet he'll respond similarly."

In short, those who possess an accurate Theory of Mind can model the intentions of others and profit thereby. And it is at least possible that the more conscious you are, the more accurate is your Theory of Mind, since cognitive modelers should be more effective if they know, cognitively and self-consciously, not only what they are modeling but also *that* they are doing so. It is also worth noting that an accurate ToM can be useful in ways beyond the self-serving Machiavellian model. Thus, most people in most societies value "considerate" behavior on the part of themselves and others, and being considerate typically involves literally considering the interests, needs, and inclinations of other people. (Of course, a persistently cynical outlook would also suggest that even considerate behavior is itself fundamentally self-serving and thus, in a sense, manipulative and Machiavellian in its own way, but that's another matter.)

Earlier, we considered the hypothesis that the human fondness for stories may be a consequence of the adaptive value of experiencing various social scenarios but without the risks of actually living through them. It is hard to imagine that anyone could read, hear, or watch a story without being conscious that he or she is doing so, and that what is being attended to is in fact a story. It is equally hard to imagine that there haven't been adaptive benefits to our ancestors who took such stories seriously, all the while knowing that they were doing so.

Just as consciousness doubtless derives at the proximate ("how") level from material events occurring among neurons, the "why" of consciousness is unquestionably a matter of its evolutionary significance, occurring at the level of organisms, ecology, and natural selection. Nonetheless, many are convinced that consciousness (even more than intelligence) can only have come to us as a gift from God, an endowment enabling His chosen species to glorify the divine and do so with full, aware—that is, conscious—commitment to the saving of their souls. Similarly, there are those who maintain a mystical conception of the power of "cosmic consciousness" to move mountains, or at least, as the Yippies attempted in 1967, to levitate the Pentagon via concentrated psychic energy (an effort that, as I recall, never got off the ground), and/or an unshakeable confidence that we are surrounded by disembodied "morphogenetic fields" or other ineffable manifestations of some cerebral happening of which the merely material is only a pale semblance.

"But we are not here concerned with hopes or fears," wrote Darwin, at the end of *The Descent of Man*,

> only with the truth as far as our reason allows us to discover it. . . . [W] e must acknowledge, as it seems to me, that man with all his noble qualities, with sympathy which feels for the most debased, with benevolence which extends not only to other men but to the humblest living creature, with his god-like intellect which has penetrated into the movements and constitution of the solar system—with all these exalted powers—Man still bears in his bodily frame the indelible stamp of his lowly origin.

To this I would add that we also bear this stamp—of biology— not just in our bodily frame but also in our minds (including our consciousness), and not just when it comes to "how" but also "why."

This chapter reviews the last of the human evolutionary mysteries that we'll cover, but it certainly doesn't exhaust the possibilities, even if we restrict ourselves to "mental mysteries."

For example, in addition to considering why we became so darned smart, we might ask: Given the fact of cross-species organic continuity (which, after all, is the greatest single take-home message of evolutionary biology), why is there such a gap in mental capacities between people and other animals? One possible answer is that the gap isn't really all that large. In fact, there is a burgeoning field known as "cognitive ethology," which has demonstrated remarkable learning capacities on the part of other species, including African gray parrots, Caledonian crows, and dogs, as well as the ever-reliably surprising chimpanzees.

Another way of framing the question is, "How great is the divide between human mental functioning and that of other animals?" Are the intellectual worlds of *Homo sapiens* and other species continuous or discontinuous? Clearly there is a difference, but is it qualitative (a difference in kind) or merely quantitative (in extent)? And what are the implications of possible answers . . . for our self-perception, for the way we interact with other living creatures, and for the fraught question of which species—if any—has a soul?

Notes

1. Attwell, D., & Laughlin, S. B. (2001). An energy budget for signaling in the grey matter of the brain. *Journal of Cerebral Blood Flow and Metabolism, 21,* 1133–1145.
2. Hamilton, J. A. (1935). *The association between brain size and maze ability in the white rat.* Ph.D. dissertation, University of California at Berkeley.
3. Premack, D. (2004). Is language the key to human intelligence? *Science, 303,* 318–320.
4. Calvin, W. H. (1994). The emergence of intelligence. *Scientific American, 271*(4), 100–107.
5. Alexander, R. D. (1971). The search for an evolutionary philosophy of man. *Proceedings of the Royal Society of Victoria, Melbourne, 84,* 99–120.
6. Bailey, D. H., & Geary, D. C. (2009). Hominid brain evolution: Testing climatic, ecological, and social competition models. *Human Nature, 20,* 67–79.
7. Calvin, W. H. (2002). *A brain for all seasons.* Chicago: University of Chicago Press.
8. Rozsa, L. (2008). The rise of non-adaptive intelligence in humans under pathogen pressure. *Medical Hypotheses, 70,* 685–690.
9. Hamilton, W. D., & Zuk, M. (1982). Heritable true fitness and bright birds: A role for parasites? *Science, 218,* 384–387.
10. Hopcroft, R. L. (2006). Sex, status, and reproductive success in the contemporary United States. *Evolution and Human Behavior, 27,* 104–120.

11. Charlton, B. G. (2009). Why are women so intelligent? *Medical Hypotheses*, *74*, 401–402.

12. Sandiford, P., Cassell, J., Sanchez, G., & Coldham, C. (1997). Does intelligence account for the link between maternal literacy and child survival? *Social Science and Medicine*, *45*, 1231–1239; Čvorović, J., Rushton, J. P., & Tenjevic, L. (2008). Maternal IQ and child mortality in 222 Serbian Roma (Gypsy) women. *Personality and Individual Differences*, *44*, 1604–1609.

13. Nettle, D., & Pollet, T. V. (2008). Natural selection on male wealth in humans. *American Naturalist*, *172*, 658–666.

14. JoVe, T. H. (1997). Social pressures have selected for an extended juvenile period in primates. *Journal of Human Evolution*, *32*, 593–605.

15. Jolly, A. (1966). Lemur social behavior and primate intelligence. *Science*, *153*, 501–506; Humphrey, N. K. (1976). The social function of intellect. In P. Bateson & R. Hinde (Eds.), *Growing points in ethology*. Cambridge, UK: Cambridge University Press.

16. Byrneand, R. W., & Whiten, A. (1988). *Machiavellian intelligence: Social expertise and the evolution of intellect in monkeys, apes and humans*. New York: Oxford University Press.

17. Alexander, R. D. (1990). How did humans evolve? Reflections on the uniquely unique species. *University of Michigan Museum of Zoology Special Publication*, *1*, 1–38.

18. Cheney, D. L., & Seyfarth, R. M. (2007). *Baboon metaphysics*. Chicago: University of Chicago Press.

19. Silk, J., Alberts, S. C., & Altmann, J. (2003). Social bonds of female baboons enhance infant survival. *Science*, *302*, 1231–1234.

20. Mercier, H., & Sperber, D. (2011). Argumentation: Its adaptiveness and efficacy. *Behavioral and Brain Sciences*, *34*(2), 94–111.

21. Dunbar, R. (1997). *Grooming, gossip and the evolution of language*. Cambridge, MA: Harvard University Press.

22. Cosmides, L., Clark Barretta, H., & Tooby, J. (2010). Adaptive specializations, social exchange, and the evolution of human intelligence. *Proceedings of the National Academy of Sciences*, *107*, 9007–9014.

23. Cosmides, L. (1989). The logic of social exchange. *Cognition*, *31*, 187–276.

24. Wrangham, R. (2009). *Catching fire: How cooking made us human*. New York: Basic.

25. Kaplan, H., Hill, K., Lancaster, J., & Hurtado, A. M. (2000). A theory of human life history evolution: Diet, intelligence, and longevity. *Evolutionary Anthropology*, *9*(4), 156–185.

26. Gottfredson, L. S. (2007). Innovation, fatal accidents, and the evolution of general intelligence. In M. J. Roberts (Ed.), *Integrating the mind*. Hove, UK: Psychology Press.

27. Aarssen, L. W. (2010). Darwinism and meaning. *Biological Theory*, *5*(4), 296–311.

CHAPTER TEN

Digging for Treasure

S OCRATES WAS TOLD BY the Delphic oracle that he was the
wisest of men—not because of how much he knew, but
because one of the few things he knew was how much he did
not know. By the same token, the more you have read *Homo
Mysterious*, the wiser you have become, as you learned more and
more about what we do not know!

College students undergo a similar Socratic transition.
Beginning their studies as freshmen, they are convinced that they
know a great deal. As their education proceeds—especially if it is a
really good education—they become increasingly aware of the
gaps in their knowledge and wisdom, until, when ideally they have
been helped to see that they know hardly anything at all, they
graduate.

The current tour of what we do not know has been limited to
but a small subset of our ignorance, its goal being to illuminate
just some of the dark places on the human evolutionary map.
Paradoxically, by shining a light on darkness, we have not abolished that darkness, but rather, rendered it more identifiable, even
as it remains essentially obscure: not unknowable, mind you, just
currently unknown. Isaac Newton famously wrote that if he had
seen far, it is because he stood on the shoulders of giants, which
was both an exercise in undue modesty (Newton was himself one

of the greatest such giants) and nothing less than the truth. In *Homo Mysterious*, instead of looking far, we have looked nearby—at ourselves—using a giant's microscope: the principles of evolution by natural selection, as elaborated by that greatest of biological giants, Charles Darwin.

We haven't come close to exploring all of our own evolutionary mysteries. In at least one such case—the question of the so-called missing link—this is because on closer examination the presumed mystery self-destructs. The phrase "missing link" has in the past been interpreted as a serious challenge to the evolutionary narrative of human phylogeny, implying that the key connector between modern human beings and our ancestral "apes" has not been found, ostensibly because it doesn't exist. In fact, the concept of missing link is altogether misleading: There are lots of links, some as yet missing, many found. And the more we find, the more there are: Picture two points and draw a line between them. One point is the ancestor we share in common with modern apes; the other is *Homo sapiens*. Next, let's posit that along this line there exists a "missing link." Imagine, now, that you have found such a point, perhaps roughly intermediate between the initial two. As a result, you now have two missing links, one on either side! Find another of these "links" and—voila!—three are now missing. Paleontologists have discovered a large litany of "found links," each of which creates the opportunity, by definition, to find yet more. As this happens, the gaps between the various links grow ever smaller. We are all linked, no mystery here.

On the other hand, there are numerous small-scale peripheral mysteries, such as why we laugh, cry, and yawn. And what about Mark Twain's observation that we are the only species that blushes . . . or needs to? Psychologists and biologists have come up with numerous explanations for these largely autonomic responses, most of them involving variations on a social theme: Only rarely do people laugh, cry, yawn, or blush when they are alone, so presumably these unconscious actions serve to communicate . . . but what? And what about other hidden and unintended communicative signals, such as pheromones that indicate ovulation status and other hormone conditions, unconscious sensitivity to gene combinations (especially the major histocompatability complex) that are unconsciously used to assess mate suitability, and pupillary dilation and the concomitants of galvanic skin response (monitored in lie detector tests)? Why do our bodies give us away when we are—consciously, at least—trying to convey a different message? Along the same lines and, if anything, more perplexing is the question, "Why do we have an unconscious?" Or emotions?

And what about morality? Some theologians—and a significant number of laypersons—argue that people are not naturally good, so that without God, human beings would live according to Thomas Hobbes's grim prediction that in the absence of an overbearing (albeit secular) "Leviathan" to keep us in line, *Homo sapiens* would experience lives that are "nasty, poor, brutish, and short." Others maintain that in view of the fundamental selfishness of natural selection, the very fact that most human beings remain decent, ethical, and moral is itself an argument for the existence of a deity. Yet others follow the lead of evolutionary biologists in pointing to a variety of altogether natural, selective pressures that seem likely to induce people to behave in ways that appear altruistic—but which, at the level of individual genes, are actually selfish nonetheless.

Selfish genes do not necessarily create selfish people. In fact, quite the opposite: One of the primary ways that genes see to their own selfish propagation appears to be via inducing their bodies to behave "altruistically" toward other bodies, especially those harboring identical copies of precisely those "selfish" genes. Moreover, there can be a huge self-serving payoff in being perceived as generous and altruistic.

Then there is suicide. According to French existentialist Albert Camus, it is the only serious philosophical question. Perhaps so. But in any event, suicide is also a serious evolutionary question: As with homosexuality, any genetically influenced inclination in this particular direction should be selected against and quickly disappear, especially if it manifests early in life. (Suicide among postreproductive individuals would experience much less negative selection.) There are many animals that engage in extreme forms of altruism that are tantamount to suicide—for example, honeybees whose sting in defense of their hive causes them to die—but no cases in which individuals take their own life without a clear benefit to others, such as their offspring or other close relatives. The question of inclusive fitness theory arises here once again, and it would be gratifying (at least, scientifically) if human suicide correlated with payoffs to surviving relatives. But it doesn't, so it isn't.

An evolutionary consideration of suicide would also require a close look at the possible adaptive significance of depression, itself strongly correlated with suicide. Here is an especially rich trove of theory and data, compiled by psychologists and psychiatrists, providing alluring and sometimes even compelling explanations, but as yet, no "closure." Ditto for schizophrenia and other psychiatric diseases that have a distinct genetic component and that also tend to reduce reproductive success.

Yet another unresolved mystery concerns our own evolutionary future. Here, at last, we confront an enigma that is not only unanswered but also genuinely unanswerable. That is, we cannot predict with any reliability the precise course of our future evolution—where our species will end up, at any given time in the future—although we can have substantial confidence as to the force (natural selection) that will be powering our journey. Not long ago, it was widely thought that future human beings will have small bodies (because with the advent of technology, people aren't as physically active as they used to be) and large heads (because, presumably, they will be thinking more). In H. G. Wells's *Time Machine*, humanity in the distant future consists of the rapacious, bestial Morlocks (troglodytic descendants of industrial workers) and naïve, childlike Eloi, upon whom the Morlocks feed. More recently, the movie *Wall-E* portrayed bloated humanity, as a result of the obesity epidemic and excessive reliance upon machines.

None of these images is likely to be even close to accurate, because each is based, unknowingly, on assumed Lamarckian inheritance: the old, discredited notion that, for example, giraffes evolved long necks because their ancestors stretched those necks to reach food, after which their extended anatomy was somehow passed on to their descendants. Or that body builders, as a result of developing large muscles in their lifetime, would pass such traits to their offspring.

But in fact, the only way future human beings would have large heads or obese bodies is if people with large heads or obese bodies (based on their genetic makeup, not their dietary or exercise habits) had proportionately more than their share of children. Unlikely.

And in view of enhanced communication and transportation, it is overwhelmingly probable that gene exchange among different ethnic and socioeconomic groups will keep us one species (good-bye to any dichotomous future, á la Morlocks and Eloi).

On the other hand, evolution by natural selection definitely has not ceased, in our own species as in all others. Evolution is, in fact, unavoidable whenever some people are more effective than others in projecting their genes into the future; what changes are the "selection pressures," the factors that convey benefit or liability to particular traits, not the reality of differential reproduction and with it, the inevitability of natural selection and evolutionary change. In the distant past, for example, selection favored bipedalism, large brains, consciousness, etc., for reasons we have just speculated about. What will it favor in the future? Maybe the ability to reproduce despite strontium-90 in our bones and PCBs in our fat. Or perhaps a susceptibility to fundamentalist religious teaching. If resource scarcity becomes increasingly severe, maybe natural selection will smile upon smaller, more efficient human beings, who can thrive and reproduce using fewer calories and requiring less space, or who are not especially stressed by an increasingly polluted, globally overheated world with greatly diminished biodiversity. With increasing in vitro fertilization— not to mention cloning—it is conceivable (and perhaps, desirable) that males may eventually vanish altogether, or at least, that the various traits that have evolved in the service of human "mate selection" will disappear, to be replaced by . . . who knows what.

Stay tuned. (Note to my editor at Oxford University Press: Maybe we should start thinking about a follow-on book, *Homo Mysterious* v.2.0, to cover the "missing link," crying, laughing, yawning, blushing, suicide, morality and ethics, the unconscious, the evolution of emotions, and our evolutionary future, as well as some of the other mysteries that must, for now, remain especially mysterious.)

"just as people find water wherever they dig, they everywhere find the incomprehensible, sooner or later." So wrote Georg Christoph Lichtenberg, 18th-century physicist and satirist. More than two centuries later, it isn't at all clear that people will find water *wherever* they dig. Nor is it certain that wherever we dig in the realm of life, we shall find the incomprehensible. The point of this book, in fact, has been just the opposite: that we ourselves *are* comprehensible, even though we aren't at present altogether comprehended.

The alternative to mystery isn't triviality or boredom. Rainbows are no less beautiful when we understand that they are produced by sunlight separated into its spectral components, just as life is not rendered tedious when seen as structured by nucleic acids rather than as *élan vitale*. Or when evolution is seen as the ultimate force behind that structuring. Or when human beings are seen as inextricably connected to the whole business. Rather, as Darwin famously wrote at the conclusion of *The Origin of Species*, "There is grandeur in this view of life."

There is a chilling moment toward the end of Ray Bradbury's science fiction classic, *The Martian Chronicles*, when a human family, having escaped to Mars to avoid impending nuclear war, looks eagerly into the "canals" of their new planetary home, expecting to see Martians. They do: their own reflections. It wasn't terribly long ago that reputable astronomers entertained the notion that there really were canals on Mars. From our current vantage, this is clearly fantasy, and yet, Mars has not become any less intriguing for its becoming known, just as the moon didn't lose any appreciable panache once it became undeniably made of rock rather than green cheese.

The same applies to ourselves. Unlike Bradbury's fictional family, we really *can* see ourselves, if we simply look hard enough. Just as the philosopher Immanuel Kant once proposed *Sapere Aude* ("Dare to Know") as a motto for the Enlightenment, *Homo Mysterious* has proposed a modification: "Dare to Know How Much We Don't Know." And in the process, perhaps you have been inspired to dare even more: to help diminish the existing quantity of Unknown, or at least to cheer those who are struggling to do so, all the while knowing that more unknowns will arise, and that complete "success" is therefore impossible.

This can lead, unfortunately, to a more cynical perspective, which for obvious reasons I have elected to mention only here, at the end of our current intellectual journey. Put forth by the Polish philosopher Leszek Kolakowski, it has been called the Law of the Infinite Cornucopia: For any belief, it is always possible to come up with a seemingly unlimited amount of supporting evidence.

By the same token, perhaps it will always be possible to come up with plausible but ultimately unsatisfying explanations.

Unlike Sisyphus, however, who was condemned to spend eternity pushing a huge rock up a steep hill only to have it roll back down again, the scientific push for greater knowledge doesn't slip backward (at least, not for long)—although it never reaches a safe, secure, tedious, and satisfactory stopping point. There are always more hills to climb.

It might also help to recall a different parable, in which two brothers are told to dig for treasure in the family vineyard. They found neither gold nor silver, but their labors greatly enriched the soil.